TEACHING
ENGLISH
GRAMMAR

What to Teach and How to Teach it

Jim Scrivener

Contents

About the series

Macmillan Books for Teachers

Welcome to Macmillan Books for Teachers. The titles are written by acknowledged and innovative leaders in each field to help you develop your teaching repertoire, practical skill and theoretical knowledge.

Suited to both newer and to more experienced teachers, the series combines the best of classic teaching methodology with recent, cutting-edge developments. Insights from academic research are combined with hands-on experience to create books with focus on real-world teaching solutions.

We hope you will find the ideas in them a source of inspiration in your own teaching and enjoyment in your professional learning.

Adrian Underhill

Titles in the series

500 Activities for the Primary Classroom
Carol Read

700 Classroom Activities
David Seymour & Maria Popova

An A–Z of ELT
Scott Thornbury

Blended Learning
Pete Sharma & Barney Barrett

Beyond the Sentence
Scott Thornbury

Children Learning English
Jayne Moon

Discover English
Rod Bolitho & Brian Tomlinson

Learning Teaching
Jim Scrivener

Sound Foundations
Adrian Underhill

Teaching Practice
Roger Gower, Diane Phillips & Steve Walters

Teaching Reading Skills
Christine Nuttall

Uncovering CLIL
Peeter Mehisto, David Marsh & Maria Jesus Frigols

Uncovering EAP
Sam McCarter & Phil Jakes

Uncovering Grammar
Scott Thornbury

About the author

Jim Scrivener has worked in many different countries, including Kenya, Russia, Georgia and Hungary. He has been Head of Teacher Training for International House Hastings, Director of Education for IH Budapest and is currently Head of Teacher Development for Bell International, where he designed the Online Delta course. He was leader of the team that designed the Euro exams and has been actively involved with Cambridge ESOL exams including design of their online teacher portfolio. He is married to Noémi and has two adult sons, Alex and Ben, and a young daughter, Maisie. He can be very boring about Bob Dylan if you give him half a chance.

Foreword

Teachers frequently need to present new grammar to learners and grammar presentations are often at the heart of language lessons. This is part of the current general 'communicative' methodology, and is embodied or assumed in most current materials. Coursebooks usually provide 'ready-made' presentations, but teachers often want to strengthen or supplement the grammatical explanations in order to meet the particular learning events in their own classrooms. And when other materials like a reading text or an online activity are being used, there can be multiple situations in which further elucidation of a grammatical structure may be required. When this occurs a teacher has to decide whether it is appropriate to deal with this and if so how to insert it elegantly into ongoing work, and whether to do it now or later.

This places a constant demand on teachers to identify quickly:

1) the new structure and its possible forms

2) the meanings imparted by the structures in context

3) the core of what the student needs to learn

4) and then, crucially, ways to present and practise the structure and to check that the core concepts are understood.

Teaching English Grammar aims to help teachers meet these demands by offering quick access to key aspects of structures, ready-to-use presentation ideas, contexts for first and subsequent exposure to new language and insights on checking understanding.

Teachers with less experience often struggle with providing contexts for the new language they are presenting, and the activities here aim to provide simple and effective situational contexts for such language at this point in the lesson. This is important, because if the situation is chosen so that the human meanings conveyed within it are compelling and transparent, then the meaning of the grammatical point can almost 'teach itself', reducing the need for verbal re-explanation from the teacher, and allowing the teacher to attend to the practice of the forms of the structure.

At this point the teacher faces a second challenge: incisive checking of learners' understanding of the language point. The agile selection and use of concept questions to do this is also a crucial and often elusive skill for a new teacher to develop, the lack of which easily leads instead to a habitualised over-reliance on the misleading question 'Do you understand?' The illustrative concept questions in this book aim to help teachers to develop their confidence and facility in using these to check understanding.

More experienced teachers will be able to use the material here to review and overhaul the texture and elegance of their repertoire of presentation activities and approaches, streamlining their approach and developing their confidence and effectiveness.

Adrian Underhill
Series Editor

Introduction

This book gathers together practical teaching ideas and key information about language in order to help you prepare and teach grammar lessons. I hope that it will save you time, energy and stress and help you to feel more confident, well-informed and one step ahead of the students. Modern coursebooks are generally excellent but sometimes we (and our students) feel the need to step away from their texts and exercises. Rather than using coursebook material to introduce a new grammar point, you may want to do a 'books closed' presentation on the board – or add in an extra practice activity. You will find lots of ideas here to help you present and practise grammar points.

Presentation

The Presentation ideas in this book usually involve the teacher upfront, introducing and modelling language items, possibly using the board. They are particularly suitable for working with language items your class has not met or studied before. Many of them involve creating a context or situation which will help to exemplify the meaning and use of the target items.

Practice

The Practice ideas are based around students using the language themselves. These sections list a range of possible ideas you could use to practise various features of meaning and form. They are not intended as a sequence of activities to be used in a single lesson. Select the idea most relevant for your lesson and your class.

It's worth noting that this division into presentation and practice is somewhat arbitrary. Many teachers prefer to introduce new items through activities that involve lots of student language use and less teacher modelling or explanation. Depending on your own teaching approach, you may find that you prefer to use ideas from the practice sections to introduce new language.

All the teaching ideas are given as quite brief notes. There are many steps that I do not mention and I have to assume that you will fill in missing details yourself – and in doing so you can start to make the ideas your own and more relevant for your class. For example, to avoid repetition I have not usually stated that you need to use concept questions in presentations or that it's important to focus on form – but please assume that both of these steps are usually necessary. The Presentation sections mainly describe situations or contexts to help you present the meaning and use of the language. However, you will invariably also need to focus on the way that the item is structured, even if that is not explicitly stated.

You may find that some ideas seem unsuitable for your class as they stand – but I hope that they can still inspire you to think of other related activities that are suitable.

Some key notions in presentation and practice

Contexts

Many of the presentations in this book make use of a context. These are simple, easy-to-convey situations, scenes or stories that will help to clarify the meaning or use of a language item. You can create the context by drawing pictures on the board, holding up flashcards of photos or sketches or by creating a mini-situation in class using students to act out simple roles following your instructions. A really good context will seem to lead inevitably to natural use of the target language. Typically, after creating a context, you might elicit language from the students to see if they already have any idea about the target language. If they don't, it allows you to model the new language yourself.

Eliciting

You elicit by giving cues (asking a question, miming, showing a picture, giving a keyword, etc) that encourage the students to say something themselves – perhaps in order to draw out their ideas or to see what they know of the target language you are working on. This may help to involve students in a lesson, as they will be doing more than simply listening to you speaking. They can also show what they already know and this can help you to adjust the level of the work. Eliciting can help to reduce the amount of unnecessary teacher talk in class.

Modelling

You model by saying something aloud once or a number of times because you want the class to hear a well-pronounced example of a language item. You should take care to speak as naturally as possible and not artificially exaggerate any features.

Drilling

You drill by modelling a sentence (perhaps to exemplify a specific grammatical item) then getting the students to repeat – often *chorally* (ie as a whole class). Alternatively, you could also ask different individuals to repeat – or pairs to say the sentence(s) to each other. Drilling is a very restricted use of language to help students notice, focus on and improve things like verb endings, word order, pronunciation etc. If a student repeats incorrectly during a drill it is usually helpful to correct. Don't worry too much about drilling being an unrealistic or 'non-communicative' use of language – or that the students might be rather unnaturally over-using target items. This type of controlled manipulation of language items is very useful.

Story / Dialogue building

You can build a short story or dialogue that includes examples of language you want the students to learn. Use the board or pictures to introduce the context and characters and then model (or elicit) lines of the story / dialogue, one by one – which the students can repeat. As the story / dialogue gets longer, students can recap and practise saying the whole thing.

Pair work

Students do pair work when each student in class works with one partner. Often the students in each pair are referred to as A and B. Pair work allows lots of students to speak and work simultaneously, maximising interaction time in class.

Mingling

In a mingling activity, each student in class stands up and walks around the room, meeting and talking to a number of other people – and perhaps after completing a task, moving on to meet others.

Engagement

Although teachers often worry about whether their lesson is 'fun' or not, perhaps a more important consideration is whether it is *engaging*. Students will learn little or nothing if they do not find the work interesting and involving. It needs to attract them, fill their minds and hold their attention. This may be because the topic is relevant, the task is stimulating, the end result appeals to them – or for many other reasons. One key factor to bear in mind is to pitch the level of challenge appropriately – neither too high nor too low – and of course this level will vary for different people in your class and at different times. Creating the right challenge level may, for example, involve the teacher varying the difficulty of questions as they ask different people around the class.

What are timelines – and how can I use them?

Timelines are a simple visual aid that you (or a student) can quickly draw on the board. They make the flow of time visible – as a line moving from the left (past) through 'now' towards the right (the future). By adding other things to the line (eg an 'X' to indicate an event or a stick baby to show when someone was born) we can clarify when something happened and this can help learners to understand the uses of a tense or how one tense is different from another.

Timelines are valuable both as (a) a teaching tool to introduce the meaning and use of verb tenses and (b) as a checking tool (like concept questions) to find out how much learners have understood.

Use timelines as an aid when explaining the meaning and use of a tense. Ask concept questions based on the timelines. Try using incomplete timelines as a way of eliciting ideas from students (*When do you think it happened?*). Invite students to come to the board to draw their suggested timelines – and let other students agree or disagree – and make alternative suggestions. Draw wrong timelines and invite students to correct you. Timelines are a great way of clarifying and checking meaning. But just remember that their meaning may not be immediately transparent to everyone – and there may be different interpretations. Many students seem to find timelines very helpful but others may remain puzzled.

Example sentences

Where possible and appropriate, example sentences in the main text are real samples of language in use, taken from the Macmillan English Dictionary corpus. Most are exactly as listed in the corpus, but in some cases, they have been edited slightly in order to help focus on the language point being exemplified by removing or changing words that seem potentially confusing or distracting for the levels in which the lessons are likely to be taught. Even so, you may find some of the samples unusual – and may consider them unsuitable for their classes. For example, the present perfect examples include *Someone has just waltzed off with my drink*. This certainly isn't the sort of example students typically come across – but, after just a little explanation of what a *waltz* is – and of the colloquial use meaning 'steal' – this is actually a very striking and visual example – and the sort of chunk of language that students tend to love learning by heart (which is halfway to getting to grips with the language). Of course, if you are not personally familiar with the meaning of an idiomatic use, then it's sensible to avoid it – but, if you do know it, I encourage you to think about using real sentences like this as they stand (even if you do need to teach the meaning of a new verb or two) – not least because some of the odder or unexpected pictures they conjure up might be more memorable.

Feedback and correction

In order to get better at grammar, students need more than input and practice. They also need to get lots of feedback on how well they are doing. Encouragement is important, of course, but it's also vital to give clear, truthful information about how well they use language. If a learner is constantly making a mistake (or could say things better than they are doing), it's little help if the teacher keeps saying only 'Good,' 'Well done,' 'Perfect' and so on.

We can distinguish some important ways of responding to errors.

1) Simply indicating that an error has been made (eg by raising your eyebrows or shaking your head) without correcting – in the hope of the learner – or a peer – being able to correct it themselves. The thinking processes involved in such self / peer correction may help long-term learning.

2) Indicating what the mistake is – or where it is (eg by repeating an incorrect word with questioning intonation) without correcting (again, to encourage students to think and correct themselves).

3) Giving the correction, partly or wholly yourself (eg by saying a corrected verb form) and getting the learner to complete it or repeat it.

There are many different ways of offering feedback or correction. Here is one way that some teachers have found very useful to help students who never use contractions.

Finger contractions

If your students keep saying 'I am not working' (ie quite deliberately and painfully decontracting, when you really want them to speak a more fluent, contracted form) try finger correction. This technique works a treat – but it needs to be introduced and used a few times on different occasions before its power and simplicity becomes clear.

Hold up one hand, showing the number of fingers for the number of words in the student's sentence (making sure that the resulting display of fingers isn't rude in some way in the local context!). Indicate that one finger represents *I*, one represents *am,* one represents *not* and one represents *working.* You can do this by pointing at one finger and saying 'I', then the next and saying 'am', then the next and saying 'not' (and so on). From your perspective, behind the fingers, the sentence will seem to go right to left! For students sitting in front of you, it'll read in the normal left to right order.

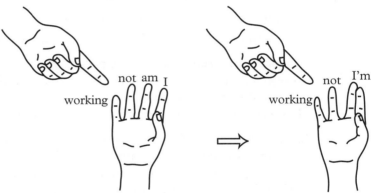

Once you have established that each finger represents a word, slowly and obviously push the first two fingers together and say 'I'm'. Repeat the action and words a few times. Get the student(s) to repeat the whole sentence.

In future classes, when students don't contract, use the same technique again. After a few times, you'll find that students quickly realise what the fingers mean even without you needing to give any instructions. This will have become a very quick and wordless way of reminding students that they need to contract the pronoun and auxiliary verb.

What are concept questions – and how can I use them?

It's easy enough to find out if students have learnt the form of a new language item – we can immediately see or hear if they say or write it wrongly. But finding out if they understand the meaning of something is much harder. Traditional teacher techniques such as asking *Do you understand?* are famously uninformative – because a student might say *yes* for various reasons (*I don't want to look stupid* or *I think I understand*). But there is a useful technique to check students' understanding – one really worth learning if you don't know it: asking concept questions.

Concept questions (CQs) are questions that you can ask students in order to check if they have understood the meaning of language items they are learning.

Well-made CQs check understanding by asking questions that:

- are simpler in form and complexity of meaning than the language item they are checking.
- can usually be answered without students needing to create long or complex answers.
- quickly reveal misunderstandings if students have trouble answering or give incorrect answers.
- help to consolidate correct understandings.
- allow all students to think and check for themselves if they understand.

CQs are often used as an integral part of presentations, especially when working on verb tenses, and especially for checking if students understand what time is referred to, but they are valuable for a number of other grammatical items. However, not everything can be easily or usefully concept checked.

In class, you can ask CQs to several students, listening to their answers and evaluating whether they have understood the meaning of the language item well or not, perhaps not confirming a student answer until you have heard from a number of them. While asking individual students, you also hope that all the other students in class are thinking through the question and preparing their own answers.

An example

In this book, I have included some concept questions for a number of grammatical items. These are ready-to-use in class – but please make sure you are clear how the entries work. Here is an example for comparatives:

- **Harry's taller than Bill.** Are Harry and Bill the same height? (*No*) One of them is 1.56 metres tall; one is 1.59 metres tall. Which one is 1.59 – Harry or Bill? (*Harry*) Make a sentence about Harry and Bill using *shorter.* (*Bill's shorter than Harry*)

The first sentence is in bold. This is an example sentence you read out to students. The concept questions to ask students (about that example sentence) then follow, with sample correct student answers in brackets.

How might this example be used in class?

1) You could use these CQs after first spending some time teaching the meaning of comparatives (from a coursebook, or using a board picture etc).

2) When you decide it is time to check if students have really understood the meaning (which could be either during the presentation or after it) say 'Listen.' Then read the starter sentence aloud (perhaps twice): 'Harry's taller than Bill.'

3) Then ask the first concept question, pause to allow all students a little thinking time, then nominate a student by name who answers the question correctly.

4) Acknowledge the answer by nodding (or saying 'thank you') but do not immediately say if the answer is correct or not until you have asked a few more students. Then ask the same question to one or more other students. This makes sure that it is not just one clever or quick student who has 'got it'. In fact, it is vital that to check a range of learner levels within class. You need to discover if the class as a whole has 'got it'.

5) After asking a few students, you can clearly confirm if the answers were actually accurate – or else correct or explain in the case of wrong answers.

6) Repeat steps 3–5 with other questions (NB some CQs include an additional contextualising sentence, eg *One of them is 1.56 metres tall.*) – and maybe even recycle some earlier questions randomly. You are aiming to see if students understand well enough to answer confidently and, perhaps, quickly.

What if students give wrong answers to concept questions?

If, at any stage, one or more students give a wrong answer to a CQ, it may be best to avoid launching straight into an explanation or correction.

When you ask CQs you may find yourself hoping for 'correct' answers – but remember that the exercise is essentially about collecting feedback. If there are wrong answers, it probably won't help to just tell them the correct answer. Wrong answers give you feedback that there is some teaching that still needs to be done to help clarify the problems!

'Make a sentence' challenge

The example CQs above include one additional technique – asking the students to make a new sentence. Note that this example is more focussed than saying 'Tell me any sentence using a comparative' which tends to lead to random and often silly, unnatural sentences. In contrast, the sentence asked for here (a) is clearly set within the context that has already been established (b) has a specific challenge to form a sentence for which the meaning is known. Little is left to chance; only a small number of sentences would answer the challenge.

Key grammatical terminology

Noun	The name of (or way of referring to) a person, thing, place, quality, concept, etc • **Countable** (or **unit**) **noun**: a noun that we can count *one book, two books, twenty sheep.* • **Uncountable** (or **mass**) **noun**: a noun that is thought of as a single mass that cannot be counted *rice, paper, air.* But we can count (a) subdivisions or containers – even if they are not stated *two grains of rice, five bags of rice, three teas, four sugars* (b) types *twenty cheeses.*
Noun phrase	A number of words that act as a noun and could be substituted by a pronoun. <u>*The man I met at the cafe*</u> *is going to phone me tonight.* The underlined words are a noun phrase which could be substituted by *he.* Strictly speaking, a noun is a one-word noun phrase!
Pronoun	A word that can replace a noun or noun phrase. • **Subject pronouns**: *I, you, he, she, it, we, they* • **Object pronouns**: *me, you, her, him, it, us, them* • **Possessive pronouns**: *mine, yours, his, hers, its, ours, theirs* • **Reflexive pronouns**: *myself, yourself, himself, herself, itself, oneself, ourselves, yourselves, themselves* • **Indefinite pronouns**: *somebody, anything, nobody,* etc • **Demonstrative pronouns**: *this, that, these, those* • **Question pronouns**: *who, which, what, whose, (whom), whoever, whichever, whatever* • **Relative pronouns**: *that, who, which, what,* **whom,** *whoever, whosoever, whomever, whomsoever, whatever*
Verb	Verbs describe actions, processes or states. They take different forms with regard to tense (present, past), aspect (progressive, perfect), person (first, second, third), number (singular, plural) and voice (active, passive).
Types of verb	• **Main verb** describes the action or state *play, kick, walk, wish, think.* • **Auxiliary verb** the 'helping' verb that goes together with a main verb to help make the tense or structure *am, was, have, did.* • **Modal verb** an auxiliary verb that adds a functional meaning to the main verb (advice, obligation, permission, etc) *you <u>can</u> play, we <u>must</u> decide, you <u>could</u> ask, they <u>should</u> leave.* Modal verbs don't have aspect and don't change for person. • **Action verb** (also called dynamic verb or active verb) describes actions or events *run, break, cook, notice.* • **State verb** (also called stative verb) describes an ongoing state or condition, *be, think, love.* State verbs are not usually used in progressive (*-ing*) tenses.

	• **Reflexive verb** has a reflexive pronoun. The subject and object of the verb are the same *I cut myself shaving.*
	• **Multi-word verb** a general term for phrasal verb, prepositional verb and phrasal-prepositional verb. It is made up of two or three words that act as if they were a single verb *get over, make do with, look after.*
	• **Intransitive verb** has a subject but no direct object ie whatever is being done is not being done <u>to</u> anyone or anything. *She walks for half an hour every morning.* (The walking happens but is not being done to something.) • **Transitive verb** has a subject and one (or more) objects. • A direct object is the person or thing that is directly affected by the action of the verb ie the verb is done <u>to</u> them. *He hit his boss.* (The action is done to the boss.) • In the sentence *She gave me some cash* the direct object is *some cash* – the thing immediately affected by the action of giving. *Me* is the 'indirect object' – it tells us who is receiving the direct object.
Verb phrase	A sequence of words (including the main verb, auxiliary verbs and / or particles) that act as a verb. In these sentences the underlined words are verb phrases: *<u>I'm going to swim.</u> Next June we <u>will have been living</u> here for ten years. She <u>ought to be able to guess</u> the answer.* Confusingly, there are different definitions of the term verb phrase but this seems to be the most widely accepted one.
	• **Base form** or **Bare infinitive** the basic form of the verb, without endings or *to*; *run, go, take, cook, wash, be, break, fly.* Typically column 1 (of 3) in a coursebook verb table. • **Present participle** the *-ing* form of a verb *running, going, taking, cooking, washing, being, breaking, flying.* Typically not listed in a coursebook verb table (but easy enough to make from column 1). The *gerund* has the same form – but refers to the noun: *<u>Swimming</u> is my favourite sport.* • **Past form** the form of a verb used in the past simple tense *ran, went, took, cooked, washed, was / were, went, broke, flew.* Typically column 2 (of 3) in a coursebook verb table. • **Past participle** the form of a verb used when making perfect tenses and passives *run, gone, taken, cooked, washed, been, broken, flown.* Typically column 3 (of 3) in a coursebook verb table.

Conditional	Conditionals express what happens if something else happens. Coursebooks often focus on: ● **First conditional** a real-world condition that is normal, possible or likely to be fulfilled *If I go to Kansas, I'll buy it for you.* ● **Second conditional** an imagined condition that is unlikely or impossible to be fulfilled *If I went to the moon, I'd buy it for you.* ● **Third conditional** a speculation about how past events might have been different *If I had gone to Kansas, I'd have bought it for you.* ● **Zero conditional** statements about truths, regular situations, rules, laws, natural phenomenon etc *If you heat ice, it melts.*
Adjective	A word which describes or tells us more about a noun *green, tall, bad.* ● **Comparative adjective** compares things *greener, taller, worse.* ● **Superlative adjective** states that something is most or least *greenest, tallest, worst.*
Adverb	A word which tells us more about a verb, adjective or adverb. Also something of a 'dustbin' class of grammar for all the awkward words we have trouble classifying. Although widely taught at lower levels, they may be classified under other headings eg time expressions. ● **Adverb of manner** tells us how something is done *slowly, well.* ● **Adverb of time** tells us when something happens *tomorrow, soon.* ● **Adverb of frequency** tells us how often something is done *usually, never.* ● **Adverb of place** tells us where something happens *outside, upstairs.* ● **Sentence adverb** used for modifying a whole clause or sentence, perhaps commenting on what is said *honestly, obviously.* ● **Adverbial** a number of words that act as an adverb. *She walked <u>with great difficulty</u>* ('with great difficulty' tells us *how* she walked).
Preposition	A word or words that help us understand the relationships between things in terms of place, movement, time or ideas. ● **Preposition of place** *above, against, across, at, behind, below, beneath, between, by, in, next to, on, on top of, outside, over, underneath, upon* ● **Preposition of movement** *across, along, around, between, over, past, through, to, under* ● **Preposition of time** *at, on, in, for, since* ● **Preposition showing relationship between ideas** *despite, except, owing to*

Collocation	Words that have a tendency to co-occur (ie be found together). For example, many nouns, verbs and adjectives have a strong link to a specific preposition. • **Noun + preposition** *love of, success in* • **Adjective + preposition** *interested in, scared of* • **Verb + preposition** *search for, argue about*
Determiner	A word that helps clarify what a noun refers to. This category includes: • **Article** *a / an, the* • **Quantifier** *some, all, few, each, any, no* • **Demonstrative** *these, that* • **Number** *seven, a hundred* • **Possessive adjective** *I, my, your, his, her, its, our, their*
Conjunction	A word that connects two words, clauses or sentences together. • **Coordinating conjunction** (*and, but, or, so, yet, for*) joins words, phrases and clauses together. • **Subordinating conjunction** (*because, although, if, since, as* etc) is used to open a new dependent clause and helps to show the relationship between the clauses. Conjunctions can work as part of a pair <u>neither</u> red <u>nor</u> white wine, <u>both</u> Jurgen <u>and</u> me.
Subject and object	• **Subject** the person or thing that does the action of the verb. • **Direct object** the person or thing the action of a verb is done to. • **Indirect object** the person or thing that receives or is affected by the direct object. *She gave him a karate chop to the neck. She* is the subject (because she did the action). *A karate chop* is the direct object (because it is the thing given). *Him* is the indirect object (because he was affected by the karate chop).

The sounds of British English

Vowels

A vowel is a voiced sound made without any closure or friction so that there is no restriction to the flow of air from the lungs.

/iː/as in _cheese_; /ɪ/ as in _hit_; /ʊ/ as in _hook_; /uː/ as in _shoe_; /e/ as in _head_; /ə/ as in _ago_; /ɜː/ as in _bird_; /ɔː/ as in _four_; /æ/ as in _bat_; /ʌ/ as in _cut_; /ɑː/ as in _farm_; /ɒ/ as in _hot_.

Diphthongs

A diphthong is the result of a glide from one vowel sound to another within a single syllable.

/ɪə/ as in _clear_; /eɪ/ as in _say_; /ʊə/ as in _pure_; /ɔɪ/ as in _boy_; /əʊ/ as in _no_; /eə/ as in _air_;/aɪ/ as in _high_; /aʊ/ as in _now_.

Consonants

In the production of a consonant sound, the air flow is restricted by closure or partial closure, which may result in friction. Consonants can be voiced or voiceless.

Consonant sounds you can recognise from the normal alphabet: /p/, /b/, /t/, /d/, /k/, /g/, /f/, /v/, /s/, /z/, /m/, /n/, /h/, /l/, /r/, /w/.

Consonant sounds that have special symbols: /tʃ/ as in _chips_;/dʒ/ as in _fudge_; /θ/as in _thin;_ /ð/ as in _these_; /ʃ/ as in _sheep_; /ʒ/ as in _vision_; /ŋ/ as in _sing_; /j/ as in _yellow_.

A voiced consonant is one made with the distinctive added 'buzzing' vibration made by the voice-box in your throat: compare _ssss_ (unvoiced) with _zzzz_ (voiced). Voiced consonants are: /b/, /d/, /g/, /z/, /v/, /m/, /n/, /l/, /r/, /w/, /ð/, /j/, /ʒ/, /dʒ/, /ŋ/.

A voiceless consonant is one made without the voice-box vibration. Unvoiced consonants are: /p/, /t/, /k/, /s/, /f/, /ʃ/, /tʃ/.

Contraction

A reduced, combined form of a sequence of two function words, represented by a spelling with an apostrophe: _do + not → don't; they + are → they're._

Uncontracted form

A possible contraction which is nevertheless pronounced and written as two separate words: _they are_ rather than _they're_.

Weak form

We pronounce many common (often short) words in a 'weak' manner. For example, for the article _a_ we usually say /ə/ rather than /eɪ/. We pronounce _for_ /fə/ rather than /fɔː/, and we pronounce _was_ /wəz/ rather than /wɒz/.

Strong form

When a word we normally pronounce with a weak form is said with its rarer full pronunciation, often for emphasis: _He WAS_ /wɒz/ _there this morning._

1 Singular and plural

Form

Singular	Plural	
an umbrella	*umbrellas*	add *-s*
a watch	*watches*	add *-es*
a dictionary	*dictionaries*	*-y* → *-ies*

Some common irregular plurals

tooth	*teeth*	*oo* → *ee*
man	*men*	change the vowel
mouse	*mice*	sound and spelling
knife	*knives*	*fe* → *ves*
potato	*potatoes*	*o* → *oes*
cactus	*cacti*	*us* → *i*
crisis	*crises*	*is* → *es*
sheep	*sheep*	no change
child	*children*	different ending
person	*people*	different word

Presentation

The farm

1) Draw a simple, small farm on the board (a house, a shed, a field). Check that students know what your drawing shows! Add in Federico, the farmer and a visitor, Isabella. Write a year from the past (2000) at the top of the board.

2) Mime to indicate that Federico is telling Isabella about his farm. Add items to the picture (a dog, a cow) and elicit sentences he's saying (*I've got a dog. I've got a pony. I've got a sheep. I've got a goose. I've got a field. I've got a tractor. I've got a child. She's got a mouse!*).

3) Erase the past year and write the current year. Explain that Federico has been very successful. Add new items to the picture and elicit the new sentences (*I've got three dogs. I've got 20 ponies. I've got 40 sheep. I've got ten geese. I've got three fields. I've got two tractors. I've got two children. They've got five mice!*). If you don't want to draw 20 ponies, just write the number next to the animal.

4) Write up the words you have used and focus on the different ways of making plurals.

5) Use separate pictures to introduce any regular or irregular plurals you wish to focus on that don't easily fit into the farm context (*dictionary → dictionaries; knife → knives*).

If you choose an alternative context, look for situations which, like a farm, allow you to bring in a wide number of different plurals (/s/, /z/, /ɪz/) and irregulars like *foot / feet, mouse / mice, sheep / sheep*.

Practice

If you are teaching at very low levels, you will need to adjust your classroom language to suit the level. Many of these ideas can be introduced by gesturing rather than giving instructions.

Counting

Bring a number of different toys, objects and pictures into the room – including more than one of many items. Place the items on different students' desks. Set little tasks and ask questions around the class such as 'Count the objects on your desk,' 'What have you got on your desk?' 'What has Pedro got on his desk?' Add more objects and mix items around to give further practice.

In my home

Tell the students 'In my home we have three bedrooms, two TVs, twelve chairs, seven clocks and two dogs. Now tell me about some numbers in your home.'

Variation

'Tell me about some numbers in this school / classroom.'

Quick choice quiz

A lively game (if you have a suitable room with sufficient floor space for movement) is a quiz in which students have to vote physically to show which answer they think is correct. On four large pieces of paper write the following in big, clear letters:

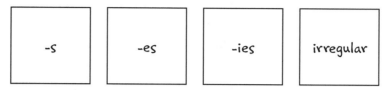

Ask all the students to come into an open space – the area at the front of class is often best. Place the four signs at different places on the walls of the room around the open space. The signs should not be too close to each other – but they should all be easily accessible for all students (no chairs or tables in the way).

Choose some singular nouns. When you say a noun, every student must decide individually how the plural is made – and move to stand in front of the correct sign. Students are allowed to change their minds when they see where other students are going! When everyone has made their final decision and stopped moving, announce the real answer – and award one point (a token) to each student in the right place. Gather everyone back in the middle again – and go on to the next noun.

Concept questions

- **The woman is in the room.** How many people are in the room? (*One*) Is there one person in the room? (*Yes*)

- **The women are in the room.** How many people are in the room? (*We don't know. More than one*) Is there one person in the room? (*No – more than one*)

Repeat the same idea with *child | children, person | people* etc.

Pronunciation

Regular -s / -es

Regular plural endings can have three different pronunciations.

- We use /s/ after unvoiced sounds   *shops* /ʃɒps/, *hats* /hæts/, *seats* /siːts/

- We use /z/ after voiced sounds   *shoes* /ʃuːz/, *dogs* /dɒgz/, *seas* /siːz/

- We use /ɪz/ after the sounds /tʃ/, /dʒ/, /s/, /ʃ/ and /z/   *watches* /wɒtʃɪz/, *boxes* /bɒksɪz/, *places* /pleɪsɪz/

Watch out for these problems . . .

- **Students avoid plurals:** ✗ *I saw three student in the corridor.*

- **Students add an -s to words that are already in the plural:** ✗ *womens* ✗ *peoples* Of course, students will have heard words such as *women's* and *people's* and may have wrongly assumed them to be plurals rather than possessives.

- **Students use singular verbs with plural nouns (or vice versa):** ✗ *The children was . . .*

- **Students mispronounce the /s/ ending as /ɪs/:** *cooks* /kʊkɪs/, *walks*/wɔːkɪs/. Help them by pointing out that words like *cooks* and *walks* are one syllable but they are using two.

Teaching tip: memory practice

Some methodology books may give the impression that the only worthwhile classroom activities are ones which involve realistic communication between students. However, while communicative practice is essential, there are some things that are probably best learnt by fairly traditional techniques involving simple input, memorisation, reminders and recall. Plurals is one area where some memory practice (helping students to know what the plural of *child* is) can be helpful – alongside chances to actually use language with lots of singulars and plurals in realistic tasks, dialogues and situations.

2 Countable and uncountable nouns

Form

Countable

We can count things that we think of as individual items, such as *cars, fish, sheep, people, cans, shoes, bottles, books, toes, clouds, grains of rice, bottles of milk, plates of food.*

Uncountable

We can't count things that we think of as a single mass rather than as individual items. These include:

Some foods	*rice, wheat, flour, mashed potato, jam, chocolate*
Liquids	*juice, water, wine, glue, milk, coffee*
Materials / substances	*steel, paper, silicon, air, coal*
Qualities	*honesty, cowardice, trust, patience, kindness*
Emotions and feelings	*love, anger, warmth, relief*
Abstract concepts	*information, fun, help, music, news, death, noise*
Generalised activities	*travel, hitchhiking, work, sport, support*

Some nouns can be countable (when we think of them as individual items) or uncountable (when we think of them as a mass). These include *space, food, glass, cake, sauce, sugar, light, Coke, bread, curry, class, yoghurt, lamb, wine, business, perfume, football, glue, cheese, deodorant, juice, paint, salad, whisky.*

Sometimes, the countable and uncountable nouns have very different meanings.

paper (U) = the material; *a paper* (C) = a newspaper

wood (U) = the material; *a wood* (C) = a small area filled with trees

Presentation

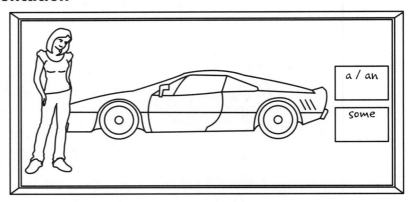

Supermarket trip

1) Draw two columns on the board and add two separate boxes at the top. Write 'a / an' in one box and 'some' in the other.

2) Draw Anna standing next to her car. Explain that she is going to the supermarket.

3) Say 'She wants to buy some rice' – but instead of reading the word *some* tap the table, ring a bell or substitute a humming noise. Point at the two boxes on the board and ask students what word they think should go in the space. When they agree, draw an icon representing rice into the *some* column.

4) Continue saying more sentences about Anna – each time substituting your noise instead of the word *a / an* or *some* (*Anna wants to buy a newspaper. She needs to get some petrol. She's got some money in her purse. In the shop she asks for some information about special offers*).

5) Ask students if they know why you sometimes use *a / an* and sometimes *some*. Explain briefly about countable and uncountables. In English it is possible to count some nouns. Others cannot be counted. We think of uncountable nouns as a mass of stuff or as a single concept that cannot be divided up into separate items / units. Uncountable nouns have no plural form. You always use a singular verb with uncountable nouns (*There is some snow on the upper slopes*).

6) Erase the lists of items from the board. Check if students can correctly recall the sentences about Anna.

Practice

Countable and uncountable nouns are often introduced alongside a focus on *some* and *any*. In fact, it's hard to introduce uncountable nouns without using these.

Other situations

In a similar way to the supermarket trip presentation above, other situations can be used to inspire sentences using specific countable / uncountable nouns – for example:

Student coming to study in UK

A student is preparing to come and study in the UK for six months. What do they need to think about (example uncountable nouns: *accommodation, family, food, news*)?

Bold explorer

Tell the story of Carla the explorer who is going to the South Pole (example uncountable nouns: *luggage, clothes, ice, courage*).

Tired househusband

A man at home struggles to do the housework (example uncountable nouns: *polish, washing-up liquid, air freshener, patience*).

Countable or uncountable?

Write the names of about 20–30 different items on the board, including singular and plural countable nouns as well as uncountables (*hat, clock, rice, orange juice, coat, air, pop song, sunshine, father, happiness, phone*). Draw two large boxes on the board labelled 'countable' and 'uncountable'. Invite students to work in groups to decide which words go into which box. After some time, invite students to come up one by one and write words into boxes. Other students can agree or disagree with their decisions.

Can you count . . . ?

An even simpler teaching and checking activity is to ask questions to see if students can distinguish between nouns that can be counted and those which can't. Ask them 'Can you count rain?' (*No*) 'Can you count teeth?' (*Yes*) 'Can you count information?' (*No*).

You can use simple icons to contrast some countable / uncountable things – for example, draw two lakes and ask 'Can you count lakes?' (*Yes*) 'Can you count water?' (*No*).

Picture differences

On one sheet of paper (sheet A) draw sketches of about fifteen countable and uncountable food items (apples, loose rice, milk in a bottle, potatoes). On another sheet of paper (sheet B) draw many of the same items – but with a few variations (flour instead of apples). Make photocopies of sheet A and B. In class, make pairs, A and B. Give sheet A to As and sheet B to Bs. Students should keep their sheets secret from each other and by describing what is on their card, attempt to find out which items they both have (*I've got some rice. I've got an egg. I've got some apples. So have I* etc).

I went to the market

If your students need a reminder, start by writing the alphabet on the board. Say 'I went to the market and I bought an apple.' Invite a student to repeat your sentence and add a new purchase beginning with the next letter of the alphabet

(*I went to the market and I bought an apple and some bread*). Continue with other students trying to remember the list so far and then correctly adding their own item. As the list gets longer it will get harder and students will make more errors (which results in more laughter). Make sure you encourage students to use a mix of both countable and uncountable nouns.

→ Unit 9 *Some* and *any*

Concept questions

- **Hiro wants to buy three books.** What does Hiro want to buy? (*Some books*) Do we know how many? (*Yes, three*) Can we count books? (*Yes*)

- **Sara wants to buy some rice.** What does Sara want to buy? (*Some rice*) Do we know how much? (*No, we can't say*) Can we count rice? (*No*)

Watch out for these problems . . .

- **Students confuse countable / uncountable with plurals:** Countability is a separate issue from whether a word has a different plural or not. For example, *sheep* is the same word for singular and plural – but sheep are countable. Be careful. Some uncountable nouns have an *s* ending and may look as if they are a plural countable noun eg *tennis, news, politics, chess, physics, snakes and ladders, linguistics, athletics, measles, billiards, aerobics, economics, diabetes.*

- **Other languages may count items that are uncountable in English:** Here are some words that often cause problems: *homework, information, news, money, advice, furniture, hair, knowledge, research, pasta, equipment, weather.* We can count *suitcases* but not *luggage* or *baggage, rooms* but not *accommodation, cars* but not *traffic.*

- **Students use *a / an* with uncountable nouns:** ✗ *I saw an interesting news tonight.*

- **Students use a plural countable noun when they should use an uncountable noun:** ✗ *You have beautiful hairs.*

- **Students use uncountable nouns as if they can have plurals:** ✗ *Have you got any informations about the concert?* ✗ *I forgot my homeworks.* ✗ *Can you give me some advices?*

3 Containers, quantities and pieces

Form

Containers + uncountable noun

a bottle of lemonade
a cup of coffee
a glass of orange juice
a can of beer
a packet of cheese
a plate of food
a box of printer paper
a bag of rice
a tube of toothpaste
a carton of milk
a case of wine
a tank of petrol
a jar of jam
a pack of soap powder
a spoonful of sugar

These containers can also contain countable nouns eg *a packet of cigarettes*.

Container + *-ful*

a tankful of petrol = a tank of petrol

This emphasises that the container is completely filled.

Parts or weights + uncountable noun

a piece of cheese
a slice of bread
a grain of sand
a drop of water
a lump of meat
a pile of rubbish
a scrap of paper
a sheet of paper
a bit of French
two kilos of beef

Presentation

bottle	tootpaste	a box of matches
bar	wine	a bottle of cheese
packet	cheese	
case	rice	
tube	tea	
teaspoon	shampoo	
can	ketchup	
glass	chocolate	
piece		
cup		
slice		
jug		
cube		

Counting uncountable nouns

1) Make a set of word cards, each with a container or quantity (*bottle, bar, packet, case, tube, teaspoon, can, glass, piece, cup, slice, jug, cube*). Make a second set of cards of uncountable foodstuffs (*toothpaste, wine, cheese, rice, tea, shampoo, ketchup, chocolate*).

2) Draw three columns on the board. Stick up the container cards on the left in a list going down the board. Stick up the food cards in the middle column to make a separate list.

3) Ask the class if they can see any from the left hand list that go with an item from the middle. When someone makes a suggestion, move the cards together in the right-hand column. Elicit the phrase *a bottle of cheese* and ask the class if they think it is a good combination or not. If you and the class agree that it is wrong, replace the cards to their original lists. If you agree that it is good (*a box of matches*), leave them there.

4) Continue to check more combinations.

5) Hand out a photocopy of similar lists. Students should work in pairs to match up as many foodstuffs with a possible container / quantity, without using any container / quantity more than once.

This task might be a useful preparation for the Shopping lists activity.

Practice

In my cupboard

Make pairs, A and B. Students start sentences for their partner to complete. A says 'In my cupboard I've got a bottle of . . .' B has to reply with a suitable item (*orange juice*). B then says a new sentence with a new container or quantity 'In my cupboard I've got two kilos of . . .' and A has to complete the sentence suitably (*sugar*). Partners continue to challenge each other in this way.

Shopping lists

Shopping lists are always good for this language point. Students can prepare for a party, first discussing and agreeing what they will need (*We must get eight bottles of lemonade*), then writing a shopping list, then role-playing going to the shop (*Two kilos of flour, please*). Perhaps it should be a small village shop to allow for personal service; there isn't much conversation practice of countable and uncountable nouns in supermarkets!

Shopping phonecalls

Prepare a set of flashcards showing foods and other shopping items. Give five or six to each student. They then have to 'phone' a partner and ask them to get some shopping for them (*I need half a kilo of chicken, a box of chocolates, three bottles of sunflower oil . . .*). The listener should write down the list. When all students have given their lists, ask students to hide the new lists they wrote down and 'phone' a third student with the list (which this time they will have to remember).

What do I need?

Ask students to write a list of ingredients for a dish they know (*pizza*) but leave out the quantities. They then meet up with other students and orally explain how to make the dish, adding in quantities (*Take half a kilo of flour. You need ten slices of pepperoni. Add a pinch of salt*).

Concept questions

- **Fernando drank two glasses of apple juice.** What did Fernando drink? (*Some apple juice*) Do we know how much? (*Yes, two glasses*)

- **Faisal ate two slices of bread.** What did Faisal eat? (*Bread*) Do we know how much? (*Yes – two slices*) Did he eat the whole loaf? (*No*)

Teaching tip: countable <u>and</u> uncountable

Students are often puzzled to hear people say things like *Could I have two milks?* They have learnt that *milk* is uncountable and believe that this must be wrong. But it isn't. Like many foodstuffs, milk can be both countable and uncountable. The same is true of many other nouns although food and drink are probably the most common.

When it is countable we are usually counting the container or quantity (*two glasses of milk*, or *two packets of milk* or *two litres of milk*) – but we are not actually saying the container or quantity. The container is implied rather than stated. *I bought two teas* means *I bought two cups of tea*. Ordering *two teas* is only possible if the listener will unambiguously understand what container is referred to.

Similarly, you can count collections, pieces, parts, bits, quantities or weights of things (*ten packs of paper, five bundles of wheat, two kilos of rice, three pieces of information, four news items, a few drops of whisky, a bit of good luck, a little rain, enough pasta*).

Countable	Uncountable
Two coffees, please. (= two cups of coffee)	*We need some more coffee.* (= ground coffee beans)
I found three grey hairs. (= three separate items)	*Your hair feels so soft.* (= all the hair on your head)
The potatoes need to cook for 20 minutes. (= the actual potatoes you will use)	*Finish with a layer of mashed potato and grated cheese.* (= a quantity of cooked potato)
Do you want a chocolate? (= one single separate sweet made from chocolate)	*Would you like a piece of chocolate?* (= the sweet brown substance)

4 Subject and object pronouns

Form

Pronouns refer to nouns and noun phrases. We use them to avoid repetition.

The machine's broken. It isn't working properly.

Subject pronouns

The subject of a sentence is the person or thing that does the action of a verb.

> *__I__ woke up at about 3 am.*
> *__You__ need a dictionary.*
> *__He's__ / __She's__ a member of the team.*
> *__It__ isn't working.*
> *__We__ lived in the room above the shop.*
> *__They__ offered her a job.*

Object pronouns

Direct objects

The direct object of a sentence is the person or thing that the action of a verb is done to. It often comes directly after the verb.

> *She hit __me__.*
> *I heard __you__.*
> *I called __him__ / __her__.*
> *We bought __it__.*
> *They saw __us__.*
> *Let's ask __them__.*

Indirect objects

The indirect object of a sentence is a person or thing that the action of the verb is done for or given to – but not the person or thing.

> *Bring __me__ the towel.*
> *I gave __you__ the book.*
> *She bought __him__ an MP3 player.*
> *I showed __her__ the rules.*
> *We threw __it__ a biscuit.*
> *They sang __us__ a new song.*
> *Give __them__ a chance.*

For example, *Bring me a towel*. What did he bring? *A towel* – this is the direct object. Who did he bring it to for? *Me* – this is the indirect object.

Presentation

Handing objects round the room

Direct objects

1) Hand something such as a pen to student A. Give an instruction using a direct object (*drop it, throw it, hide it, punch it*). Do a little mime to help the student follow the instruction if they have a problem.

2) Continue with other students, giving more instructions using *it*.

3) Continue giving other instructions with personal direct object pronouns (*push him, call them, help her*).

4) After a while, encourage students to start giving instructions to each other.

Indirect objects

In the same lesson . . . or maybe a later one, start to add in some instructions with indirect object pronouns.

1) Hand something such as a pen to student A. Indicate student B and give an instruction to student A using an indirect object (*Give her the pen*). Student A must follow the instruction and hand the pen on to Student B.

2) Model a new instruction (*Throw him the pen*) and encourage student A to say it to student B. B then throws the pen to C.

3) Slowly add in more instructions. Use the verbs *give / throw / show* and the pronouns *me / him / her / us / them*. When possible, encourage students to use the instructions themselves without prompts.

4) Extend with other instructions using new nouns for students to follow (*Show her your book*).

Jobs and roles

Subject pronouns

1) Hand flashcards showing various locations (*a hospital, Moscow*) to different students. Explain that the pictures show their lives.

2) Use the flashcards to help elicit or model simple sentences about students (*You're a doctor. They live in Moscow*). Get students to repeat sentences.

3) Go round again, but get the sentences wrong (*She's a nurse. They live in Vienna*). Encourage students to correct you (*No, she's a doctor*).

Practice

Subject pronouns

These are typically introduced very early on in a Beginner's course when students don't have much other vocabulary or grammar. Learning the meaning and use is often integrated into teaching other things like meeting and greeting people (*Hello. I'm Anna. She's Claudia*).

Reference

At higher levels, the biggest problems tend to come with recognising what a particular pronoun (especially *it*) refers to in a complex sentence or text. To tackle this, get students to go through a text, drawing boxes around all instances of a pronoun (every *it*) – and then drawing lines back to the word or words that the pronoun refers to.

Concept questions

Subject pronouns

Write these notes on the board.

	a doctor	a good cook	a good singer
Adam	✓	✓	✗
Andrea	✓	✗	✓
Me	✗	✗	✗

- **True or False:** She's a doctor. (*True*) He's a good cook. (*True*) He's a good singer. (*False*) They're both good cooks. (*False*) They're both doctors. (*True*) I'm a doctor. (*False*)

- **Finish these sentences:** She . . . He . . . They . . . You (= the teacher) . . .

Object pronouns

Write these notes on the board.

	cooking a meal for Andrea's parents	writing an email to Andrea's grandfather
Adam	✓	✗
Andrea	✗	✓
Me	✗	✗

- **True or False:** They are cooking a meal. (*False*) He's cooking a meal for his parents. (*False*) He's cooking a meal for her parents. (*True*) He's cooking a meal for them. (*True*) She's writing to his grandfather. (*False*) She's writing to her grandfather. (*True*) She's writing to them. (*False*) I'm cooking a meal. (*False*)

- **Finish these sentences:** She . . . He . . . They . . . You (= the teacher) . . .

Meaning and use

Backward reference

Pronouns generally refer backwards to things that have already been mentioned.

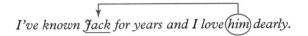

I've known Jack for years and I love him dearly.

The word *him* refers back to *Jack*. We don't need to repeat the name.

Forward reference

Pronouns can also (more rarely) refer forwards to things that have not yet been mentioned.

He was standing with his back to her. 'The name's Tony' he whispered, without turning round.

He refers forward to *Tony*, which has not been given before this point.

Pronouns are only useful if it is absolutely clear what they refer to. In the following short text, the referent (ie the person or thing that is referred to) of the pronoun is not entirely clear. Is it the snake, the bedcover or the arm?

The snake slid over the bedcover and curled round his arm. I carefully lifted it up.

Other uses

Apart from the standard meanings, pronouns have some other important uses.

- The pronoun *it* acts as an impersonal empty pronoun.
  It's raining
  Isn't it a pity?
  I really like it in this café.

  It would be hard to say precisely what the *it* referred to in these sentences.

- We can also use the pronouns *you* and *they* to talk about unknown people or people in general.
  You never see men at these conferences any more.
  They knocked it down in 1998.

- We can use the pronouns *they* / *them* / *their* etc with a singular meaning instead of *he* or *she* when we don't know the sex or want to avoid any sexual bias.
  When the interviewee comes in, give them a copy of the test.

- We can use the pronoun *one* to make things sound more impersonal, to generalise an idea or to refer to people in general. This may be to avoid saying things that might seem personally embarrassing but this use of *one* is a little old-fashioned.
One doesn't like to complain.

- Using *one* also makes a document more formal, by removing personal references. This use is unlikely to be encountered by beginners.

Watch out for these problems . . .

- **Students use a male pronoun for a female (and vice versa):** ✗ *I saw Eva and he told me* . . . Idea: Place two silhouette images on the classroom wall – a male and a female figure. When students use the wrong pronoun, simply point at the wrong image, look worried and wait for them to correct themselves!

- **Students use a pronoun when it isn't needed:** ✗ *Mr Salmon he gave it to me.* ✗ *The picture it is very nice.* Idea: use finger correction to show the sentence with the number of words they said – then 'throw away' (ie remove the finger representing wrong word) the unnecessary word.

Teaching tip: spotting the direct object

Be careful – if there are two objects, you need to take care that students identify them correctly. In the sentence *She gives the man some cash* the direct object is *some cash* – the thing immediately affected by the action of giving. Confirm this by asking 'What does she give – some cash or the man?' This means that *the man* is an indirect object as it tells us who is receiving the direct object.

5 Reflexive pronouns

Form

Reflexive pronouns

I cried ***myself*** *to sleep.*
I rewired the house ***myself***.
*Make **yourself** comfortable!*
He repaired the window ***himself***.
My brother does all the paperwork ***himself***.
She locked ***herself*** in.
The door opens by ***itself***.
*We'll do it **ourselves**.*
*Help **yourselves** to more wine.*
*I hope the **children** behave **themselves**.*
The twins are only three, but they can already dress ***themselves***.

These refer back to the subject of the verb. Reflexive pronouns can be used when the subject and the object of a sentence are the same (*I cried myself to sleep*) or to emphasise the subject (*We ate all the cake ourselves*).

We use *each other* or *one another* to say that each person does something to the other or others.
They talk to each other on the phone every night.

After *feel, lie down, concentrate, sit (down), hurry, wash, shave, dress* we do not normally use reflexive pronouns unless we want to emphasise that the action is surprising or unexpected.
Our youngest boy can already dress himself.

Presentation

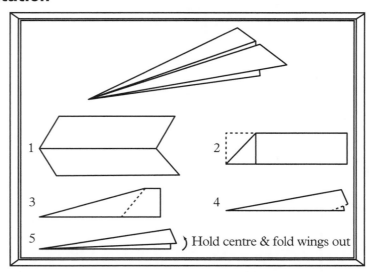

1
2
3
4
5   ) Hold centre & fold wings out

I did it myself!

1) Show students how to make a very simple origami model (a paper dart).

2) When all have made it, hold yours up, look proud, and say 'I made it myself.' Get students to hold up their models and 'boast' to their neighbour.

3) Get everyone to hold up their models and model / drill 'We made them ourselves.' Get half the class to hold up their models while the other half points and says 'They made them themselves.'

4) Get students to practise questions and responses with lively intonation. Model each sentence yourself first, get students to repeat and then try saying it in pairs as question and answer.

    Did Georgi do your homework?

    No. I did it myself!

    Did the other class arrange the chairs like this?

    No. We did it ourselves!

5) Get students to think of and ask new questions themselves.

Practice

This item is quite hard to practise communicatively. It may be best to focus on traditional pen and paper exercises, finding the correct pronoun to fill in the gap in a sentence.

Planning decisions

Ask students to imagine that they are working on a big project (changing to a different classroom). Brainstorm a list of about ten tasks that need to be done (*move all the books*). Decide who will do which task, aiming to use reflexive pronouns as much as possible (*We'll put the posters up ourselves. The teachers can move their stationery themselves. Mary will design the floor plan by herself. You can do that yourself!*).

Concept questions

- **Sharzia did the homework herself.** Who did the homework? (*Sharzia*) Did she do it with someone else? (*No*) Did she have any help? (*No*)

- **Darina asked Miguel some questions and then repaired the car herself.** Who repaired the car? (*Darina*) Did Miguel repair the car? (*No*) Did Darina repair the car? (*Yes*) Did she do it with someone else? (*No*)

Meaning and use

We use reflexive pronouns when the subject and the object are the same.
I cleaned myself up and got ready for dinner.
In this sentence *I* and *myself* are the same person.

Using a reflexive pronoun can dramatically change the meaning.
He tried to kill him describes an attempted murder.
He tried to kill himself describes an attempted suicide.

In imperatives, the subject *you* is understood but not said.
Phone him yourself.

We can use many verbs that take an object with a reflexive pronoun.
He cut himself shaving.

If we want to emphasise that someone does something without help, we use a reflexive pronoun at the end of a clause.
I decorated the whole room myself!

We use *by* + reflexive pronoun to mean on your own or alone.
Since his wife died, he's been living by himself.

We use reciprocal pronouns to say that each person did the same action to another or others.

Jacques and Frida painted pictures of each other means that Jacques painted a picture of Frida and Frida painted a picture of Jacques.

Jacques and Frida painted pictures of themselves means that Jacques painted a picture of Jacques and Frida painted a picture of Frida (or they both painted pictures of both of them).

Watch out for these problems . . .

- **Students omit a reflexive pronoun when it is needed:** ✗ *I was starting to enjoy* (myself). ✗ *The two men introduced* (themselves) *and shook hands.*

- **Students use reflexive pronouns after *feel*:** ✗ *I feel myself very comfortable at the moment.* ✗ *They felt themselves quite ill.*

- **Students use *themselves* when they mean *each other*:** ✗ *People were hugging and kissing themselves.* Idea: use concept questions to help here, ask 'Who did they kiss?' For a funny demonstration, use mime to show the difference in meaning between hugging yourself and hugging someone else.

6 Possessives

Form

my birthday	*His birthday is after **mine**.*
your dog	*Is that dog **yours**?*
his CDs	*Those CDs are **his**.*
her money	*The money is all **hers**.*
its legs	*–*
our laptop	*You can borrow **ours**.*
their friends	*They introduced some friends of **theirs**.*

My, your, his, her, its, our, their come before a noun phrase.
my best answer

Mine, yours, his, hers, ours, theirs replace a noun phrase and answer the question
Whose?
your dog → yours

- Its (NO apostrophe) = possessive
  The United States and its European allies.

- It's (WITH apostrophe) = *it + is / it + has*
  It's time to get aboard.

Presentation

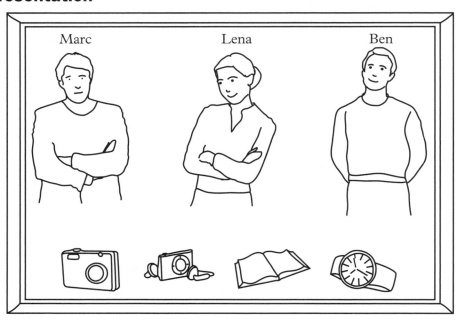

People's presents

1) Place some cartoon pictures of three people on the board (Marc, Lena and Ben). Explain that it is Marc's birthday. Add a picture of a shop with some desirable items (an iPod, a camera, a book, a watch).

2) Tell a story about Lena buying an item, giving it to Marc, who didn't like it (!) and who later gave it secretly to Ben. As you tell the story, keep pausing and interrupting yourself (as if you are forgetting the story) to ask lots of little questions (*Is it his? Is it hers now? Whose is it?*).

3) Once you have got as much mileage as you can from the first item, repeat the idea a few more times with new stories about other possessions (*Lena buys a book for Ben*). Get students to ask questions like yours.

4) At the end recap all the items by taking all the item pictures off the board and asking students whose they are.

Practice

Circle practice

Ask everyone to stand in one large circle (or, if your class is too large, keep them at their desks). Give each student a flashcard or small object (*a pen*). Model 'This is my pen'. Pass it on to Student A who looks at you and says 'This is your pen' and then holds up their item and adds 'This is my phone'. They then pass on the items to Student B (not someone standing or sitting next to them) who says (to you) 'This is your pen', (to Student A) 'This is your phone' and then adds 'This is my dictionary' – and so on. Continue adding more items.

More complex circle practice

You can fairly easily vary or extend the simple drills in the idea above to make use of more complex sentences and possessive pronouns as well as adjectives (*Is this your pen? No, it's his. Give it to him. Is this your pen? Yes, it's mine. Don't give it to her; give it to me*). For maximum confusion, you could also have different objects being passed simultaneously!

Variation

Teach a number of different verbs (*pass, throw, give*) and some adverbs (*slowly, angrily, secretly*) and get students using them to pass on the items in this manner (passing secretly, throwing quickly).

Flashcards: famous people, possessions and relations

Find colour pictures of celebrities, pop groups or politicians who your students will know and their possessions, parents, friends. Cut the pictures up so that possessions are separated from the people. Students work to match pictures and describe the relationships (*This is hers. That's theirs*).

The museum

Collect one or two personal possessions (calculators, gum, pencils, cough sweets) from each student. Students should not see what others contribute. Make a museum on a large table at the front of the room by displaying the items in an interesting way. Write up useful sentences on the board – or model them if you want to (*I think that's hers. Is that his? Is that your pen? Yes, that's mine. I know that's hers*). Invite pairs of students to visit the museum. They can walk around and look at objects and discuss the objects. Encourage them to guess which items belong to which students. Tell them they can point or gesture but cannot use anyone's name when talking.

When students have had some discussion in pairs, lead a whole class discussion still using the pronouns to agree which objects belong to which students.

Variation: Lost property

As a variation on the museum, have students come up to the 'Lost Property office' to see if they can find their lost items. Students could perhaps script and / or role play conversations to practise the language (*I think that's my umbrella. That's not yours. It's mine. Is that yours? No, mine's yellow*).

Story building

Bring in lots of small real objects or pictures of them and pictures of some people. Distribute a number of pictures / objects to each group. Tell groups to prepare a short story called 'The Argument' involving the people and objects – using at least ten possessive pronouns and ten possessives. If they find it tough, suggest that they include dialogue in their story.

Concept questions

- **This is hers.** Is this my book? (*No*) Is this your book? (*No*) Is this his book? (*No*) Is this her book? (*Yes*) Who does the book belong to? (*her / Maria*) Is it correct English to say 'This is her book'? (*Yes*) How can I say the same thing in only three words? (*This is hers*)

Adapt this model for *This is mine, This is ours* etc.

Meaning and use

Belonging

Possessives often tell us who things belong to.
That's my diary.
Ours is the third house on the left.

Relationship

They can also be used to indicate a relationship.
Isn't that your Uncle Gunter?
That friend of yours – what's her name again?

We use possessive adjective + *own* to emphasise that something is related to or belongs to someone.
I do my own cooking and food shopping.
This letter is in her own handwriting.

Connection

Sometimes they indicate other types of connection or association (knowing something, having responsibility, doing an action, special occasions etc).
Does he know his ABC?
His birthday is two days after mine.

Time of life

We use possessives to talk about people's general age.
Our guide was a quiet man in his forties.
The couple who booked into the hotel were both in their twenties.

Body parts

We use possessives to talk about parts of the body.
Her lips met mine.

Comparisons

We can use possessives to compare possessions, qualities, attributes etc between different people.
There was barely a scratch on his car, but mine was wrecked.
Your system is completely different from ours.

Watch out for these problems . . .

- **Students use object pronouns instead of possessives:** ✗ *I want you to meet a friend of me* (= mine). ✗ *This great country of us* (= ours).

- **Students use the wrong gender or number:** ✗ *'Is this Mary's book?' 'Yes, It's his.'* ✗ This may be more common for students whose languages have the possessive agreeing with the object not the subject, or for languages that do not distinguish between male and female in pronouns.

7 *This, that, these, those*

Form

Before a noun

We use *this* and *that* with singular countable nouns and uncountable nouns.
this evidence
that cup

We use *these* and *those* with plural nouns.
these cars

If we use *some, any, enough, more, many, few* etc we must also use *of*.
Some of these children . . .
For most of this month . . .

As pronouns

We can also use *this, that, these* and *those* on their own, as pronouns substituting for a noun or noun phrase.
Aargh! Not this again!
That was a real surprise.

Presentation

That's my scarf!

1) Ask students to lend you one or more objects each. Place these visibly in different locations around the room. Some things should be close to individuals or groups of students and some further away.

2) Get a student who has their own object on their desk in front of them to say 'This is my calculator.'

3) Nominate a new student in another part of the room. This student should recap what the previous student said (changing the demonstrative if necessary) and then adding to it (*That's Dmitri's calculator and that's my scarf*). Students will need to change *this / that / these / those* as appropriate to reflect distance and singular / plural.

4) The game continues with a growing list as students try to recall every item that came before them.

Practice

Open spot the difference

Find two pictures of the kind that are commonly used for pair information gap exercises ie two similar but slightly different pictures. Place picture A on the board (blow it up much larger if possible – or project it on a computer, interactive whiteboard or OHP). Give a copy of picture B to each pair of students. Their aim is to discuss the differences, then write down them in a list, using *this, that, these, those* (*This table has five apples on it but that one only has four. These people are wearing hats but those aren't*). Students will need to use *this* and *these* for the picture closest to them and *that* and *those* are for the more distant board picture.

Tell me

Say to students 'Tell me about the things on your desk' (*This is my notebook and this is my favourite pen*) and 'Tell me about the things on the desk over there' (*That's Helen's mobile phone*).

Describing

Tell students 'Come over to the window. Tell me what you can see' (*Those people are sitting on the wall*).

Concept questions

● **That's my pen.** Am I holding my pen when I say this? (*No*) Is my pen very near me? (*No*) Is my pen in another town? (*No*) Is my pen in another room? (*No*) Can I see my pen? (*Yes*) Can I point at my pen? (*Yes*)

● **These are my friends.** Do I have one friend or more than one friend? (*More than one*) Are my friends in another building? (*No*) Are my friends in the same room? (*Yes*) Are my friends on the other side of the room? (*Probably not*) Are my friends standing or sitting near me? (*Yes*) Do I move my hand when I say the sentence? (*Probably, indicating the people near me*)

Meaning and use

This and *that*

We use *this* and *that* to refer to singular items.

These and *those*

We use *these* and *those* to refer to plural items.

Identifying

We use *this / that / these / those* when we want to identify which person or thing we are talking about. They usually identify things visible to the speaker which could be pointed at or indicated. We often do this when showing pictures or objects or when introducing people to each other. We choose which word to use depending on how near to us we think an item is. We use *this* and *these* when something is considered close. We use *that* and *those* when something is further away. This is a subjective choice rather than a factual measurement and either form can often be used without substantially changing the meaning.

This is the total price of your holiday.
That's me, in the bottom right-hand corner of the picture.
These are my friends Claudia and Jack.
Those must be our seats over there.

Reference within text conversation

We can use demonstratives to refer backwards or forwards to things that are mentioned in other parts of a conversation or text.

'What about transport?' 'That's all arranged.' (*that* refers back to the earlier-mentioned *transport*)

'Right – this is what we are going to do.' (*this* refers forward to the speaker's plan)

Watch out for these problems . . .

* **Students use *this / that / these / those* without verb *be*: ✗** *This my friend.* ✗ *Those books mine.*

* **Students have trouble clearly forming distinct pronunciations of *this* and *these*: ✗** *this* /ði:s/ (instead of / ðɪs /) ✗ *these* /ði:s/ (instead of / ði:z /)

Teaching tip: telephoning

When students do telephone role plays, remind them that *this* is normally used to refer to the speaker's end of a conversation and *that* to the other end. For example, a speaker can confirm who they are with *Yes, this is Lito speaking* and ask someone on the other end *Who's that?* or *Is that Maya?*

Later in the conversation, the comment *That's a really good idea* would usually be about something said at the other end of the conversation, whereas, *This is a really good idea* is more likely to refer to something the speaker says.

8 Articles

Presentation

> Every day I walk to ____ town centre. There are always lots of ____
> people there. I usually buy ____ ice cream, ____ packet of ____ sweets
> and ____ newspaper. Then I go to ____ beach and sit on ____ bench
> reading ____ newspaper. Sometimes I look up at ____ clouds in ____ sky
> and watch ____ seagulls flying over ____ sea.

Board gap-fill

1) Prepare a short text containing *a, an, the* and Ø (zero article), see above for an example. Construct the text carefully so that the article usage exemplifies the points you wish to teach.

2) Write up the first sentence on the board, substituting any articles with gaps.

3) Ask students to think about which words are missing on their own and then comparing in pairs. Discuss and confirm answers. Elicit or state reasons for article choice as issues come up.

4) Continue with the rest of the sentences from the text and get more answers.

Answers

Every day I walk to <u>the</u> town centre. There are always lots of <u>Ø</u> people there. I usually buy <u>an</u> ice cream, <u>a</u> packet of <u>Ø</u> sweets and <u>a</u> newspaper. Then I go to <u>the</u> beach and sit on <u>a</u> bench reading <u>the</u> newspaper. Sometimes I look up at <u>the</u> clouds in <u>the</u> sky and watch <u>the</u> seagulls flying over <u>the</u> sea.

Practice

The classic practice activity for articles has always been the humble gap-fill text (made either on a computer or with correction fluid). Students then work individually or in pairs to fill in the missing articles.

Text reordering

Many teachers will be familiar with tasks in which students are asked to reorder a text that has had its sentences mixed up – but may have been unsure as to exactly what the point of such tasks might be. Well, one really sound purpose is to help students focus on the use of articles to shape a conversation or text.

Write up the following sentences on the board (or photocopy them) and ask students working in pairs to find the best order. Tell them that sentence (a) is in the correct position at the beginning of the story.

a) I had an accident this morning in the kitchen.
b) Suddenly, I dropped the book on the floor.

c) And the egg went all over my trousers.
d) I was eating an egg and reading a book.
e) When I picked up the book I knocked the food off the table.

When they have got the correct answer (a), (d), (b), (e), (c) ask them to reflect a little on how they worked it out. Obviously, the logic of the story is an important factor – but draw their attention to the importance of articles by asking questions like 'Could B be sentence 2?' (*No*) 'Why not?' (*It uses the book, not a book* – ie the book has already been mentioned earlier in the story.)

New → Known

This activity focuses on the key use of articles to introduce new information or to refer to known information. Check that students know the word *lion* (maybe show a photo of one). Write the following frame on the board and tell students that it is a conversation in a zoo. Ask pairs to fill every gap with either *lions*, *a lion* or *the lion*.

Dad: *Hey, look. There's . . .*
Child: *Where? I can't see it. Where did . . . go?*
Mum: *It's over there by the tree – with three other . . .*

When you check answers at the end, discuss why each form is used. Get students to practise acting the dialogue, encouraging them to use lively intonation.

Afterwards, challenge students to write a new short dialogue set in a new location that uses all the nouns in one of these sets of words: *eggs, an egg, the egg* or *books, a book, the book*.

Concept questions

- **The baby wants a toy.** What does the baby want? (*A toy*) Does it matter which one I give it? (*No, any toy is fine*)

- **The baby wants the toy.** What does the baby want? (*The toy*) Does it matter which one I give it? (*Yes, it wants a specific one – possibly one that it can see now*)

Meaning and use

There are two key reasons why a speaker or writer may choose indefinite or definite articles.

General or specific?

The indefinite articles *a* and *an* show that we are talking about things in a general way – without saying precisely which people or items we are referring to (to a whole type, class, species or variety of something).
It stands out in a crowd (ie any crowd – not a specific crowd).
You need a dictionary (ie any dictionary, not a specific one).
Children must be accompanied by an adult (ie any adult, not a specific one).

The definite article *the* shows that we are talking about something specific – when we know precisely who or what is being referred to (an individual person or thing).

The food smells wonderful (ie not food in general, but the particular food we can smell now).

New focus or known focus?

Most students will be able to understand the difference between *Give me a biscuit* and *Give me the biscuit*. The first sentence means that you can pass me any biscuit – it doesn't matter which. The second means that I want a specific biscuit, and both listener and speaker know exactly which one is referred to.

But, what about this short text?
Round the corner was a ruined barn – and, next to the building, a tall oak. The tree had lost all its leaves. The brown and orange litter covered the flowerbeds.

Would your students know . . .

• why is it *a* ruined barn but *the* building?

• why is it *a* tall oak but *the* tree?

In many conversations and text, there will be different articles used at different points in the text. You will find that there is often a movement as shown in this diagram:

First mention		Further mentions
New		Known
General	→	Specific
A / an		*The*

The first time a new noun is mentioned, it will often be introduced using an indefinite article *a ruined barn / a tall oak*. After that, the noun or a synonym for that noun is already known by the reader / listener – ie it is no longer a general thing – but a specific, known example of the thing – and further references will use definite articles *the building / the tree*.

The may be used on a first mention if it is a unique or shared piece of knowledge (*the park, the Moon, the nine o'clock news*) or if the writer / speaker can assume that the listener / speaker will be able to imagine or create the idea of something without it being explicitly introduced *round the corner, the ceiling*.

Other guidelines

Sadly, the two important points above don't explain everything as the rules for use of articles are extremely complex. Here are further guidelines:
We can use *a / an* . . .

1) to mean *one*.
a thousand years
The team earned over a million pounds.

2) with singular countable nouns to talk about a whole species or type of a thing.
A dog needs regular exercise.

3) for actions where the noun carries more meaning than the verb.
Did you have a shave this morning?

4) after the verbs *be, seem, become,* (and others) to give more information (job, status, character, behaviour) about a person or thing.
He's a liar and a cheat.
Her husband seemed a very pleasant man.
Easton became an American citizen.

We can use *the* with . . .

1) known things: things that are local and / or very familiar to most people in the context and do not need to be introduced or explained.
Suddenly all the lights went out.
I looked up at the ceiling.

2) unique things: ie there is only one.
the back of my neck
the main entrance

3) groups: nationalities, groups of people, family names.
the police
the Welsh
the Browns

4) some geographical terms: with some mountain ranges, island groups, areas of water, regions and places with *republic, kingdom, states* etc in the name.
the Alps   *the Middle East*
the Channel Islands   *the United Kingdom*
the Pacific Ocean

5) ordinal numbers, dates and periods of time.
the seventh
the first of January
people who were born in the nineties

6) nouns made from adjectives to describe a whole class or type.
the poor
the well-informed
the unemployed

We can use zero article with . . .

1) proper nouns ie the names of people, places, products, languages, publications, events etc.
Ø Kiran   *Ø Swahili*
Ø New York   *Ø Christmas*
Ø Suzuki   *Ø Hamlet*

2) uncountable nouns referring to something in general.
   I like Ø chocolate.

3) plural countable nouns referring to things in general.
   Chinua loves Ø fast cars.

4) entire groups or classes of things.
   How do Ø whales communicate?

5) some places we go to for a purpose: school, hospital, church, home etc.
   He switched off the television and went to Ø bed (ie to sleep).
   She doesn't go to Ø church (ie to attend mass) *very often.* Compare *She's gone to visit **the church*** (as a tourist).

6) names of school and college subjects, sports, meals, medical conditions, illnesses, ways of travelling.

Ø physics	*Ø tonsillitis*
Ø volleyball	*by Ø bus*
Ø breakfast	

7) sometimes with times and periods of time.
   in Ø summer
   at Ø midnight
   But times are also possible with *the.*
   She wouldn't need her swimsuit again until the summer.
   We don't watch TV in the daytime.

This

In contemporary UK English the word *this* is sometimes used as a sort of indefinite article in personal stories and jokes.

I met this really cool girl last night (= a really cool girl). The meaning is slightly different from *a.* The word *this* seems to have the effect of identifying the person as an important character in the story.

Pronunciation

Initial sounds

- Some words written with *h* are pronounced with an initial vowel sound (and therefore take *an* rather than *a*).
  an hour
  Some are arguable.
  a / an historic town

- Some words that start with *u* or *eu* are pronounced with an initial /j/ sound (as if written *yu*) and therefore take *a* rather than *an*.
  a university
  a Euro

- Names of some alphabet letters (*f, h, l, m, n, r, s,* and *x*) are pronounced with an initial vowel sound and go with *an*.
  Friday starts with an 'f.'

Stress

Articles are usually unstressed and pronounced with weak forms.

- *a* /ə/

- *an* /ən/

- *the* /ðə/ or before vowel sounds /ði/ NB there is typically an intrusive /j/ sound *the apple* /ðɪ j æpəl/.

You would normally only use strong forms when you want to emphasise something. Stressing *a* or *an* (possibly with /eɪ/ or /æn/pronunciation) would normally emphasise that it was only one item you were referring to, not many.
No, not 'turkeys' I said 'a̲ turkey' – just one.

Stressing *the* (probably with /ðiː/ pronunciation) would emphasise the uniqueness or importance or high quality of the thing referred to.
No, he's not a boss. He's t̲h̲e̲ boss.

Don't model and teach the strong forms /eɪ/, /æn/ and /ðiː/ as the standard, correct pronunciations. These pronunciations are rare but mis-teaching of them is a key reason why students' language often sounds unnatural and odd. So for example, if you teach nouns like *fire* or *orange* – make sure you model /ə faɪə/ and /ən ɒrɪndʒ/ rather than /eɪ faɪə/and /æn ɒrɪndʒ/.

Watch out for these problems . . .

- **Students omit articles:** ✗ *Give me pen.* ✗ *Have you done homework?*

- **Students omit *a / an* with jobs:** ✗ *Peter is businessman.* ✗ *I want to be history teacher.*

- **Students use *a / an* with plurals:** ✗ *What a beautiful photos!*

Teaching tip: create your own exercises?

The main problem with creating your own exercises is that you can unwittingly put in questions that are very problematic to answer or explain yourself. Articles, while being necessary right down to beginner level, also have some truly advanced-level complexities. When asked why a certain answer is *the* not *an*, I have found myself on more than one occasion saying 'It just is' or words to that effect. When teaching lower levels, if you are unsure of your linguistic ground, this is one language area where you may do best to stick to published sources for exercises. If you do decide to make your own, watch out for the complexities!

9 *Some* and *any*

Form

We use *some* for affirmatives.
I've got some bad news.

We use *not . . . any* for negatives.
I haven't got any qualifications.

We can use *some* or *any* for questions.
Have you got any money on you?
Did she give you some money?

Affirmative

	uncountable	singular countable	plural countable
some	paper *I've got some paper.*	✗⋆	books *I've got some books.*
any	✗	✗⋆	✗

Question

	uncountable	singular countable	plural countable
some	paper *Have you got some paper?*	✗	books *Have you got some books?*
any	paper *Have you got any paper?*	✗⋆	books *Have you got any books?*

Negative

	uncountable	singular countable	plural countable
some	✗	✗	✗
any	paper *I haven't got any paper.*	✗⋆	books *I haven't got any books.*

⋆not usually . . . but see notes on pages 54–55

Presentation

Shopping list

1) Find pictures of a number of countable and uncountable items (eggs, wine, batteries, pens, rice).

2) Write 'My shopping list' on the board. Add the first picture (eggs) to your board and say 'I haven't got any eggs. I need to get some eggs.' Get students to repeat.

3) Continue with more countable items (*I haven't got any potatoes. I need to get some potatoes*) and then introduce some uncountable ones (*I haven't got any rice. I need to get some rice*).

4) On the board present a short dialogue in which two characters prepare a shopping list (*We need some flour and some eggs. Have we got any lemonade? Yes. I think there's some in the cupboard*). Get students to repeat sentences and practise the conversation. You could continue the conversation with an exchange in a shop (*Have you got any rice? Yes. There's some on that shelf*).

5) Continue using Shopping trip (below) as a follow-on practice.

Practice

Shopping trip

Photocopy pictures of about 20–25 different shopping items (cheese, beer, matches, carrots, tea). Write a list of all items on the board. Divide the class in half. One half will make 'shops'. Give each student in this half a random selection of four or five of the pictures. Ask the other half, the 'shoppers', to choose five items they want to buy from the board and make a short shopping list. The shoppers now go to one of the shops and ask questions (*Have you got any eggs?* or *Do you have any eggs?*). If the shop has the item, they give the picture to the shopper. After a while, swap groups and repeat the activity.

Variation: real items

Use real items rather than pictures (a small bag of rice, beans, small portion packets of ketchup).

Celebrity TV chef

Students work in groups. Tell them that they are the production team for a TV food programme. One student in each group will be the 'cook' and another student will be the TV presenter (who will ask questions to the cook). The cook will tell the TV audience the recipe for an unusual dish. The team must prepare the show's script. (Presenter: *Do you need any flour? Any eggs?* Cook: *Well. You need some white flour – about two kilos. But you don't need any eggs*).

Allow time for writing – and then get the students to perform their TV show for others to enjoy.

Spot the difference

Find a set of two spot the difference pictures that include a large number of separate countable and uncountable items (the contents of a fridge, some shop shelves or a table with things on it). Students work in pairs A and B. Without looking at their partner's picture they ask questions to find out what their partner has that they don't – and vice versa. You might want to require that students keep to *Have you got any . . .?* questions.

Meaning and use

Some in affirmative sentences

Some refers to a part which is less than the whole or a quantity which is less than all. We typically use *some* when we are not sure of a quantity, when we are asking to find out a quantity or when we are being vague, maybe because we do not consider the quantity important.

Some in questions

You can use *some* in questions, especially . . .

- if you anticipate a positive response.
  Did you get some nice Christmas presents this year?
  Did she give you some money?

- when you are offering something and want to encourage the other person to accept.
  Would you like some dessert?

- when you are requesting something for yourself or that you want to be done.
  Can you get some milk?
  Can we have some quiet please?

Some with countable nouns

With countable nouns, you can think of *some* as the plural of *a / an* – meaning an imprecise small number.

I can see a tree. → *I can see some trees.*

We can sometimes use *some* with a singular countable noun (NB this is colloquial usage).
Some fool drove into the back of my car.

Any in negative sentences

In negative sentences *any* refers to a zero quantity / amount. Sentences can often be rewritten as an affirmative sentence with *no*.
There weren't any complaints = There were no complaints.

Any in questions

In questions *any* is used to ask whether an item exists or doesn't exist. It is typically used to ask if either a small amount or nothing exists.
Are there any biscuits left? = Are there still a small number of biscuits left or none?
There may be more uncertainty than when asking a question with *some* – and there may be an expectation that the response will state that there are few or none.

Any in affirmative sentences

We can use *any* with countable nouns (singular or plural) in affirmative sentences to say that it is not important which specific individual item is referred to.
Pick any design you want – they're all the same price.
Press any key.
She can talk on any subject.

We can also use *any* in affirmative sentences, especially those with conditional / if meanings.
If there is any delay . . .

There would be no difference in meaning if you changed the word *any* for *some*.
Any often comes after *if* + verbs: *have, want, need, require, get, hear, see, be* etc.
If you need any help, just ask.

Some and *any* as pronouns

Some and *any* can behave as pronouns, substituting for a noun.
Won't you have some?
There wasn't any.

Pronunciation

Compare:

I'll bring you some grapes.	/səm greɪps/	When *some* is used as a determiner before a noun, the noun is typically stressed, while *some* has a weak pronunciation.
I'll bring you some grapes.	/sʌm greɪps/	*Some* may be stressed if the quantity is the most important thing in the message (some but not all the grapes).
I'll bring you some.	/sʌm/	When *some* is used as a pronoun, it is likely to have a strong pronunciation.

Any does not have different weak and strong forms, but can still be stressed or unstressed.

Can I be of any use?	/enɪ ˈjuːs/	When *any* is used as a determiner before a noun, the noun is typically stressed, while *any* is unstressed.
Can I be of any use?	/ˈenɪ juːs/	*Any* may be stressed when the questioner has already had or is expecting a negative answer (*I expect that I will not be of use*).
Did you have any?	/hæv enɪ/	When *any* is used as a pronoun, it may be stressed or unstressed.

Watch out for these problems . . .

- **Students avoid *some* or *any* when they might be more natural:** *I'd like cheese, please. Have you got ideas?*

- **Students use *some* or *any* with an article:** ✗ *I want some the paper.*

- **Students use *any* in requests:** ✗ *Could you pass me any salt, please?* Students make this error because they think 'use any in questions.'

- **Students wrongly assume that *any* is always negative:** For example, students may not see a difference between the sentences *Any student can go there* and *No student can go there*.

Teaching tip: misleading exercises

Many exercises on *some* / *any* ask students to choose between the two items by filling in the correct word in a gap-fill sentence. Unfortunately, in quite a few exercises, many supposedly wrong answers are actually possible.

What's the answer to this student task?
Have you got ___ bread?

As a teacher, you need to decide what you would do with a question like this. If a student filled in the gap with *some*, would you mark it wrong? It is often 'wrong' in coursebook exercises and tests. What explanation would you give? At lower levels, is it better to give students some handy, simple guidelines (use *any* for questions) – rather than tell them everything? Would it confuse students to tell them all the exceptions? This tricky balance between only-partly true simplicity and potentially mind-bogglingly complex truth is a tightrope that the practical language teacher is walking all the time.

10 *Much, many, a lot of, lots of, plenty of, a great deal of*

Form

Many

- We use *many* with plural countable nouns.

- We usually use *many* in questions and negative sentences.
  How many brothers have you got?
  I haven't got many CDs.

- We can also use *many* in affirmative sentences, especially as the subject.
  Many families come back to our hotel year after year.

Much

- We use *much* with uncountable nouns in questions and negative sentences.
  How much money do you have in your purse?
  You haven't got much coffee in your cup.

- We also use it after *so* in affirmative sentences.
  There was so much food.

A lot of, lots of, plenty of, a great deal of

- We use *a lot of* + uncountable noun + singular verb.
  A lot of their money is in property.

- We use *a lot of* + plural countable noun + plural verb.
  A lot of cars are parked on the pavement.

- Students should generally avoid *much* and *many* in affirmative sentences and should use *a lot of*, *lots of*, *plenty of* (more informal) or *a great deal of* (more formal) instead.

Presentation

The rich boyfriend

1) Draw a picture of Sophia and her friend Nadine. Explain that both women have just met new boyfriends. Sophia's boyfriend is a millionaire and Nadine is asking her lots of questions about him.

2) Use picture cues to elicit questions that Sophia is asking (*How many houses has he got? How much money does he have? How many cars has he got? How many friends has he got?*). Get students to repeat the questions.

3) Use picture cues to elicit answers to the questions (*He's got two large houses. He's got lots of money. He's got three expensive cars. He hasn't got any friends*).

4) Get students to practise the questions and answers in open and closed pairs.

5) Explain that Nadine is now asking Sophia about her (much poorer) boyfriend. Elicit Sophia's answers to the same questions (*He's only got one house. He hasn't got much money. He's got a lot of friends*).

Concept questions

- **Jin has got plenty of maize.** Has he got a small quantity or a large quantity? (*A large quantity*) Has he got lots of maize? (*Yes*) Has he got a great deal of maize? (*Yes*) Has he got more than enough maize? (*Yes*) Can I say 'He has much maize'? (*No*) Why not? (*Because maize is uncountable*)

Practice

Simple sorting

Basic sorting tasks are useful for work in the area of countable and uncountable nouns and quantifiers. Draw three columns on the board. In the left hand column place word cards with different countable and uncountable items (*bottles, juice, birthday cards, heaters, heat, gas, suitcases, rice, hair*). At the top of the second column write 'How much . . . has he got?' At the top of the third column write 'How many . . . has she got?' Invite students (either individually, in groups or as a whole class) to come up and place cards from the left-hand column into the correct column.

Watch out for this problem . . .

- **Students use *much* in affirmative sentences:** ✗ *I have much cheese.* ✗ *I spent much money this afternoon.* Offer practice by getting students to transform negative sentences with *much* and *many* to positives with *a lot of* etc. *I didn't spend much money.* → *I spent a lot of money.*

11 *Few* and *a few*; *little* and *a little*

Compare:

| 1 | (a) *There's little hope of recovery.* | Sentence (a) is very pessimistic. |
| | (b) *There is a little hope of recovery.* | Sentence (b) has some optimism. |

| 2 | (c) *There is little time to prepare for the exams.* | Sentence (c) suggests that it is almost too late. |
| | (d) *There is a little time to prepare for the exams.* | Sentence (d) suggests that we still have some time. |

A few / a little

Both mean small amount or quantity and have a positive connotation.
I've got a few contacts = although it is a small number, I do have some.

We use *a few* + plural countable noun, *a little* + uncountable noun.

These items are often taught at Elementary levels.

Few / little

When we use *few / little* the meaning is similar to *not many* or *not much*.

We use *few* + plural countable noun, *little* + uncountable noun.

Both have a negative connotation that suggests a very small, perhaps insufficient, number or quantity.
I've got few contacts = I have a very small number of contacts (perhaps not enough).

Both can have a positive meaning. If the noun itself is a negative concept eg *difficulties, headaches, obstacles, disputes, complaints, problems* etc, having few of them may be good.
We get very few complaints of racial discrimination.

These items are often not taught until Intermediate levels.

Presentation

The strange planet

1) Draw a rocket landing on an alien planet – then add an explorer coming out of the spaceship and looking around. Elicit from the students what the explorer is doing.

2) Draw a geographical feature (a few lakes) and elicit what the astronauts are saying to their mission control (*There are a few lakes*).

3) Introduce other pictures to elicit further sentences (*There is a little oxygen. There are a few green aliens. There are a few large mountains. There is a little snow on the mountains*).

4) Finally get students to recap the whole description to each other.

Concept questions

- **He saw a few policemen.** Did he see some policemen? (*Yes*) Did he see a large number of policemen? (*No*) Did he see only one policeman? (*No*) How many did he see? (*A small number – maybe three or four*) Exactly three or four? (*We don't know exactly how many*)

- **He saw few policemen.** Use the same questions as above – with the same answers – but add: Did he see as many policemen as he expected? (*No*)

We can use the same concept questions to contrast *few* and *a few*. Note that all the answers are the same except for the last one.

12 Other quantifiers

Form

We use these before nouns in noun phrases and as pronouns substituting for nouns.

Have we got enough money?
I've had enough.
'Are there any problems?' 'None'
All enquiries should be put in writing.

Quantifiers are used instead of an article. We cannot say ✗ *I wanted some the cake* (but when a quantifier is followed by *of*, we often need to use *the*, *these* or another determiner or pronoun).

Some quantifiers . . .

- can only be used with plural countable nouns: *few of, a couple of, both of* etc.

- cannot be used with plural countable nouns: *much of, little of, the whole of, large amounts of, a bit of* etc.

- cannot be used with singular countable nouns: *some, plenty of, masses of, several of, a number of, a couple of, both of, each of, none of.*

- are not usually used in affirmative sentences: *much, many.*

- are not typically used in negatives or questions: ✗ *Wasn't there no paper?* ✗ *Weren't there no books?*

- sound more formal: *a great deal of, a quantity of* etc.

- sound more informal: *a bit of, masses of, heaps of, loads of* etc.

→ Unit 9 *Some* and *any*
→ Unit 10 *Much, many, a lot of, lots of, plenty of, a great deal of*
→ Unit 11 *Few* and *a few; little* and *a little*

Presentation

The restaurant kitchen

1) Find a suitable picture with many different quantities of different things (a restaurant kitchen with *lots of flour, a few potatoes, several carrots*). Show the picture on the board.

2) Point at one of the items (*flour*) and ask students a question about the quantity (*How much flour is there?*). If students use numbers in their answer (*about ten kilos*) ask them if they can think of a way of describing the quantity without using any numbers. Elicit or model a suitable answer (*There's a lot of flour*).

3) Continue eliciting ways of describing the quantities of other items, introducing as many different ways of quantifying as you wish to.

4) Recap by getting students to describe the picture to each other in pairs.

Practice

Describe the differences

Select a pair of spot the difference pictures containing quantities of different things. The quantities should differ between picture A and B. For example, a park with lots of ducks / no ducks, a few children / lots of children, a great deal of litter / no litter etc. Make pairs A and B. Hand picture A to As and B to Bs. Challenge students to work on their own and to make a list of what they can see in their own picture, using as many different ways of quantifying as possible. When they are ready they should describe to their partner what they can see in their own picture – and note as many differences as they can.

Plenty or none?

Get students to prepare a set of (non-embarrassing) statements, some true, some false, about how much / many they have of certain things in their bag, pockets, or at home (*We have plenty of rice at home. There are no paper clips in my bag*). When lists are ready, students can read statements to each other. Partners guess which are true or false.

Shopping

Quantifiers naturally lend themselves to practice via shopping situations. For example, try getting students to prepare general shopping lists, shopping lists for a particular meal, lists in preparation for a party or big event such as a wedding.

Concept questions

You will need to use different concept questions for each item. These are just examples.

- **Angela has a couple of cats at home.** Does Angela own cats? (*Yes*) Does she have lots? (*No*) How many cats does she have? (*Two*) Does she have more than two? (*No*) Exactly two – not more or fewer? (*Yes – exactly two*)

- **We haven't got a great deal of rice in the cupboard.** Is there some rice in the cupboard? (*Yes*) Is there a lot? (*No*) Is there a small amount? (*Yes*)

Meaning and use

The most precise way to refer to a quantity is to use a number.
three new employees

Quantifiers are other words (or phrases) that tell us how much or how many of something there is (or isn't) – usually with less precision than a number. The table below summarises the main ones.

Meanings	Quantifiers
complete quantities	*all (of), the whole of*
large quantities	*lots of, a lot of, a great deal of, large amounts of*
more than a small number	*several (of), a number of*
a quantity more than sufficient	*plenty of*
a quantity sufficient for a purpose	*enough*
two	*a couple of, both of, each of*
a small quantity	*a few (of), few (of), a little (of), little (of), a bit of*
absence / zero quantity	*no, none of*
(in questions) unknown, unspecified quantities	*much, many, any*

Watch out for these problems . . .

- **Students mismatch quantifiers with countable / uncountable nouns:** ✗ *I need to borrow a few money.* ✗ *How much points did you win?*

- **Meaning errors:** these can be hard to spot as sentences may seem grammatically well-formed but be used inappropriately for a specific situation. Particular problems may occur with: *enough, plenty, few / a few, little / a little, all / the whole.* Make sure you use concept questions thoroughly to check.

13 Adjective order

Form

When used together, adjectives tend to come in a certain order.
her large, blue eyes not ✗ *her blue, large eyes*

Personal opinions	Before	General qualities				Before	Type				
		size	physical	age	shape		colour	origin	material	purpose	
beautiful		*large*	*heavy*	*old*	*square*		*red*	*English*	*wooden*	*garden*	*chairs*

We generally put:

- qualities before colour before type.
  pretty, red, ceramic tiles

- size before shape.
  a *small, square garden*

- personal opinion before fact.
  a *beautiful, deep red sunset*

- bigger general overview picture before specific focussed individual details.
  a *famous Italian painter*

- These are only guidelines not rules and variation is often possible.
  yellow, diamond-shaped signs
  a *tall, attractive blonde*

Presentation

I bought this   book.

Adding adjectives

1) Write up 'I bought this . . . book' (leaving a long space where the dots are). Ask students for suggestions of an adjective that could go in the space. Choose one and write it in the middle of the gap (*I bought this interesting book*).

2) Now ask for another adjective from students (*old*) and then ask them to decide where they would put it – before or after *interesting* (*I bought this interesting old book*). Elicit a third adjective and again agree on where to place it. Clarify any guidelines as you go.

3) Repeat the activity a few times with new sentences (*She bought a / an . . . dress* or *It was a / an . . . building*).

Practice

Card order

Make small groups of between three and five students. Prepare a set of about 20 cards with different adjectives for each group (*delicious, large, Thai, friendly, square*). On the board write up a short sentence with a gap where the adjective(s) should be (*I saw a . . . cat last night*). The groups should try to use one, two, three or more of their adjective cards to fill in the gap. Tell them that they will get one point for each adjective that you agree is suitable and well-used. But also warn them that they will get zero if the adjectives seem to be in an unlikely order! In this way, students will have to balance the hope of getting lots of points for a long sequence of adjectives with the risk of losing it all if the order is incorrect. After some working time, get a suggestion from one group, write it up and collect opinions as to whether the sentence is good and possible. Do the same with other groups' ideas.

Adverts

Bring in about ten interesting or unusual objects from your home or find pictures on the Internet or in catalogues. Tell the class that you want to sell your items on an Internet website and need their help in describing them. Get students to work in groups, passing objects from group to group. Each group should produce a phrase to describe each object (*a long, red, hand-knitted woollen scarf*).

Teaching tip: too complicated?

The adjective order guidelines are listed here because you need to be able to check them in answer to questions. But the truth is that students find them hard to make use of. There are some kinds of grammar rules and guidelines which are just too complicated to apply on the spur of the moment as you are writing or speaking a sentence. I think the reality here, as I suspect with much grammar, is that students learn this simply by being exposed to language and internally, subconsciously, working out what to do, rather than by applying guidelines. So, don't worry if your students can't produce this immediately. This could be one language area where it's enough to raise their awareness.

Also remember, that it is actually very rare to have more than two adjectives together. Yes, even three is quite rare! However for fun, we can construct a highly unlikely noun phrase that makes use of lots of adjectives (*That wonderful, huge, solid, old, round, red, French, wooden dressing table*).

14 Comparatives

Form

<table>
<tr><td colspan="5">Common sentence pattern:</td></tr>
<tr><td>Someone /
Something</td><td>verb
(in correct tense)</td><td>(much)
(far)</td><td>comparative
than</td><td>something
else or clause</td></tr>
</table>

Regular (short words)

adjective + -*er*:
Ben is taller than Isaac.

- We add -*r* to adjectives ending in -*e*.
  fine → finer, late → later, safe → safer

- We double the final consonant and add -*er* to adjectives ending in vowel + consonant in a single syllable word.
  big → bigger, hot → hotter, fit → fitter

- We change -*y* to *i* and add -*er* to two-syllable adjectives ending in -*y*.
  brainy → brainier, noisy → noisier, windy → windier

Regular (longer words)

more / less + adjective:
Travelling by plane is more expensive than travelling by train.

- We can use either -*er* or *more / less* with some regular comparative adjectives.
  tastier / more tasty, simpler / more simple

- We can use either -*er* or *more / less* with some adjectives with negative prefixes.
  He was unkinder to her / He was more unkind to her.

Irregular

good	*better*
bad	*worse*
far	*farther / further*
well (= in good health)	*better*

Than introduces the thing the subject is being compared with.
This is older than that.
Beethoven's Ninth is much longer than his other symphonies.
The new machine is far more efficient than the old one.

Presentation

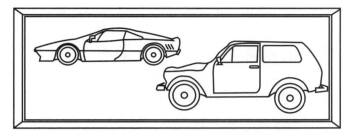

Cars

1) Bring in two contrasting toy cars or display pictures on the board. Name the types (*This is a Lada / This is a Ferrari*). Line them up on the table. Explain that their owners are arguing with each other about whose car is better.

2) Ask which one the students think is better. Use the discussion to elicit some comparisons using adjectives such as *faster, more economical, less luxurious, older, less comfortable* (*The Ferrari is faster than the Lada*). Elicit some sentences the owners might say (*My car's more expensive than yours*).

Cars do seem to be particularly productive for inspiring a range of good comparisons!

Practice

Quick drawings

Draw two simple items on the board (a large building and a small building). Ask students to tell you about one of the items. Some of the things can be visible and some imagined (*It's bigger. It's more expensive. It's less popular. It's emptier*).

Cities

Think about Moscow and New York (or any two contrasting towns the students know). Ask students 'Are they similar?' (*No*) 'OK – tell me some differences.'

Table

Write up some numerical information in a table form (two tourist sites: how many visitors, size, distance from the capital, entrance cost). Invite students to make comparisons.

Real objects

Bring in a number of similar but contrasting real items: different toiletries (perfumes, soaps, deodorants) or different gadgets (iPad®, mobile phone, PDA, calculator). Elicit and drill comparisons (*Shampoo is more expensive than soap*).

Flashcards

Use pictures of famous people or famous places instead of real objects.

Personal comparisons

Say to students 'Tell me a food / song / film that you like. Now tell me one you don't like. Compare them'.

My family

Tell students 'Think of a person in your family. Find ten ways that you are different from them' (*He's older than me*).

Boasting party

Students imagine that they are at a party of very rich people. Students mingle and meet up in pairs. Each person must make a statement – and the other should make a boast that he / she has something better / bigger (A: *My house has twenty rooms.* B: *Only twenty? My house is much bigger than that!*).

Joined-up comparisons

Write the names of 10–15 different but related items randomly around the board (animals: bears, rabbits, ants, ducks, snakes, mice, tigers). Ask a student to come to the board and draw a line connecting two of these. Elicit a good comparison between the two things (*Tigers are more ferocious than ants*). Repeat the game again and again with new pairs of items.

Variation

Students are not allowed to re-use an adjective that another student has used.

Concept questions

- **The Suzuki is much cheaper than the Rolls Royce.** Which car has a very high price? (*The Rolls Royce*) Which car has a low price? (*The Suzuki*) One car costs £30,000 pounds. One car costs £12,000. Which car costs £12,000? (*The Suzuki*) I have £15,000. Which car can I buy? (*The Suzuki*) Why? (*It's cheaper.*) Make a sentence about the cars using *expensive*. (*The Rolls Royce is (much) more expensive than the Suzuki*)

- **Our new classroom is worse than the old one.** Is the new classroom good? (*No*) Which do I prefer – the new one or the old one? (*The old one*) Why? (*It was better*) Make a sentence about the classrooms using *better* (*The old classroom was better than the new one*).

Meaning and use

We use comparatives to compare things (nouns or noun phrases) to say how one thing is different from another, or has more or less of a feature or quality than another thing.

Comparisons may be with the same thing at different times – ie we are saying that there is a change in something over a period of time.

Grammar books and coursebooks often say that comparatives are used when <u>two</u> things are being compared and that superlatives are used when more than two things are being compared – but this is not strictly true.

The leopard is faster than the gazelle and the zebra.
This milkshake's tastier than all the other drinks in the world.

→ **Unit 15 Superlatives**

More advanced points

Quantities

We can add quantities before comparative adjectives.
This is ten times better than the old one.

Verb + comparative

We can use comparative adjectives after some verbs (*become, appear, seem,* etc).
It looks bigger.

Comparative + *and* + comparative

This shows a change over time.
The night became colder and colder.

More and more + adjective

This shows change over time (this is an interesting example of *more* used with a one-syllable adjective!).
We're getting more and more lost.
They were getting more and more desperate.

Adverb + comparative

We can use adverbs with comparative adjectives.
It was considerably colder in the mountains.
It was definitely hotter than any place in the tropics.

Than

We can use *than* before an object pronoun.
She's quieter than him.
We can leave *than* out – especially when it is clear what something is being compared to or when the sentence ending is obvious.
A: *Here's a good card.*
B: *This one's better.*
Food is getting saltier (. . . than it used to be).

Pronunciation

We usually stress the comparative adjective. A typical sentence stress pattern would be: subject – comparative – thing being compared.
The <u>wa</u>ter's <u>col</u>der than <u>yes</u>terday.

If we use *than*, it is weak in British English pronunciation ie /ðən/ rather than /ðæn/.

Watch out for these problems . . .

- **Students use *more* with one-syllable adjectives:** ✗ *He's more big than me.*

- **Students use *-er* as well as *more*:** ✗ *Katerina drives much more faster than me.*

- **Students use *as* instead of *than*:** ✗ *This bridge is 200 m longer as the one to the island.* ✗ *Helmut's taller as me.*

- **Students use *very* with a comparative:** ✗ *Her new home is very bigger.*

Teaching tip: using 3D examples

In general, consider using 3D aids rather than 2D aids where possible in your teaching. They offer a richer context for comparisons than 2D illustrations on a board. They also allow for different perspectives, since each student in the room will see things slightly differently.

If you have a set of Cuisenaire rods in your school, there's no better time to try using them! At its simplest, you can get students to compare two rods (*longer, darker* etc). Better still, you can get the rods to 'be' other things (cars, buildings, people etc) and compare these.

15 Superlatives

Form

Someone / Something	be (in correct tense)	the / my / his etc	superlative	noun phrase	(ever) (in a place) (of a time / period)

Kate is my best friend.
It's the longest tunnel in Europe.
That is my least favourite song ever.

Regular (short words)

the + adjective + -*est*
I'm the oldest.

Almost all one-syllable adjectives are this type.

- We add -*st* to adjectives ending in -*e*.
  fine → finest, late → latest, safe → safest

- We double the final consonant and add -*est* to adjectives ending in vowel + consonant.
  big → biggest, hot → hottest, fit → fittest

- We change -*y* to *i* and add -*est* to two syllable adjectives ending in -*y*.
  brainy → brainiest, noisy → noisiest, windy → windiest

Regular (longer words)

the + *most* / *least* + adjective
Carmen wears the most beautiful clothes.

All adjectives with three or more syllables are this type.

- We usually put the word *the* in front of superlatives but other words such as possessives are also possible.
  the most important items
  my best friend's wedding

- We use *in* to relate the superlative to a location.
  We have the cleanest diesel fuel in the world.

- We use *of* (or *in*) to relate the superlative to a time or period.
  My time in the navy was by far the most exciting period of my life.
  It was the worst storm in nearly a century.

(continued)

Some two-syllable adjectives can use either *-est* or *most / least*.
clever → *most clever / cleverest*
polite → *most polite / politest*

Irregular

good	best	It was the best meal I'd ever had.
bad	worst	It was the worst storm in nearly a century.
far	farthest / furthest	Who can jump farthest / furthest?
old	oldest / eldest	He's the oldest man in the world. Her eldest sister.

Superlative adjectives can be compounds.
She's the best-qualified person in the family.

Presentation

	Population	Distance from Beijing	Average winter temperature	Average summer temperature
Harbin	Approx 10 million	1,221 km	−18 °C	23 °C
Chengdu	Approx 11 million	1,813 km	6 °C	25 °C
Qingdao	Approx 7.5 million	687 km	−1 °C	24 °C

Three cities

1) Write up a small table of numerical information about three cities in your country (their population, distance from the capital, average summer and winter temperatures).

2) Invite students to tell you about one of them. If students try to make a superlative, help them. If not, model some examples yourself (*It's the largest. It's furthest from the capital*).

3) Repeat with different kinds of information in a table (animals, houses).

Practice

Many of these are just variations on the earlier ideas for working with comparatives!

Quick drawings

Draw three or more simple items on the board (a large bottle, a medium-sized and a small bottle). Ask students to tell you about one of the items. Some of the things can be visible and some imagined (*That one is the tallest. It's the most expensive. It's the least popular. It's the most delicious*).

Boasting dialogue

Build or elicit a dialogue in which three people are discussing and boasting about their homes, their schools, their cars. Include lots of superlatives (*Yes, but my car's the biggest*).

Real objects

Bring in a number of similar but contrasting real items: different toiletries (perfumes, soaps, deodorants) or different gadgets (iPod, mobile phone, PDA, calculator). Elicit and drill some superlatives (*Shampoo is the most expensive*).

Opinion questionnaire

Prepare a questionnaire with two or three questions about people's favourite celebrities (*Who is the worst Hollywood actor? Who is the most handsome sports star?*). Ask students to work in pairs and write five more questions in the same style. Students can then get up, mingle and survey different people.

Comparing in the classroom

Get students in small groups to make superlative sentences about themselves (*Greta has the cleanest shoes. Paula's bag is the oldest*). You could help inspire by giving out a list of possible nouns + adjectives (shoes / clean, bag / old).

Flashcards

Same as above – but use pictures of famous people or famous places.

Cars

Bring in three or four contrasting toy cars. Name the types 'This is a Volkswagen / Ferrari / Rolls Royce' and get students to make comparisons (*the fastest, most economical, least luxurious, oldest*). Extend into a story with three people who boast that their car is better than the others (*My car's the most exciting!*).

Crazy records

For imaginative classes, show students a book of records listing longest, tallest, fastest etc. Ask students to invent and write some unusual new short entries (*largest potato in the world, person who had the longest sleep, funniest joke*).

Quiz

Make small groups. Ask two or three questions in a superlatives quiz (*Which animal is the fastest runner? Which building is the tallest in the world?*). Now get groups to prepare five more questions themselves. When ready, continue the quiz using questions from different groups.

Personal opinions

Say to students 'Tell me some foods / songs / films etc that you like. Now tell me some you don't like. Compare them.'

Family

Say to students 'Who's the youngest person in your family? OK – now tell me about someone else. Who is the oldest, tallest, quietest, most interesting?'

Concept questions

- **Abdul's the tallest.** There are three friends – 1.56, 1.57 and 1.59 metres tall. Are the three friends the same height? (*No*) Which one is the tallest? (*Abdul*) How tall is Abdul? (*1.59 metres*)

- **The Suzuki is the cheapest.** There are three cars – a Suzuki, a Ferrari and a Volkswagen. Which car has a very high price? (*The Ferrari*) Which car has a low price? (*The Suzuki*) One car costs £150,000. One car costs £12,000. Which car costs £12,000? (*The Suzuki*) I have £15,000. Which car can I buy? (*The Suzuki*) Why? (*It's the cheapest*) Make a sentence about the Ferrari. (*The Ferrari is the most expensive*)

Meaning and use

We mainly use superlatives to compare one item with two or more others – and to say that the item is at an extreme – the most or least of something.

The tallest

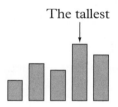

We can sometimes use the superlative to compare just two things.
Usain and Ichi are both fast – but Usain is the fastest.

There are some words which already have an extreme meaning where we wouldn't normally use a superlative (✗ *most favourite* ✗ *most unique* ✗ *least dead*).

We use the structure superlative + noun + *'ve / 'd ever* + past participle to say that something is an extreme in a person's whole experience.
That's the most pathetic excuse I've ever heard.
Davis is the most brilliant man that I've ever worked with.

We use the structure *one of the* + superlative to say that . . .

● there is a group of people or things that represent the extreme of something (a group of the most or least).

● one person / thing is a member of that group.

● but the person / thing is not actually the most or least within that group.

It's one of the prettiest villages on the south coast means that (a) there are a number of extremely pretty villages on the south coast (b) this village is part of this group (c) but it is not the prettiest (or it isn't possible to decide which is the prettiest).

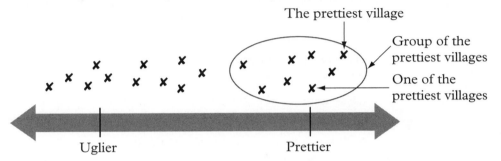

She's one of Britain's coolest young designers.
It's one of the most popular restaurants for miles around.

Common expressions

We use the superlative in many common expressions.
In business, it's the survival of the fittest.
Ken's a hard act to follow, but I'll do my best.
They were very late, and I was beginning to fear the worst.
This is cutting edge television at its best.
If the worst comes to the worst, we'll cancel the lecture.

Watch out for these problems . . .

● **Students use both *most* and *-est* with the same adjective:** ✗ *The music in there is the most loudest.*

● **Students omit *the*:** ✗ *It was best in the world.*

16 Comparisons: *as . . . as, not as . . . as, the same as, like*

Form

as . . . as

Someone / Something	verb (in correct tense)	(*not*) (*just*) (*nearly*) (*twice*)	*as* adjective / adverb *as*	something else or clause

I'm working as fast as I can.
He's not as good as Amis.

We sometimes omit the first *as* in colloquial use.
It's hot as hell in here.

After *not*, we can use *so* instead of the first *as*.
It's not so late as I thought.

like / the same as

Someone / Something	*is / looks / tastes / sounds / smells / seems / feels / appears / behaves / acts*	*like*	something else or clause
		the same as	

She sounds like her mother.
You behaved like a complete idiot!
Doesn't he look like Marco?
One centimetre is the same as ten millimetres.
The house is exactly the same as it was 20 years ago.

Presentation

Use ideas from comparatives but vary images or examples so that the things being compared are similar (the same height, same speed, same cost).

→ **Unit 14 Comparatives**

Concept questions

- **Zira is as tall as Graciana.** Is Zira taller than Graciana? (*No*) Is Graciana taller than Zira? (*No*) Is one person taller than the other? (*No*) Who is the tallest? (*No one. They are the same height*)

- **The cake's good but it isn't as tasty as the pie.** Are the cake and the pie both tasty? (*Yes*) Which is better – the cake or the pie? (*The pie*) Is the cake tastier than the pie? (*No*) Is the pie tastier than the cake? (*Yes*)

Meaning and use

as . . . as

We use *as . . . as* to say that something is identical or very similar to something else.
Her skin was (as) *white as snow.*
The base of your bed is as important as the mattress.
We often use the structure *as* + adjective / adverb + *as possible* (or similar expressions) to emphasise the distance, speed, condition or other characteristic quality of something.
They agreed to conclude negotiations as soon as possible.
I try to keep as healthy as possible.
Her son ran as fast as his little legs could carry him.

not as . . . as

We use *not as . . . as* to say that something is different from (usually less than) something else.
This job is not as easy as it may appear.
The exam wasn't as hard as I expected.

just as . . . as

We use *just as . . . as* to suggest that the similarity is very close or that the things being compared are equal.
The fish tasted just as good as it looked.
Animals feel pain just as much as we do.

We can modify the comparison with *quite, almost, about, nearly* etc to say that things are (a) similar but not quite identical or (b) not quite an extreme.
Sam's almost as tall as his mother.
The damage wasn't quite as bad as expected.
Redmond is about as far west as you can go.

as . . .

If we compare something to another thing that is visible or obvious in some way or has already been stated, we can omit the concluding part of the *as . . . as* structure.
No laptop? Well, my phone's just as useful. (= *as a laptop*)

X times as . . . as

We use *X* times *as . . . as* to say that something has significantly more or less of the adjective.
There were twice as many visitors as usual last weekend.
A house in London costs twice as much as a similar house in Liverpool.

Metaphorical uses

As . . . as turns up in many proverbs, sayings, idioms, etc:
It's as old as the hills.
They walked in holding hands, as bold as brass.
A few days in bed and you'll be as right as rain.
His explanation was as clear as mud.

like / the same as

We use *like* to say that something is very similar to something else. We use *the same as* to say that something is identical or almost identical (with only minor differences). The expressions are often used to compare things metaphorically.
The interview went like a dream.
The dress fitted her like a glove.
Tom has been like a father to me.
That bike is the same as mine.

The comparison is often with a currently visible item or currently existing situation using *this* or *that*.
Why are you staring at me like that?
In a situation like this, anything could happen.

You can also compare to a well-understood situation using *the same* + adverbials *always, as usual* etc.
'How is Eva?' 'Oh, she's still the same as always.'
'How are things?' 'Much the same as usual.'

Pronunciation

as . . . as are both weak in British English pronunciation and so we stress the adjective that comes between them.
as <u>old</u> as / əz əʊld əz /

Watch out for this problem . . .

- **Students use a comparative form after *as*: ✗** *He is as faster as me.*

17 Comparisons: *too* and *enough*

Form

too + adjective

He's too ill to come in today.
The crates were much too heavy to carry.
I was too shy to ask her to dance.
The water was too cold for a shower.

too + adverb

He ran much too slowly.
She played too dangerously.

adjective + *enough*

He wants to join the army when he's old enough.
The teachers aren't strict enough for this class.

adverb + *enough*

He told me I hadn't been working hard enough to pass the exam.

enough + noun

We have enough food for everyone.

Presentation

Excuses, excuses

1) Draw two characters on the board: a girl and her lazy boyfriend lazing on a sofa.

2) Use the pictures to help elicit and build a dialogue in which one person keeps asking for help and the other always has a reason to refuse.

A: *Could you help me move this box, please?*
B: *It's too heavy to lift.*
A: *Could you bring me the pen from that shelf, please?*
B: *It's too high for me to reach.*
A: *I want to watch the news. Turn the TV on, please.*
B: *It's too late for the news.*
A: *Make me a cup of coffee, please.*
B: *I'm too tired to get up.*

3) Get students to practise repeating and acting out the dialogue. Encourage lively intonation.

Variation

You can adapt the conversation to also include examples of *enough* (*Could you help me move this box, please? It's too heavy to lift. I'm not strong enough*).

Practice

Why can't he do it?

Find pictures showing people in problem situations (a small child trying to reach a sweet on a high shelf). Ask why he can't do what he is trying to do (*The shelf's too high. He's not tall enough*). Hand out some new pictures to pairs and get them to discuss and agree reasons.

Anecdote

Tell an anecdote about yesterday including all the things that went wrong. Get students to guess the missing *too / enough* sentences. 'I went to the bank but it was shut' (*You were too late*). 'I saw a nice new widescreen TV that I wanted but I didn't buy it' (*It was too expensive. It wasn't cheap enough*). 'I bought a cup of tea at a stall but it was horrible' (*It was too cold. It wasn't hot enough*).

Mime

Mime different mini-situations and get students to say the sentences: wipe your brow and shade yourself from the sun (*It's too hot*), try and fail to pick up a bag (*It's too heavy*), look at your watch and look panicky (*It's too late*), run for the bus and fail (*I can't run fast enough*), look worn out (*I'm too tired*). Hand out cards with sentences for students to mime for each other to guess.

Offers game

Ask students to offer you things spontaneously – or they could prepare a list first – or you could provide one. Refuse each offer with a *too* sentence (*A book*) 'No, thanks. It's too boring.' (*A free holiday in Barbados*) 'No, thanks. It's too far away.' (*Money*) 'No, thanks. It's too little.' Afterwards, reverse roles, offering things to students – then get students to repeat the game in pairs.

Questions

Ask 'Can you pick up an elephant?' (*No*) 'Why not?' (*It's too heavy*) 'Can you run a hundred kilometres?' (*No*) 'Why not?' (*I'm not fit enough*) 'Can you eat twenty hamburgers?' (*No*) 'Why not?' (*My stomach isn't big enough*)

Reasons

'Tell me a place in this town / country / world that you don't like. Give me some reasons why you don't like it.'
'Tell me a kind of food you don't enjoy. Give me some reasons why you don't enjoy it.' etc.

What's wrong

Think of ten reasons that a class might complain about a course (*The lessons are too long. The exercises are too boring. The room isn't big enough*).

Variation

Imagine you are in a terrible restaurant / museum / shopping mall / sports centre / hotel. Ask to speak to the manager and complain about lots of things.

Concept questions

- **It's too hot.** Is the weather hot? (*Yes*) Is it very hot? (*Yes*) Are you happy that it's hot? (*No*) Is it hotter than you like? (*Yes*) Would you prefer it to be cooler? (*Yes*)

- **It's too heavy for me to carry.** Is it heavy? (*Yes*) Is it very heavy? (*Yes*) Can I carry it? (*No*) Why not? (*It's very heavy*) Can someone else carry it? (*Perhaps*) Who might be able to carry it? (*Someone stronger than me!*)

- **Bob is old enough to join the army.** Can Bob join the army now? (*Yes*) What is the minimum age to join the army? (*18*) Is Bob 18 or older? (*Yes*) Is he younger than 18? (*No*) Is he too young to join the army? (*No*)

Meaning and use

Too

We use *too* to say that something has more of something (an adjective or adverb) than is good, suitable or normal. In most cases, the sentence has a negative meaning.

- If Mary says that a suitcase is *too heavy* – she means that it has more weight than is good (and, for example, she isn't able to pick it up and carry it).

- If Janos says that the lecturer spoke English *too quickly* – he means that the speed of the lecturer's English was faster than was good (and, for example, he couldn't easily understand it).

Using *too* adds an element of personal opinion to a statement. *It's hot* sounds like a reasonably objective description of the weather. Compare that with *It's too hot.* This also says that the weather is hot but adds in a strong personal opinion that the quantity of heat is more than is good (for the speaker).

The word *much* intensifies the adjective or adverb. Each of these sentences is stronger than the one before.
It's crowded.
It's too crowded.
It's much too crowded.

Too . . . to sentences can be used with positive meanings but this is rarer.
That dessert was too delicious to leave on my plate.

We use *too* to . . .

- give reasons why you don't want to do things – or can't do things.
  I can't help you – it's too difficult.

- give reasons why things didn't happen or happened in a certain way or to make excuses.
  We left early because it was too hot.
  I thought I could do it but it was too difficult for me.

- make complaints.
  This food is too dry.

- show that you are angry, upset or disappointed.
  It's much too hot in here. Can't you turn the heating down?

- explain that things didn't match your predictions or live up to your expectations.
  Sorry I'm late. The bus left ten minutes too early and I missed it.

Enough

We use *enough* to say that something is sufficient – as much as you need. In negative sentences, it means that there is not sufficient – less than you need.

Many positive *too* sentences can be changed into negative *enough* sentences.
The shirt was too small → The shirt wasn't big enough.

Similarly, you can often express a parallel meaning.
The box was too heavy for him to pick up → He wasn't strong enough to pick up the box.

Pronunciation

The pronunciation of *too* and the strong form of *to* is the same – /tuː/. The weak form of *to* is pronounced /tə/.

If *much* isn't used, the main stresses are likely to be on *too* and the main verb.
It's <u>too</u> hot for me to <u>drink</u>.

The main stress could be on the adjective / adverb and on the main verb.
It's too <u>hot</u> for me to <u>drink</u>.

If *much* is used, it is likely to take a main stress.
It's <u>much</u> too hot for me to <u>drink</u>.

Taking secondary stresses into account, many sentences using this structure have a definite on / off rhythm.
It's <u>much</u> too <u>hot</u> for <u>me</u> to <u>drink</u>!

Watch out for these problems . . .

- **Students use *too* instead of *very*: ✗** *I liked your food too much.* ✗ *She is too happy.* Students often wrongly assume that *too* is used to make an exaggerated positive meaning. Consider this sentence: ✗ *The museum was too interesting.* Although this is a possible English sentence, it may sound strange from a student. Learners often use sentences like this with a positive intention, but to a listener it sounds as if the museum was more interesting than was good and that the speaker had a problem with this. The sentence would sound more natural if the speaker added to the sentence: *The museum was too interesting to visit in just one hour.* Now it is clear that the negative meaning is associated with having to leave the museum, not with the museum itself.

- **Students use *too much* instead of *too*, *really* or *very*: ✗** *I like this ice cream too much.* (*I really like this ice cream.*) ✗ *She was too much rude to me.* (*She was too rude to me* or *She was very rude to me.*)

- **Students get the word order of *much too* mixed up: ✗** *He's too much tired to go out.*

18 Prepositions of place

Form

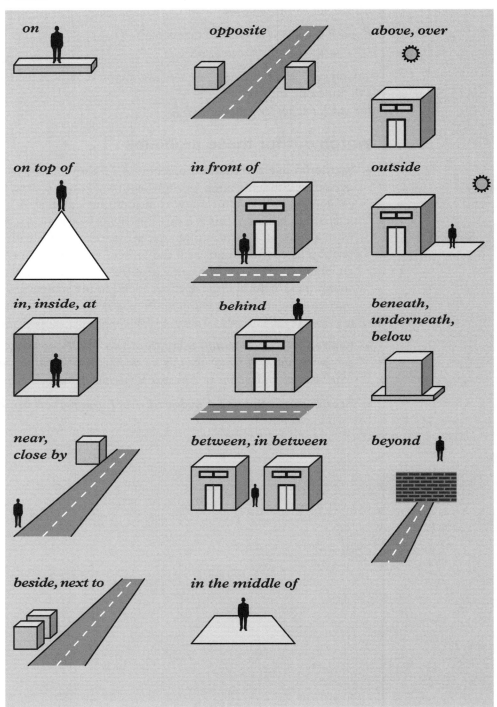

on

opposite

above, over

on top of

in front of

outside

in, inside, at

behind

beneath,
underneath,
below

near,
close by

between, in between

beyond

beside, next to

in the middle of

Presentation

Scenes

1) Use Cuisenaire rods, Lego bricks, action figures or other toys to create a little scene that illustrates a preposition of place (*Hugo's standing on top of the car*). Briefly name the nouns in the scene – for example pointing to Hugo and saying 'Hugo' and then the car and saying 'car'.

2) Invite students to describe what they see and if they use the wrong preposition, briefly change the scene to show the meaning of what they said – then make the original picture again and model the correct sentence yourself, getting students to repeat it. Continue with more scenes (*The cinema is next to the post office. The dog is in front of the school*). If you use Lego, you don't need to actually make the items, you can simply use single bricks – or blocks of bricks – to represent things - for example holding a red brick and saying 'This is a car'.

3) When you have focussed on all the prepositions you wish to introduce, reverse the process. Say a sentence yourself (*Jules is sitting opposite Mira*) and ask students to make or draw a picture to illustrate it. When they have made the image, ask others if it is a good illustration or not – and if useful, get others to change it. Continue with more sentences.

Practice

Labelling

Draw or copy diagrams like those on the board (opposite) but remove the words. See if students can put back the missing labels.

Stories

Tell a simple story with a lot of prepositions in it. 'When the robot walked into the room he saw a desk. In front of the desk was a green bucket. There was a chicken in the bucket. On top of the desk there were three eggs . . .' After telling the story once, start again and see if students can help you by telling you where things were.

Teacher picture dictation

Find a picture that lends itself to lots of use of prepositions of place. Do not show the picture to the class. Instead, describe it, slowly, item by item 'There is a tree next to the building' and ask them to draw what they hear. At the end, let students enjoy comparing their various pictures – and then show them your original. Who got closest?

Pairwork picture dictation

Same idea – but get students to work in pairs. Each is given a 'secret' picture to dictate to their partner.

Real things

Ask students 'Tell me where Olaf's desk / Lin's car / your book / the ladder is?'

Real places

Ask students 'Where is the supermarket / the Internet café / our school?'

Concept questions

The best way to concept check prepositions of place is to use Cuisenaire rods, bricks, toys (or quick sketches on the board) and ask students to create and 'show me' a picture that physically demonstrates the meaning. Alternatively, get them to draw a board picture illustrating it.

- *Show me:* **Amin's house is opposite Erich's.** (To do this students would probably need to create a road, with two houses on either side. It is easy to see they haven't understood the concept if they place two houses *next to* each other!)

- *Show me:* **The case is on top of the wardrobe.**

Meaning and use

We use prepositions of place to . . .

- describe where things are – after verbs *be, be situated, live, remain, sit, stand, stay, put* etc.
  She was sitting under a shady oak tree.

- describe where activities or events happen – after verbs *meet, take place, happen, hold, dance, eat* etc.
  They met outside the cinema on their first date.

Watch out for these problems . . .

- **Students use *in front* of when they mean *opposite*:** *The park is in front of the cinema.*

- **Students omit words that are part of a preposition:** ✗ *It is next the supermarket.* ✗ *The post box is in front the post office.* ✗ *She stood on top the hill.*

- **Students use prepositions of movement when prepositions of place would be more suitable:** ✗ *I arrived into the station.* ✗ *The children were sitting towards the teacher.* ✗ *There was a beautiful painting through the corridor.*

Teaching tip: the trouble with diagrams

Teachers and books often characterise the meanings of prepositions with simple diagrams such as those on page 84. While these can be very helpful, you will need to remember that all diagrams like these have problems.

- Sometimes the meaning or use is very hard to capture in a simple picture. What exactly is the difference between *on* and *on top of* as shown in the diagrams?

- Although the core meaning may be clearly captured, it is hard to imagine a realistic, likely sentence that would match the diagram *He's standing on top of a pyramid.* (?)

- Sometimes students may make a completely different interpretation of a diagram than the one we expected – they think *outside* means 'on the grass' or only refers to sunny days.

- Sometimes a diagram only makes sense once you already know what it means, which isn't much use for initial teaching purposes – though it may help memorisation.

We could try to make our diagrams more precise and / or more reflective of real world sentences.

There were stacks of books on the floor.

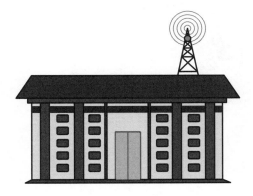

A mobile phone mast had been sited on top of the school building.

You'll have to decide for yourself which kind are most suitable for your students.

19 Prepositions of movement

Form

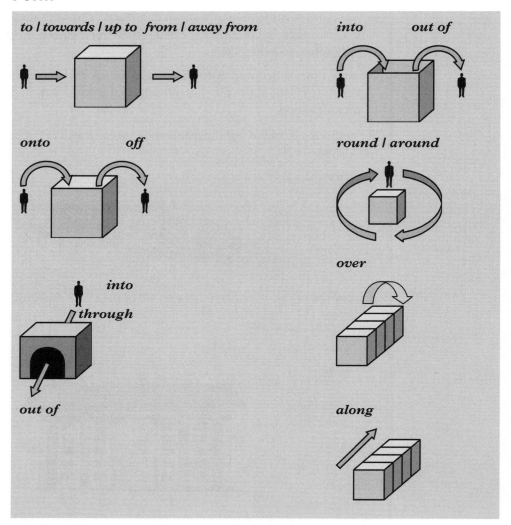

to / towards / up to from / away from

into   out of

onto   off

round / around

into
through

over

out of

along

Presentation

The tightrope walker

1) Use Cuisenaire rods, Lego bricks, action figures or other toys to tell a story about a tightrope walker or another story with lots of movement. As you tell the story, use your props, mime or draw pictures to demonstrate what happens.

Yvette is a tightrope walker. She lives in a small wood near the circus. Every evening she walks to work. She goes out of her house, down the garden path, through the gate, through the wood, over the bridge, along the river, round the circus tent and in through a door. When it's her turn, she walks out of the dressing room, along the corridor, into the ring, onto the ladder, up the ladder to the top. She climbs onto the step and then steps off onto the rope. She walks very carefully along the rope to the other end. She never . . . falls off.

Change or shorten the story as appropriate to the prepositions you wish to teach.

2) When you have finished, start telling the story again, but pause before each preposition, as if you have forgotten it. Let students help you by suggesting the right words. Repeat the correct preposition and say the sentence again, with the rod movement.

3) When the story has been retold once (or maybe more times) invite a student to come up and try to tell the story themselves with rod movements. As before, the class can help.

4) Get students to tell the story to each other in pairs.

5) Give a handout with gaps where the prepositions are. Students can fill them in.

Practice

Many ideas for prepositions of place are re-usable with adaptation.

Fairy stories

Fairy stories seem very suitable for preposition practice as they tend to have a lot of movement into different locations. Try '*Goldilocks and the Three Bears.*' 'Goldilocks jumped out of bed, ran across the room, down the stairs, through the front door, down the path, through the gate.'

King Kong

I don't know why – but I keep returning to this scenario for prepositions of place and movement lessons! I build a scene (in my case using Cuisenaire rods – but I'm sure there are other ways) and tell the story of King Kong (*the ship sails to the island, explorers walk through the jungle, King Kong climbs up the Empire State Building*). It seems to work well – and because many people know the story you can elicit lots of help in telling it and making sentences!

Personal prepositions

'How do you come to school? What it the best way to go to the park?'

Teacher Robot

Tell your students 'Imagine I'm a robot. I can only do exactly what you tell me. How can I walk across this room to the door? Give me precise instructions.'

Concept questions

As with prepositions of place, the best way to concept check prepositions of movement is often to ask students to create and 'show me' a picture of the meaning. Do remember that the meaning involves a movement – so get students to show you the characters moving – not just a static picture.

- *Show me:* **He walked through the forest.** (To do this students would probably need to make a forest – perhaps using a number of 'trees' and then have a character to take the walk.)
- *Show me:* **She walked past the shop.**
- *Show me:* **It flew under the bridge.**

Meaning and use

We use prepositions of movement to describe the direction that things are moving in – often after movement verbs *go, walk, ran, take, travel, drive, fly* etc.
One man had climbed onto the roof of his car.
She walked ahead of him along the corridor.
A blast of cold air swept through the house.

Place and movement

Some prepositions can describe either place or movement *over, above, in, outside* etc.

Some prepositions of movement are closely related to prepositions of place.

	Movement		Place
When you . . .	walk to / towards the station	→	you arrive in / at the station
	have climbed onto the roof		you are on / on top of the roof
	have crept into a classroom		you are in / inside the classroom
	have come out of a shop		you are out of / outside the shop
	stroll along a river bank		you are beside the river
	drive through a tunnel		you are inside the tunnel
	fly over / above the town		you are over / above the town

There are also many metaphorical or idiomatic meanings.

Watch out for these problems . . .

- **Students use the wrong preposition:** ✗ *Gabi walked between the forest* (through).
- **Students confuse** *place* **and** *movement:* ✗ *I'll meet you into the kitchen* (in).

20 Prepositions of time

Presentation

Teacher's pictures

1) Bring in a variety of personal photos and photos of news events and encourage your class to bring some in too.

2) Discuss when things happened and how long for. Use the pictures to elicit sentences exemplifying the prepositions you wish to teach (*Natasha went there last summer. I go there in winter. Marcin lived there for twelve years*).

3) Distribute three or four new pictures randomly to pairs. Students need to walk around and ask questions to find out what their pictures show, then write some sentences about each.

Practice

Call-out quiz

This is a good language area for snappy, shout-out quizzes and games. Prepare a list of times that collocate with *in, on* or *at* (*Saturday, the weekend, summer*). Read the times out one at a time and ask students to call out the complete collocation (*on Saturday, at the weekend, in summer*).

Variation (1)

Get students to prepare three cards with *in, on, at* written on them in thick pen. When you call out, they lift up and show the correct card.

Variation (2)

Write *in, on* and *at* on posters and place in different parts of the room. When you call out a time, students must walk to the correct part of the room.

Gap-fill exercises

It is often useful to do simple gap-fill exercises with prepositions of time – filling in the missing preposition in sentences (*We are going to stay in New York . . . three weeks*). They usually reveal many misunderstandings and confusions.

Calendar

Bring in a large calendar. Ask students to tell you when things happened / will happen. Ask follow-up questions about times, how long things lasted, when they ended.

Diary

Similarly, give students a blank diary grid and ask them to fill in past and future events. They can then meet up and chat, perhaps also trying to agree a future meeting, date or outing.

Personal questions

Ask questions (*When did you visit the zoo? How long will you study in this school?*) and get short answers (*last winter, for six months*).

Concept questions

These are examples. You'll need different questions for different meanings.

- **Ariel's worked in London since October.** Did Ariel work in London in September? (*No*) Did Ariel work in London in November? (*Yes*) When did Ariel start working in London? (*October*) Is she still working in London now? (*Yes*) What did Ariel do in October? (*She started working in London*)

- **Jens said 'I'll finish the work by midday.'** Will Jens finish the work in the afternoon? (*No*) Will he finish the work in the morning? (*Yes*) Will he finish the work before midday? (*Yes*)

Meaning and use

We use prepositions of time to describe when things happen and how long they last.

on, at and in

We use *on* with days and dates.
on Thursday
on Christmas Day
on January the first

We use *at* with specific times, some parts of the day and with periods of time imagined as a unity.
at midnight
at night
at the weekend

We use *in* with years, months, seasons, some parts of the day and to mean 'at the end of a period of time after now.'
in 2007
in March
in winter
in the morning
in two years

by, until / till (British English) / through (American English)
We use *by* to mean 'before an end time.'

by New Year
by Tuesday

We use *until* (*till*) to mean 'up to an end time.'
until 6 pm

In American English we use *through*.
through Sunday

after and *before*

We use *after* to mean 'following a time.'
after the meeting
after Easter

We use *before* to mean 'earlier than a time.'
before January
before midday

during and *through*

We use *during* to mean 'within a period of time.'
during the meeting
during summer

We use *through* to mean 'for a whole period of time from beginning to end.'
through the war

for and *since*

We use *for* to mean 'the length of a period of time.'
for the winter
for two nights

We use *since* to mean 'from a beginning time.'
since 1963
since he arrived

→ **Unit 42 Time words: *for* and *since***

Teaching tip: how many to present at once?

Although this unit has looked at many time prepositions in one go, it would probably not be sensible to teach more than a few at once. Teachers often present these prepositions in pairs or groups – as in the Meaning and use section above – eg *for* and *since* are often taught together and contrasted, as are *at*, *on* and *in*. Keep an eye open for problems and errors in future lessons. Students often find these meanings easy to confuse, even some time after first meeting them.

21 *Have* and *have got*

Form

Have

Affirmative

I have an idea.
He has two classes this morning.

Question

Do you have an email account?
Does he have any brothers and sisters?

Negative

I don't have time.
He doesn't have any money.

Short answers

Yes, I do. / No, I don't.
Yes, he does. / No, he doesn't.

Have is a normal main verb. We don't usually contract the verb when the meaning is ownership or relationship.

✗ *He's a cat.* (because it sounds like *He is a cat*!)

We don't normally use *have* in progressive forms.

✗ *She's having two houses in Switzerland.*

The normal question form is *Do you have . . .?* The form *Have you . . .?* is possible but rare.

Have got

Affirmative

I've got classes all afternoon.
She's got a lot of work to do.

Question

Have you got a girlfriend?
Has she got any money?

Negative

I haven't got all day!
She hasn't got any money.

Short answers

Yes, I have. / No, I haven't.
Yes, she has. / No, she hasn't.

Have got is an unusual two-word verb formed like a perfect tense.

The *got* part never changes but the *have* part changes to match the person (*You have, she has* etc) and time (*We have got, We had got, We will have got* etc).

We don't use *have got* in the progressive (*-ing*) form.
We normally abbreviate the *have* to *'ve* or *'s*.

Presentation

Secret treasures

1) Prepare multiple photocopies of some everyday objects (*a watch, a phone, a dictionary, a pen*). You can decide whether you only want to include singular countable nouns or also have plurals and uncountables. Give each student one random picture.

2) Hold up your picture. Model 'I've got a dictionary' (or whatever it is you have). Get individual students to say a true sentence about their own picture.

3) Ask students to swap pictures with other students. Tell them to keep their new picture secret.

4) Pick one student. Ask 'Have you got a pen?' Sneak a look at their picture and help the student to make the correct answer (*Yes, I have* or *No, I haven't*). If it was a *no* answer, continue asking questions (*Have you got a watch?*) until you get a *yes* answer. You can also include *Wh*-questions if you wish (*What has Joan got? What have Pierre and Poli got?*).

5) Repeat the same game with other students. When you think the class are ready, get one confident student to ask the questions to another student still in front of the whole class.

6) Ask students to swap pictures with other students again – then stand up, mingle and play the game together.

Practice

Possessions

Hold up flashcards of people holding or using different objects. Get students to make sentences (*She's got a red handbag*).

Personal characteristics

You can also use flashcards to elicit descriptions of people (*He's got beautiful hair. She's got a lovely smile*).

Lies

Hold up a flashcard of a person and describe him / her. Include one wrong fact (*She's got a blue handbag*). Students should see if they can spot your mistake.

Rooms

Find and copy a magazine photo of a room, if possible belonging to a famous person. Give a copy of the photo to each pair of students. Tell them if the room's owner is a *he* or *she*. Ask them to look at the picture and write some sentences about what the owner has got. Give an example or two (*He's got a television. He's got an old clock*). When students are ready, collect answers on the board – ask if students can guess who the owner is – then reveal the answer.

Meaning and use

We use *have got* and *have* . . .

1) to show ownership.
    I've got some stamps.

2) for things people attend according to a plan or timetable.
    I have a meeting at two o'clock.

3) to talk about relationships with other people.
    She's got two brothers.

4) to talk about illnesses or medical problems.
    I have a terrible sore throat.

5) to talk about personal appearance or characteristics.
    He's got long hair.

Have got is more informal and is also used more often in speech.

Have is potentially a confusing verb for students – and at the root of many errors. As well as the uses looked at above . . .

- it is an auxiliary verb used to form perfect tenses: *We've lost the argument.*

- it features in the modal verb *have to: They had to run.*

- it is part of the causative structure *have something done.*

- it is a delexical verb in formations such as *have a bath, have a walk* etc.

- it features in many idioms *I've had it up to here with Pierre.*

- and more!

It is worth spending some time in class helping raise students' awareness of the different uses they have met. One way of doing this is to write two sentences on the board, labelled (a) and (b) (eg (a) *Kay had a green bath* (b) *Kay had a bath last night*) and ask students questions to check that they can distinguish between them (*Which sentence is about something Kay owned?*).

Watch out for these problems . . .

- **Students make '*Have you . . .*' questions:** ✗ *Have you your bags?* Although *Have you . . .* is a possible grammatical form, we rarely use it. Encourage students to use *Have you got . . .* or *Do you have . . .* for questions.

- **Students mix *Have you got* and *Do you have* together:** ✗ *Do you have got an answer?* ✗ *Do you got some money?*

- **Students use *have* in the progressive to talk about ownership or relationship:** ✗ *She's having three older sisters.* Note that *She's having trouble, She's having a meeting* etc are all fine as it isn't possession or relationship.

22 Present simple: *be*

Form

Affirmative

Noun / pronoun + *be* + noun phrase or adjective

I am / I'm	*He is / He's*	*We are / We're*
You are / You're	*She is / She's*	*They are / They're*
	It is / It's	

I'm a quick learner.
It's a small hotel.
They're beautiful designs.

Negative

Noun / pronoun + *be* + *n't / not*

I'm not. . . .	*He's not . . .*	*We're not . . .*
You're not . . .	*She's not . . .*	*They're not . . .*
	It's not . . .	

It's not fair.
We're not married.

Question

Invert noun / pronoun and verb.

Am I . . . ?	*Is he . . . ?*	*Are we . . . ?*
Are you . . . ?	*Is she . . . ?*	*Are they . . . ?*
	Is it . . . ?	

Is he happy?
Are you upset?

Short answers

The most common response to a simple information question such as *Is he a receptionist?* would be a short answer:

Yes, I am.	*No, I'm not.*	—
Yes, you are.	*No, you're not.*	*No, you aren't.*
Yes, he / she / it is.	*No, he / she / it's not.*	*No, he / she / it isn't.*
Yes, we are.	*No, we're not.*	*No, we aren't.*
Yes, they are.	*No, they're not.*	*No, they aren't.*

(continued)

> ### *There is / there are*
>
> We use *there + is / are* as a way to talk about things that exist or happen.
> *There are four bridges across the River Danube.*
> *There's a concert on Sunday night.*

Presentation

Job pictures

1) Show a picture of a person in an easily identifiable job. Model a sentence (*He's a doctor*) and get students to repeat.

2) Show more pictures and elicit or model more sentences (*She's a teacher. They're police officers*). Review and test by pointing at earlier pictures for students to say the sentences.

3) Distribute some new pictures for students to add to the board and make new sentences (*She's a housewife*).

4) Ask students to choose one job. Students mingle and tell each other about themselves and others (*I'm a doctor. She's a taxi driver*).

Variation (1) Mood / Situation pictures

Use pictures of people or faces representing different situations and moods (*She's angry. They are cold. He's tired*).

Variation (2) Adjectives

Use pictures of people and objects representing sizes, shapes, colours, etc (*He's tall. The car's red*).

Practice

Names

Write cards with the names of people the students will know (classmates, people in the school, politicians, TV stars). Hand one card to each student. Each student now writes five sentences using *he / she's* (*She's old. She's a politician*). When ready, students read out the sentences and others guess who is being talked about. You could use negatives as well (*She isn't a teacher*). Extend the activity by allowing students to ask questions (*Is she old? Is she a politician?*).

Matching descriptions

Prepare a set of about ten pictures and a matching set of cards with short descriptions on them (a picture of a diamond necklace with a card description: *It's very expensive,* a picture of a successful pop star with a description: *He isn't poor*). Mix the cards and pictures up and photocopy a set for each group. In their groups students must try to match up pictures and descriptions. When they have finished, give them a new set of pictures and blank cards. They now write the descriptions for each picture – and other students can play their game.

Mime game

Write out some cue cards that students will be able to mime for others (*I'm cold, I'm hungry, I'm a shop assistant, We're friends, We're doctors*). Invite students up individually or in pairs to read a card (secretly) and then mime the sentence for the rest of the class to guess. The students who are watching can practise asking questions (*Are you cold?*).

Guess the subject

Choose an interesting picture of a person or animal (*a rabbit*) and write some sentences that the person / creature might be thinking or saying (*I'm quite small, My fur is white. Carrots are my favourite food. My ears are very long*). Stick the picture face-down on the board. Write the sentences up one by one and elicit ideas for what the picture might show. Don't reveal the picture (even if anyone guesses correctly) until students have heard and considered all the sentences. At the end, show the picture and let students see if they were correct.

Estate agent

Students work in pairs. A is an estate agent. B is a potential house buyer. A shows B round an imaginary house (using the classroom) and describes features (*This is the kitchen. There are two windows*).

Meaning and use

Main verb or auxiliary verb?

Make sure that students can distinguish between . . .

- *be* as a main verb.

- *be* as an auxiliary verb (one that helps form the tense of another main verb).

In each of these sentences, *be* is a main verb.
Brie is a soft creamy cheese.
Most of our accommodation is self-catering.
When the sauce is thick, add the cheese.

Compare those examples with the following:
Marianna's cooking dinner for me tonight.
It's made of very thin material.

These examples include *be* but in each case it is an auxiliary verb, not a main verb. The second verb is the main verb. In the first example, the verb *be* is used as part of the present progressive. Note that there is also a main verb in the *-ing* form. In the second example, the verb *be* is used as part of the passive voice of the present simple. The main verb is a past participle.

Watch out for these problems . . .

- **Students omit the verb *be* completely:** ✗ *She doctor.* Some languages do not have an equivalent verb or may not require its use in all circumstances.

- **Students make questions with *do:*** ✗ *Do you be sad?*

- **Students use incorrect combinations of person and verb form:** ✗ *You is . . .* This type of problem is known as a problem of *agreement* or *concord* (ie the correct going together of subject pronoun / noun and verb form).

Teaching tip: unnaturally long answers

Don't encourage your students to give unnaturally long answers. For example, look at this classroom exchange between student A and B who are practising question and answer exchanges using *be*.
A: *Are you a businessman?*
B: *Yes, I am a businessman.*

This is a very unnatural response. It would not be normal to repeat information that had already been stated in the conversation. The second version is much more natural.
A: *Are you a businessman?*
B: *Yes, I am.*

Teachers sometimes say that they prefer the first example because they want their students to get practise in using 'full sentences' including the structure pronoun + noun phrase. If that's what you want, the secret is finding a way of doing that which is natural and realistic. There is no point practising grammar that is superficially 'correct' (ie well-formed grammatically) but is entirely unrealistic as an example of real communication. If you want students to say sentences like *I am a businessman,* try modelling an exchange like this:
A: *What do you do?*
B: *I'm a businessman.*

23 Present simple: affirmative

Form

I / You / We / They	live	in Prague.
He / She / It	lives	

There is an -s ending on the verb for third person singular.

The -s ending and spelling

- We use -es when the base form ends in /dʒ/, /s/, /z/, /ʃ/, /tʃ/ or /z/.
  *discuss*es, *rise*s, *wash*es, *catch*es

- We use -ies (to replace the y) when the base form ends in a consonant followed by y.
  fly → *fl*ies, *carry* → *carr*ies

- Note also.
  go → *goes*, *do* → *does*, *have* → *ha*s

Presentation

Daily routines

1) Tell or elicit a story using board pictures or flashcards getting students to repeat each sentence.

    Diego wakes up every day at 7.30. He gets up at 7.45. He has a shower, brushes his teeth and puts on his clothes. He leaves his house at 8.15. He walks to the bus stop and waits for the number 166 bus etc.

2) Ask students to recap and retell the whole story at various points.

3) Elicit a second very similar story for a different character (*Brigitte wakes up every day at 10 . . .*).

Variation: weekly routines

Joanna drives to London every Thursday. She meets her mother and they play tennis together. She sleeps at her mother's house. She drives back home on Sunday morning etc.

Practice

Spelling and pronunciation

Make sure your students get some basic activities that focus on spelling and pronunciation, including all the differently spelt -*s* endings (especially -*s*, -*es*, *y* → -*ies*) and pronunciations (/s/, /z/ and /ɪz/). Simple discrimination and sorting games are often suitable; write three columns on the board labelled /s/, /z/ and /ɪz/ and call out verbs. Students should come to the board and place the word in the correct column (with discussion, listening to teacher's model again and teacher feedback where useful).

Diary

Make a diary of someone's daily / weekly routine using single words for entries (*tennis, shops*). Elicit sentences about the routine (*He goes to the shops every Thursday*). Get students to make their own diaries and repeat the task in pairs, using *I go . . .*

Soap opera

Create an imaginary 'soap opera' with varied stereotypical characters. Elicit from students the different lifestyles and routines of these characters (*Anita works at the laundrette. She smokes 50 cigarettes a day*).

Spot the lies game

Read out ten present simple sentences about yourself. Eight should be true and two false (*I read three newspapers every day*). Students must guess which sentences are false.

Guess the job

Read out sentences describing a person's life (*I walk a lot. I carry a heavy bag. I knock on doors*). Who can guess the job first? (*postman*)

Link to collocations

Teach the present simple alongside common verb–noun collocations for household routines (*She cleans the windows / tidies the toys / makes the beds*).

Concept questions

- **Ildiko works in the bank.** Has Ildiko got a job? (*Yes*) What is her job? (*She works in the bank*) Does she work there on Monday? (*Yes, probably*) Tuesday? Wednesday? etc. Is she in the bank NOW? (*Possibly, but we don't know*)

- **Henri plays football.** What sport does Henri like? (*Football*) Does he play often? (*Probably*) Is he playing football NOW? (*Possibly, but we don't know*)

- **Ice melts at 0°.** Is this a fact? (*Yes*) Is it always true? (*Yes*) Was it true last week? (*Yes*) Was it true ten thousand years ago? (*Yes*) Will be it be true in the year 3000? (*Yes*)

Meaning and use

Core meaning

Things which we think of as generally true and unlimited in time ie without a beginning or an ending. Despite its name, the present simple can actually refer to the past, present and / or future (and it isn't very simple).

Uses

We use the present simple to talk about . . .

1) habits, routines, repeated actions: things that are done *usually, often, regularly, occasionally, sometimes* etc and things done on certain days or occasions.
   I always get the eight o'clock train.
   I usually play in defence.
   The Blue Café closes on Mondays.

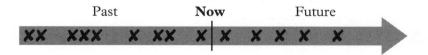

2) permanent situations, truths and things believed to be true: things that happen all the time. Things that seem permanently true and don't have any obvious beginning or end.

Here the land rises and falls in gentle hills.
The river flows in a south-westerly direction.
My sister lives next door.

3) states, senses and feelings that are generally true, using verbs such as *believe,*
know, live, have, feel, like, taste etc.
We live at 23 Brookfield Avenue.
I feel sorry for him.

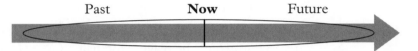

4) states, senses and feelings that are happening around now – *believe, know, have,*
feel, like, taste etc.
Your hair feels so soft.
This tea tastes funny.
I don't trust Hillary.

5) timetabled or planned events in the future.
The match starts at 3 o'clock.
The London train gets in at 10.05.

6) the future after the words *when* or *if* (when *will* cannot be used).
Just buzz me when the client arrives.
I can send it to you by email if you give me your address.

→ Unit 57 First conditional

7) newspaper headlines (to make a past event seem more 'live').
President bans Union

8) live commentary especially of sports events.
Beckham kicks to Ronaldo.

9) jokes and anecdotes.
A bear walks into a petrol station and says . . .

Using the present simple to talk about things happening NOW

Other than uses (4) and (8) above, the present simple does not usually refer to
things happening NOW. We normally use the present progressive for actions

happening NOW and for events 'around now' that are limited in duration with a beginning and end.

→ **Unit 30 Present progressive contrasted with present simple**

Pronunciation

The -s ending

We pronounce the third person singular -*s* ending in three different ways: /s/, /z/ and /ɪz/.

- /s/ when the base form ends with unvoiced consonants: /p/, /t/, /k/, /f/ (*slips, waits, likes, laughs*).

- /z/ when the base form ends in a vowel sound or one of these voiced consonants: /b/, /d/, /g/, /v/, /ð/, /m/, /n/, /ŋ/, /l/ (*sees, knows, rubs, rides, digs, gives, breathes, hums, grins, rings, calls*).

- /ɪz/ when the base form ends with /s/, /z/, /ʃ/, /tʃ/, /dʒ/, /z/. We also use the -*es* spelling (*misses, fizzes, washes, catches, judges*).

- *Does* is pronounced /dʌz/ or /dəz/. *Says* is pronounced /sez/.

Contractions

If your students are learning British English pronunciation, teach the contracted forms (*don't, doesn't*) as the standard forms – rather than introducing the uncontracted forms (*do not, does not*) first and only later showing the contraction.

Watch out for these problems . . .

- **Students use the -*ing* form instead of present simple:** ✗ *I smoking a lot.* ✗ *He living in China.*

- **Students omit the third person -*s* ending:** ✗ *Maria like chocolate.* ✗ *He work in a café.* Idea: Students <u>will</u> omit the -*s* ending. Don't worry that you taught it badly; it's simply something that takes a long time to become natural. Try gentle reminders when they forget: drawing an 's' shape in the air with your finger, saying 'ssss' or pointing at a large 's' on a poster you've placed next to the board.

- **Students add an unnecessary auxiliary verb:** ✗ *I am live here.*

- **Students use *do* and *does* unnecessarily:** When used by low level students, auxiliary *do* / *does* is usually inappropriate in affirmative present simple statements: *She does walk to school.* However, it is, in fact, possible if the speaker wants to emphasise the truth of what he is saying, especially to disagree with a previous speaker: A: *Omar doesn't live in London.* B: *He <u>does</u> live there!* NB the auxiliary verb (*do* / *does*) is stressed.

- **Students mispronounce the -s ending:** The distinction between /s/ and /z/ is not typically a problem for speakers of many mother tongues (maybe because it's actually harder to say the endings with the wrong phoneme – and it doesn't make a big difference to communication even if you get it wrong). However, the /ɪz/ ending does cause some trouble. Students may use it to pronounce many -s endings eg cooks /kʊkɪz/ walks /wɔːkɪz/. Idea: Help them by pointing out that words like *cooks* and *walks* are one syllable but they are using two.

Teaching tip: verb tables

The verb form used in present simple is the base form (also known as the 'infinitive without *to*'). Base forms are listed in the first column of a standard verb table.

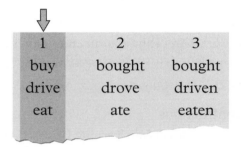

1	2	3
buy	bought	bought
drive	drove	driven
eat	ate	eaten

Draw students' attention to such verb tables in their coursebook or grammar book (they are usually in the back). Point out that the first column shows the base form and can help them select verbs, form the present simple and spell them correctly.

24 Present simple: negative

Form

I / You / We / They	don't	live	in Prague.
He / She / It	doesn't		

There is no -s on the main verb.

Negative meanings can also be made with *never*.
They never work on Fridays.

Presentation

Describing a person

1) Bring in a flashcard of an unusual looking person. Say some interesting things about him / her (*He usually wears purple trousers. He doesn't like TV*). Include a number of negative sentences. Ask students to repeat the sentences.

2) In pairs, students think of some more sentences about the person.

3) Ask students to tell the class their ideas. Write the most interesting on the board.

4) Hand pairs a new picture. They should write a similar description of this person.

Practice

My negatives

Ask students to write down four true *I don't . . .* sentences about themselves (*I don't like loud music. I don't know German. I don't eat chocolate*). Collect in the lists and read them out. Can other students guess who wrote each list?

Daily routines

Students work in pairs to write a present simple description based on pictures or flashcards. They must include things that the character doesn't do (*Lara walks to the park every day. In the park she looks at the ducks but she doesn't feed them. She doesn't walk home. She takes the bus*).

Reasons

Say 'Come to my party!' Students must respond with *I don't . . .* sentences to explain why they won't come to the party (*Sorry. I don't like dancing. I don't drink. I don't eat chips*). Repeat with other situations (*Let's go to the gym. I'll cook dinner for you*).

Quick negatives

Read out some affirmative sentences. Each time the students must suggest a negative sentence using the same verb, on the same topic, about the same person. You read 'Heidi lives in Paris' (*She doesn't live in Rome* or *She doesn't live in London*). You read 'Heidi likes chocolates' (*She doesn't like tomatoes*).

Watch out for these problems . . .

- **Students use *not* without auxiliary *do*: ✗** *She not drive to school.*

- **Students keep the 's': ✗** *Yukiko doesn't works here now.*

- **Students decontract:** The normal, natural spoken forms are *don't* and *doesn't*. While not incorrect, in many situations it will sound unnatural to say *do not* or *does not*: ✗ *I do not want to go out tonight.* ✗ *She does not use make-up.* Having said that, in many varieties of English as an International Language, it is quite normal to decontract.

Teaching tip: 's'

Crossing out the 's'

Just as students need reminding to add the *he / she / it* 's' ending in affirmative statements, they will also need to be reminded not to add it in negatives (and questions). When you write sentences or a substitution table, it may help to add a crossed-out 's' to make the point (*Rajiv doesn't often eats chips*).

Moving 's'

One way of introducing the lack of *-s* ending on the main verb in negatives and questions is by using the board to show the 's' moving from the main verb to the auxiliary verb.

She doesn't works in the City.   Does she works in the City?

Teaching tip: example sentences

If you write up some example sentences for your students to copy, don't only use the bare minimum (*I don't walk, You don't walk, He doesn't walk*). Although grammatically possible, short sentences like this will be rare – so they're not very useful as models for students. It's more helpful to make a realistic short sentence, perhaps including an adverb of frequency (*I don't often walk downtown*) or a time expression (*I don't walk in the park after seven at night*).

25 Present simple: questions

Form

Yes / No questions

Do	I / you / we / they		
Does	he / she / it	*live*	*in Prague?*

There is no -*s* on the main verb.

Wh- questions

Wh- question word	+	do	I / you / we / they	+	base form
		does	she / he / it		

Where do they live?
What does Henry do?

Is *who* the subject or the object?

- *Who does John meet?* (*who* refers here to the object of *meet*)

- *Who meets John?* (*who* refers here to the subject of *meet*)

Negative questions

Present simple negative questions are surprisingly common – especially using
Why don't you . . .
Why don't you join us for dinner tonight?

Short answers

Yes,	I / you / we / they	do.
	he / she / it	does.

No,	I / you / we / they	don't.
	he / she / it	doesn't.

We often use short answers when we respond to present simple questions.
A: *Do you go by bus?*
B: *Yes, I do. / No, I don't.*

Presentation

> Do you eat lunch before 13.00?
>
> Do you watch the TV news every day?
>
> Do you . . . newspapers in school?

Survey

1) Make a ten-question *yes / no* survey (*Do you eat lunch before 13:00? – yes / no Do you watch the TV news every day? – yes / no*). Add five more questions without verbs (*Do you . . . newspapers in school? – yes / no Do you . . . to music at home? – yes / no*).

2) Get students to read the questionnaire and fill in their own answers to the first ten questions.

3) Put them in pairs to ask each other the questions and make notes of the answers.

4) Focus on the structure of the questions – then ask pairs to fill in the verbs in questions 11–15, and afterwards, think of five new questions to add to the survey.

5) Pairs meet up with other pairs and ask questions 11–20.

6) Students report back to the class (*Sayid watches the TV news every day*).

Practice

You may want to focus on only *Yes / No* questions initially before introducing and focussing *Wh-* questions later on.

Yes / No questions

Rapid questions

Hand students a long list of *Do you . . .* questions about their lives (*Do you eat meat? Do you eat fish? Do you eat mice?*). In pairs students should ask their partner some random questions from the list. The partner may only reply either 'Yes, I do' or 'No, I don't.'

What I'd like to know about you

Make pairs. Ask students to prepare some *Do you . . .* questions to ask their partner. (*Do you like school? Do you play football?*). Pairs then ask each other their questions.

Celebrity interview

Choose a well-known celebrity. Tell students that this person will arrive at the airport for a visit to their country. They should imagine that they are a TV interviewer and prepare some *Do you . . .* questions to ask the star

(*Do you like our country? Do you like spicy food? Do you enjoy horror films?*).
Students then role play in pairs: celebrity and TV interviewer.

Wh- questions

Text facts

Choose a suitable table, chart, diagram, timetable, graph or leaflet – something
full of usable information. Distribute copies to students and ask questions about
it (*Do people buy suncream in June? What do the students do on Tuesday mornings?*).
Offer a new text and get students to prepare similar questions.

Mixed

Survey

Agree an interesting area to research with students (breakfast tastes or reading
habits). Students work with you to think of interesting questions. To work on *Yes /
No* questions suggest questions like 'Do you have a cooked breakfast?' 'Do you
put sugar in your coffee?' To work on *Wh-* questions suggest questions like 'What
do you usually drink?' 'How many slices of bread do you eat?' When ready, students interview a number of others (or possibly people outside class) and prepare
a report back (*Three people don't eat any bread at breakfast*).

Finding out about a person

Choose a picture of an interesting person. Students must ask you questions to find out
more about him / her (*What work does he do? Does he like travelling?*). Invent interesting
answers as you go and get students to note them. When they know a lot about the
person ask students to write a question and answer interview about the person.

Pronunciation

When speaking quickly, questions are often said with connected speech features.

- *Do you* /duː juː/ often becomes /duː jə/, /djə/ or even /dʒə/.
- *Don't you* /dəʊnt juː/ often becomes /dəʊntʃə/.
- *Does he* /dəz hiː/ often becomes /dəzɪ/.

Watch out for these problems . . .

- **Students make questions by inversion:** ✗ *Play you football?*
- **Students retain the 's' for third person:** ✗ *Does she works here?*
- **Students omit the auxiliary verb:** ✗ *What you like to do in the evening?*

Teaching tip: find out more about your students

Practise language and find out more about your students! Use present simple
questions every day in class when you chat at the start or end of the lesson. Ask
questions yourself, and – even better – get students to ask each other (*Do you like
soap operas? Do you eat pasta every day? Does your father work in the capital?*).

26 Imperatives

Form

We make imperatives by using the base form without a noun or pronoun.
Come and sit over here.
Tell me again – I wasn't listening.
Show me some identification.

We make negative imperatives with *Don't . . .*
Don't look at his answers!

Presentation

Physical stories

1) Prepare a story that the students can act out via a series of instructions (*Walk to the bus stop. Wait for the bus. Get on the bus. Pay your fare. Look for a seat. Sit down. Look out of the window*).

2) In class, get students to stand up in a clear space and follow your instructions (as if it was a drama activity). If there are any instructions that they don't understand, demonstrate the action yourself, rather than explain.

3) At the end of the story, see which instructions students can recall. Write them up. Focus on how they are made.

4) Ask students to work in a group of three to prepare a similar short story using instructions. When they are ready, they can try it out on other groups.

Practice

Recipes

Teach or revise some key cooking verbs (*chop, stir, boil, mix, add*). Get students to prepare instructions for making food that they like (*Mix the flour and milk. Add one egg*).

How to do it

In pairs, Student A tells Student B how to do an everyday task (putting on a tie, finding a story about a favourite celebrity using an Internet search engine, setting a mobile phone to 'mute', changing batteries in a smoke alarm, helping someone who has fainted). Student B mimes the actions as she is told them. You may need to review useful verbs before each activity.

Machines

Show students a picture of a machine. You could use an image from the Internet or something you have sketched yourself. Elicit ideas about what it does. Get students to write down some instructions for using it (*Pull the handle and wait two minutes*).

My life in your hands

Students give instructions (*Stop! Turn right!*) to help a blindfolded partner walk across the room. A more complex activity could involve tasks to complete on the way (picking up a book).

Directions

Many coursebooks feature units on asking for and giving directions. These make use of imperatives (*Turn left. Walk along the street*). To practise, make pairs, A and B. Photocopy the same map for each partner – but A's and B's maps should have some different places marked. For example, A may have the cinema, hairdresser's and Post Office, whereas B has the Tourist Information office, the shopping centre and a café. Starting from a common location (*the station*) the students take turns giving instructions to their partner about how to go to the new locations.

Warnings

Find a short exciting chase sequence of an action film. Tell students to watch it and make notes about all the dangers and problems the hero faces. At the end, work together to think of any warnings or advice you could shout to the hero to help them face the dangers (*Run! Duck! Jump! Hide!*). When you have worked out a good list of ideas, replay the excerpt and get students to shout out the warnings at the appropriate points.

Variation

Use the same idea with a sports film, such as a football match (*Run! Pass! Shoot! Kick it!*).

Meaning and use

Imperatives are used to give orders, commands or warnings or to give advice or make suggestions.

Orders and commands

It's fairly unusual to give orders or commands to other people, other than in specific contexts. These include . . .

- when there is a hierarchical relationship such as in military situations or when teachers are talking to students in schools.
  Stand up!
  Work quietly.

- when instructing someone how to do something.
  Push the button.

- when talking to a pet.
  Sit!
  Fetch!

- in informal social situations where more polite language (use of *please*) doesn't seem necessary.
  Pass me the bottle.
  Show me.

Warnings

We use imperatives in emergencies or situations where there is a threat or danger, to warn someone.
Duck!
Get out now!
Don't eat the salmon!

Advice and suggestions

We can give friendly advice and suggestions using imperatives.
Tell him before it's too late!
Buy the red one!
Forget her!

Pronunciation

With imperatives there is often a fine line between sounding authoritative and sounding rude. Get students to practise saying the same imperative (*Come here*), but changing the tone a little each time. Give feedback on how each sounds to you. You could demonstrate yourself. Describe a situation where you are a guest having a meal in someone's house. Say 'Pass me the ketchup' in two contrasting ways (ordering and politely requesting). See if students can hear the difference. Get them to try both. Point out how offensive the first one might seem. Also mention how the addition of the word *please* will help a lot too!

Watch out for these problems . . .

- **Students retain the pronoun:** ✗ *Martin. You stand up!*

27 Adverbs of frequency

Form

never	*sometimes*
hardly ever	*often*
rarely	*usually*
occasionally	*always*

We typically put adverbs of frequency between subject and verb.
He never eats meat.

We put adverbs of frequency after *be*.
She is usually at home in the evenings.

We can put some (but not all) adverbs of frequency before the subject.
Sometimes she cooks fish for supper.
Occasionally they come in before 9.00 but ✗ *Never he works late.*

We can put some adverbs of frequency at the end of a clause.
She cooks fish for supper sometimes.
They come in before 9.00 occasionally but NB ✗ *He works late never.*

Students typically meet six frequency adverbs in lower level courses: *always, usually, often, sometimes, rarely, never.* Adverbials such as *twice a week, every day* are also met at lower levels.

Later on, *occasionally* and *hardly ever* may be introduced as equivalent to *sometimes* and *rarely.* Other adverbs (eg *constantly, regularly, almost never, normally, routinely, seldom, sporadically* etc) could be considered 'more advanced' – and aren't usually introduced at Elementary or Intermediate level.

Adverbs of frequency are typically introduced with the present simple. We also use them with . . .

- past simple.
  They often went to the same restaurant.

- present perfect.
  I've rarely seen him at his desk.

- past perfect.
  The Prime Minister had hardly ever been questioned in this way before.

- present progressive + *always* (can be used to show annoyance).
  You're always doing that!

Presentation

Svetlanna . . . goes swimming on Tuesdays

0%   100%

Continuum

The classic presentation of adverbs of frequency involves use of the continuum (See *Meaning and use* opposite).

1) Offer a present simple sentence (*Svetlanna . . . goes swimming on Tuesdays*) and then invite the class to think of a word that could go into the gap.

2) When an adverb of frequency is suggested, write it into the gap and then draw the continuum, marking the two ends 0% and 100%, asking the class where they think the adverb should be placed in that line. After discussion, you and the class can agree and add the adverb to the continuum.

3) Then elicit other adverbs, filling them in the gap and adding them to the continuum.

Practice

Questionnaires

Surveys are a widely used practice activity. Students prepare and then ask questions about how often other students do things (*How often do you buy books?*).

Argument

Students prepare and act out a dialogue between boyfriend and girlfriend in which one complains and the other denies. Show how the first few lines might go on the board and then let students complete it (A: *You never come home early* B: *I usually come home at 6!* A: *You never bring me presents* B: *I sometimes bring presents!*).

How well do you know your partner?

Ask students to write eight sentences about things they think their partner does, including adverbs of frequency (*Julia never goes to the cinema*). Students then work in pairs to check how many of their sentences are correct.

Meaning and use

Adverbs of frequency tell us how often something is done. They can be placed on a continuum of frequency from 0% (it never happens) to 100% (it happens all the time). You can use a diagram like this when presenting the items to students.

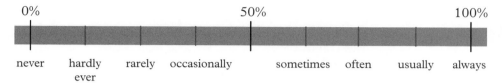

This seems relatively clear and straightforward – and this diagram is helpful to students – but note that the words are not scientifically applied. Exaggeration, generalisation and vagueness may modify the meaning. For example, when Milan complains about a friend and says *He never says what he thinks* he doesn't literally mean 'never' – but is exaggerating to make a point.

Watch out for these problems . . .

- **Students use the wrong word order:** (eg placing the adverb after the verb and before the direct object) ✗ *She drives usually her car to the sports centre.*

- **Students make a double negative with *never*:** ✗ *We don't never cook curry.*

28 Present progressive: affirmative ('now' meaning)

Form

I	'm / am		
You / We / They	're / are	watching	TV.
He / She / It	's / is		

Spelling the *-ing* form

We form the *-ing* form (also known as the present participle) by adding *-ing* to the base form.

We drop *-e* if the base form ends in a single letter *-e*.
take → taking. (This is not the case with double *e*: *see → seeing*.)

We double the consonant . . .

- if the base form ends in a single vowel + single consonant.
  sit → sitting. Exceptions are consonants *w, x, y*.
  sew → sewing, box → boxing, play → playing

- in two-syllable verbs if the base form ends in a single vowel + single consonant, and the stress is on the second syllable.
  forget → forgetting, prefer → preferring

- if the base form has two syllables and ends in *-l*.
  label → labelling (This rule doesn't apply in American English.)

We change a base form ending in *ie* to *y*.
lie → lying

We add *k* to a base form ending in *-c*.
picnic → picnicking

These are generally helpful guidelines – but not 100% solid rules. Try to include examples of each type of spelling variation in your examples when teaching.

Presentation

What are you doing?

1) Draw two people – one at each extreme of your board in different contexts (one is sitting on a beach and one is at a party). Add a mobile phone in each person's hand. Draw some other people around them, dancing, swimming, playing football etc. Make sure students understand the context and that the people are talking on the phone to each other.

2) Elicit or model some sentences they are saying to each other to describe what is happening in their location (*I'm building a sand castle. Miyuki's dancing with Haruko. Silvia's drinking a large lemonade. Sharif is swimming*). Get students to repeat each sentence.

3) Hand out a new picture showing a different pair of people (in a shop and at school). Students work in pairs to think of similar sentences they might say over the phone.

Practice

Behind my back

Turn your back to the class. Ask questions about what the students in the class are doing (*Tell me what Victor's doing now. Tell me what Hanna's doing now*). Repeat in pairs with students turning and asking questions.

Mime actions

Prepare some cue cards with actions written on them (*swimming, laughing, typing*). Student A should take a card and mime the action. Student B must guess and say what action their partner is doing (*You're swimming*).

Outside

Gather students at classroom windows and ask them to look out. Make pairs. Student A turns around away from the window. Student B chooses a person that they can see and tells their partner what he / she is doing (*This woman is looking in a shop window*). Student A then turns back to look out of the window and tries to spot which person was being described.

Pair work picture dictation

Select two interesting magazine pictures in which various people are doing different things. Photocopy them and distribute one to each person in a pair (with the instruction not to show their pictures to each other). Each student should describe their picture to their partner – who should try and draw it as accurately as possible (without looking at the original).

Team picture dictation

As a variation, make teams of four or five students. Each team appoints an artist whose job is to draw on the board. Hand out pictures. All the members of their team can see their picture except the artist. The teams must describe the picture so that the artist can draw an accurate copy on the board – or on a large sheet of paper pinned to the wall.

Storyboarding

Hand each pair a blank page divided into eight smaller rectangles, numbered from one to eight. Get students to plan an exciting 'film' by drawing a simple sketch into each of the eight spaces (the film starts at picture one and concludes at eight). When they are ready, make groups of four or six. Students can show their pictures and explain their film idea to others (*In this picture he's running away from the bank. Now the police are shooting at the helicopter*).

Concept questions

- **Jacob's playing tennis.** Is Jacob playing tennis now? (*Yes*) When did he start? (*Before now*) When will he finish? (*Sometime after now*)

- **Amanda's eating lunch at the café.** Is Amanda at work now? (*No*) Is Amanda in the café now? (*Yes*) When did she arrive at the café? (*Before now*) When will she leave the café? (*Probably when she finishes her lunch*)

Meaning and use

There are two very different time references with present progressive. This unit focuses on 'now' and 'around now'.

→ **Unit 49 Present progressive: 'future arrangements'**

Core meaning

Things which we think of as occupying a limited period of time. Temporary things – with a beginning and end – either now or around now.

Uses

We can use the present progressive to talk about . . .

1) things happening right at this moment, now.
   I'm waiting for you to answer.

I'm calling from Reception.
I'm writing on the board.

What's the most accurate time line?

If you look back at the core meaning of present progressive (above) you'll see that we think of the present progressive as having both a start time and end time. Following this idea, the 'now' meaning could equally well be characterised like this, ie showing something that started before now and will continue after now.

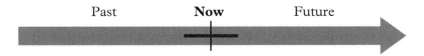

You may notice that this is essentially the same timeline as the meaning 2 below. Which timeline will you choose for the 'Now' meaning? Although this alternative diagram is probably more truthful, many teachers seem to find the simple single cross over 'now' is more immediately helpful when first introducing the present progressive.

2) things happening around the current moment, though maybe not at the precise moment of speaking. Talking about temporary states and events in progress that are of limited duration – they started *before* now and will end sometime *after* now. Although temporary, the period of time could be short or long.
   I'm reading a book about American history.
   She's serving life for murder.
   We are looking for writers.

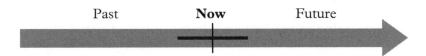

3) repeated actions over a temporary period.
   He's teaching in room 32 this month.
   We are closing at 3 pm all this week.
   She's always singing your praises.

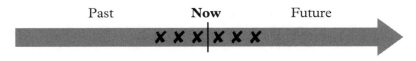

We use the present progressive (usually with *always*) for moaning or complaining about someone's annoying behaviour, habits or repeated actions. Although we use *always*, the behaviour is still perceived as happening within a specific, limited period of time, rather than really being for all time.

Pablo's always singing out of tune.

She's always complaining about her husband.

4) changes over time – for situations that are developing or changing.

> *Violent crime is increasing at an alarming rate.*
> *The situation is changing all the time.*
> *Property prices are still falling.*

Pronunciation

Contractions

We normally use contracted auxiliary verbs in most contexts other than in formal writing. The uncontracted forms are not the 'correct' or preferred forms. As with the present simple, some students get the idea that the uncontracted form is superior or more 'correct'. However, in most native speaker varieties of English, it will sound odd if the auxiliary verb is always pronounced with a 'full' value. The speaker may sound as if they are over emphatic or not fluent enough. However, in varieties of International English (eg East African English) it may be normal to decontract.

The uncontracted form can be used to emphasise a point, especially to give an answer that is in contrast to what has just been said:

A: *Silvio's not coming with us on the Priory excursion.*

Silvio: *I am coming.*

In this example *am* is both uncontracted and stressed and is probably said louder and with a facial expressions such as widening eyes or raised eyebrows.

Watch out for these problems . . .

- **Students omit the auxiliary verb:** ✗ *I swimming.* ✗ *He talking very fast.*

- **Students use the bare infinitive without an -*ing* ending:** ✗ *He is work very hard.* ✗ *We are play football.*

- **Students use the present progressive with stative verbs that normally take the present simple:** ✗ *I'm liking this very much.* ✗ *She is not believing in Father Christmas.* ✗ *They are having lots of money.*

- **Students have listening difficulties:** In normal fluent English, students may often have some difficulty hearing the pronoun in present progressive sentences because it is often pronounced in a very weak way. *He's waiting* may sound like /zweɪtɪŋ/; *I'm running* may sound like /mrʌnɪŋ/ and *We're coming now* may sound like /wɪkʌmɪŋ naʊ/. Knowing this may help students understand why they sometimes have difficulties when listening. Help raise their awareness by doing simple discrimination exercises – say a few sentences and ask students to write down the pronoun. Include examples where the pronoun is not distinct and train students to 'reconstruct' it by thinking about what pronoun could go with each auxiliary verb.

- **Students get muddled about apostrophes:** If your students get puzzled by apostrophes, remind them that one of the main uses is to indicate a place in a word where there is one or more missing letters. For example, the apostrophe in *She's leaving* indicates that the letter *i* is missing from the word *is*. So, if they can't remember where to write the apostrophe, ask them to think where the 'lost' letter was. The other main use of apostrophes is in possessives.

→ **Unit 6 Possessives**

Teaching tip: meaning and use

The teaching ideas in this unit typically involve situations where the listeners cannot see what the speaker or other people are doing or seeing. This provides a better reason for using the present progressive than just performing the action in front of the students. Compare this much-taught lesson:

- The teacher stands at the board and says 'I'm writing on the board.' The teacher walks to the door and says 'I'm opening the door.' The teacher sits down and says 'I'm sitting down (and so on).

Ideas like these may seem an obvious way of demonstrating the 'now' meaning of the present progressive. But while they may be helpful to some degree, it's worth noticing that they don't really teach how the present progressive is used.

In everyday life, we hardly ever tell someone else in the same location what we are doing at that moment; in fact, if we did, we'd probably sound slightly mad!

A: *I'm picking up my cup. I'm drinking my tea.*
B: *Yes, dear!*

Certainly, one meaning is to describe things that we are doing right now – but we would normally only say such sentences if there was a clear reason for doing so – if the listener was on the other end of a phone line and couldn't see what we were doing – or when asking someone to do something and giving a reason why we can't do it (*Can you answer the phone? I'm cooking*).

Such distinctions between 'meaning' (telling students that the present progressive refers to 'now') and 'use' (telling students that we use it when the other person can't see what we are doing) is an important one to bear in mind when teaching. Offering examples of use can be more valuable than generalised statements about meaning.

29 Present progressive: negative and questions

Form

Negative

I	'm				OR	There is no *I* form.			
You / We / They	're	not	watching	TV.		You / We / They	aren't	watching	TV.
He / She / It	's					He / She / It	isn't		

When first teaching this item, choose one of these ways of making negatives and stick to it. Otherwise it's potentially confusing for students.

Questions

Am	I		
Are	you / we / they	walking	in the right direction?
Is	he / she / it		

Wh- questions

What / When etc	am	I	
	are	you / we / they	singing?
	is	he / she / it	

Who	am	I	
	are	you / we / they	speaking to?
	is	he / she / it	

Negative questions

We quite often use negative questions, especially as a way of repeating an invitation or to encourage someone to do something.
Aren't you coming with us?
Aren't they working hard?
Aren't is used with *I*, rather than the more logical *amn't* (which doesn't exist!).

In written English always use the full uncontracted auxiliary verb.

Presentation

Lazy day

1) Draw some people on the board doing various active things and elicit what they are doing (*She's digging in the garden. They're playing football*). After all the sentences have been made, add that this was yesterday.

2) Draw a new picture showing today – with them watching TV or sleeping.

3) Get students to say all the things they are not doing today (*She's not playing football*).

→ **Unit 28 Present progressive affirmative ('now' meaning)**

Practice

Mime clues

Collect a set of photos of people doing different things. Stand in front of the class and show students that you have a picture – but don't show them what it is yet. Do a mime of the action (*swimming*) but not a terribly good one – so the class doesn't guess it immediately! Get the students to ask questions to work out what you are doing (*Are you running? Are you swimming?*). When they have guessed it correctly, reveal the picture. Get students to play the game themselves – either one student miming for the whole class – or in groups.

The hidden student

Find a place in the room where a person can't be seen (behind the door, crouching down behind the desk). Get a volunteer student to go to this place, out of sight of the rest of the class. Give the hidden student a noisy task (opening a packet of potato crisps). The student should make use of the item as loudly and noisily as possible (crinkling the packet of potato crisps). The students have to ask the hidden student questions to try and find out what they are doing. Students could also play the game in pairs.

Pair work picture difference

Use two spot the difference pictures with lots of people doing different things. Add name labels above each person (*Piotr, Christina*). Students work in pairs, keeping their own picture secret, and find out what the differences are by asking what different people are doing in their partner's picture (*What's Christina doing? Where is she swimming?*).

Suspicion

Make pairs A and B. Pairs will role play boyfriend / girlfriend or husband / wife or boss / employee. Student A is away from Student B but is very suspicious that B is not doing things properly. A must phone B and ask lots of questions (*What are you doing? Are you working hard? Are you cleaning the house?*). Allow students some time to prepare their questions – then do the activity as a role play.

The commentary

Place a TV-sized box in front of you so that only you can 'see' the (imaginary) screen. Start describing an imaginary programme (*It's night-time. A policeman is parking his car outside a building*) and then stop. Tell the class that you will tell them about the programme you are watching – but only if they ask questions. Students should ask questions (*Is he going into the building? Is anyone waiting inside the building? What is he doing now?*). Invent the story in response to their questions. When students have the idea, repeat the activity in pairs with A as a viewer and B as the person asking questions.

Variation

Use a clip from a real film downloaded on to a mobile phone. A student who can see answers questions from a student who can't see it, about what is happening.

Pronunciation

Although we always use the full uncontracted auxiliary verb in written English, when pronounced in fluent speech it will often sound contracted. In the following list, both ways of saying the example sentences are possible:

Am I winning?	/æm aɪ wɪnɪŋ/ or /maɪ wɪnɪŋ/
Are you living here?	/ɑː juː liːvɪŋ hɪə/ or /ə jə liːvɪŋ hɪə/
Is it bubbling yet?	/ɪz ɪt bʌblɪŋ jet/ or /zɪt bʌblɪŋ jet/

30 Present progressive contrasted with present simple

Presentation

A life change

1) Divide the board vertically in two. On the left, draw some pictures to establish Ivana's normal life (*She drives to work. She works in a marketing department. She has lunch in a café*). Elicit present simple sentences about her usual life (*She drives to work. She works in a shop. She lives in London*).

2) On the right of the board draw contrasting pictures to establish where she is right <u>now</u> – ie on holiday in another country. Get students to extend the original sentences with present progressive endings to show the contrast between her ordinary life and what she is doing now (*She lives in London but she's visiting India now. She usually drives to work but today she's visiting the Taj Mahal*).

Practice

A different day

Draw a picture of someone whose day is different from normal (because they are lying ill in bed or have broken their leg). Ask students to think of how today is different from her normal life (*She usually works in an office but today she's lying in bed. She usually drinks a lot of coffee but today she's drinking water*).

The teacher's life

Dictate to your class some present simple sentences about things you normally or usually do – or don't do (*I eat lots of chips. I never take exercise*). Then say that this month your life is different in a number of ways. Ask them to make sentences speculating about how it is different (*You usually eat lots of chips – but this month you're eating a healthy diet. You never usually take exercise – but this month you're going swimming every morning).* Tell them which guesses they got right. (A little teacher fibbing seems to be OK in this game; don't worry too much about telling the absolute truth.)

Concept questions

- **Ichiro usually lives and works in Tokyo but this month he's working in New York.** Is Ichiro's usual job in New York? (*No*) Where is his home? (*Tokyo*) Is he in Tokyo now? (*No*) Where is Ichiro this month? (*New York*) Which job is permanent – Tokyo or New York? (*Tokyo*) Which job is temporary – Tokyo or New York? (*New York*) Where will he sleep this evening – in Tokyo or New York? (*New York*)

Meaning and use

Many coursebooks focus on comparing these two tenses, mainly because students tend to confuse them. At lower levels, there are typically three key points that students are expected to learn:

- The present simple is for talking about things that happen always, usually, regularly, frequently, sometimes, often, hardly ever etc.

- The present progressive is for talking about things happening now or 'around now' . . .

- . . . except for state verbs (*be, hear, feel, believe, love, see, like, think, know* etc) where the present simple is used for talking about now or 'around now'.

Watch out for these problems . . .

- **Students use the present simple for things happening now:** ✗ *He walks towards the classroom.*

- **Students use the present progressive inappropriately with state verbs:** ✗ *I'm believing you.*

Teaching tip: identifying errors

It is sometimes hard to spot an error with these tenses. For example, when a student asks someone 'What do you do?' and the person replies 'I'm a shop assistant' the questioner may be embarrassed to point out that she actually wanted to ask what the person was doing at the moment. Sometimes it is useful for a teacher to ask a check question (*Are you asking about now . . . or usually?*) to help confirm the real intention of the speaker. Alternatively, keep an uncompleted timeline poster on the wall and point at 'now' with a puzzled expression to encourage students to self-correct.

31 Past simple: *be*

Form

Affirmative

I / He / She / It	was	at Sami's party yesterday.
You / We / They	were	happy about the plans.

Negative

I / He / She / It	wasn't / was not	at Sami's party yesterday.
You / We / They	weren't / were not	happy about the plans.

Yes / No questions

Was	I / he / she / it	at Sami's party yesterday?
Were	you / we / they	happy about the plans?

Wh- questions

Where	was	I / he / she / it	yesterday?
	were	you / we / they	

Short answers

Yes,	I / he / she / it	was.
	you / we / they	were.

No,	I / he / she / it	wasn't.
	you / we / they	weren't.

Be is often followed by:

- an adjective.
  She was happy.

- a noun or noun phrase.
  He was a constable.
  It was an absolutely delightful afternoon.

- an adverb.
  together, alone, alight

- a prepositional phrase.
  They were in the living room.
  The object was underwater.

Don't confuse these uses of *was / were* (ie as main verbs in the past simple) with their use as auxiliary verbs in the past progressive.
You were driving too fast.

Presentation

> When I was a baby I was . . .
>
> When I was young my sister was . . .
>
> At school I was . . .
>
> My teachers were . . .
>
> When I got my first job I was . . .

My life at different stages

1) Write up some sentence starters on the board (*When I was a baby I was . . ., On my last birthday I was . . .,When I was young my sister was . . ., At school I was . . ., My teachers were . . .,When I got my first job I was . . .*). Adjust the sentences to suit your class. Include negatives if you wish (*I wasn't very good at . . .*).

2) Talk through and write up endings for the sentences that are true for you (*When I was a baby I was very fat. On my last birthday I was 32 years old*).

3) Erase the endings and see if students can remember them.

4) Work with one student in front of the class, discussing possible true endings for them and writing them up (*When I was a baby I was very noisy. On my last birthday I was 12 years old. When I was young my sister was very annoying*).

5) In pairs students tell each other and write true sentences about themselves using the sentence starters. Stronger or more creative students could also add new sentences of their own.

Practice

Famous people

Make a list of deceased famous people that had well-known jobs or roles. Work with students to talk about them and write true sentences. (*Brandon Lee and Heath Ledger were film actors. Henry VIII wasn't King of Russia.*)

Denying

What might otherwise be dull repetition drills can be enlivened by adding small extra factors to them. This can often be achieved by contextualising the target language within a short dialogue or situation. For example, rather than just getting students to repeat 'I was at school . . . I wasn't at home' (dull!) tell them that a police officer or the head teacher is accusing them of doing something bad and asking them questions. The students have to reply by denying everything using two-word answers (*I was, I wasn't, we weren't* etc A: *You were out of school.* B: *I wasn't!* A: *You were in the shopping mall!* B: *I wasn't!* A: *Your friends were there too.* B: *They weren't!* A: *You were all very rude to the shopkeepers.* B: *We weren't!*). This sort of drill also gives students a great chance to play with intonation too. Don't allow soft, dull responses – get them to argue back.

Questionnaire

Write questions to make a questionnaire for students to ask each other and find out personal information (*Where were you born? When were you born? What was your favourite subject at school? Who were your teachers last year?*). Students mingle and ask each other the questions.

Quiz

Make quiz questions (*Who was President of the USA in 1962? Who was the Joker in Batman – The Dark Knight?*). Students can also write their own *was / were* quiz questions.

Where were you?

Write ten phrases naming different locations on the board (*at the cinema, in the bath, at the shops, on the hill, in McDonalds®*). Write up this sample dialogue:
A: *I phoned at . . . o'clock – no answer. Where were you?* (NB stress on *were*).
B: *I was . . .*

Make pairs. Students act out the dialogue giving different explanations for different times of the day (*I was in the bath! I was at McDonalds®*).

It's not always easy to practise *was / were* without bringing in other past simple verbs (*phoned* in *Where were you?* above). It may be a good idea to include such verbs without drawing close attention to them, saving a detailed focus for a presentation in a later lesson.

Meaning and use

→ **Unit 32 Past simple: regular verbs**

Pronunciation

We often pronounce *was* and *were* as weak forms: /wəz/ and /wə/.

Watch out for these problems . . .

- **Students use *was* as an all-purpose past tense:** ✗ *I was go to Berlin last year. Was* and *were* are the past simple forms of *is* and *are*. However, because they are so useful, coursebooks often teach them separately before the main focus on the past simple. This can sometimes confuse students, who may get the idea that all past sentences are made with *was / were*.

32 Past simple: regular verbs

Form

Regular verbs all end in -ed.
He walked to school.
They tidied the room.

We make regular past simple verbs by adding -ed to the base form.
walk → walked, turn → turned, watch → watched

We add -d for verbs that already end in -e.
like → liked, waste → wasted, believe → believed

We double the consonant:

- if the base form ends in a single vowel + single consonant.

  fit → fitted, stop → stopped
  Exceptions are consonants -w, -x, -y.
  sew → sewed, box → boxed, play → played

- in two-syllable verbs if the base form ends in a single vowel + single consonant, and the stress is on the second syllable.
  regret → regretted, prefer → preferred

- if the base form has two syllables and ends in -l.
  travel → travelled
  This rule doesn't apply in American English.

We change the -y to -i for some verbs that end in consonant + –y.
try → tried, fry → fried

We add k to a base form ending in -c.
panic → panicked

Time references

We often use the past simple with time references:

- *last night, yesterday, five years ago* etc.

- using *for*: *for two months, for a week or two.*

- using *in*: *in 1998, in September.*

Presentation

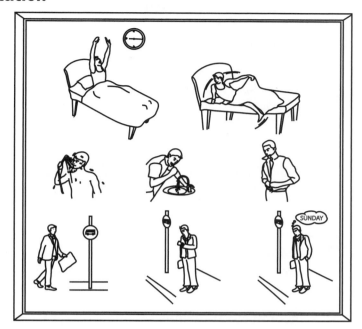

Mime story

1) Prepare a short story using only *was / were* and about ten regular past simple verbs (*opened, looked, jumped, washed, dressed, brushed, walked, waited, remembered*). Divide the story into separate small mimable chunks (indicated in the sample text by /). If you want to use pictures to help your mime you could also prepare some sketches (opening eyes, looking at clock etc).

   Yesterday morning Artur opened his eyes / and looked at his clock. / 'Oh no! 9.15!' / He was late for work! / He jumped out of bed, / washed, / dressed, / brushed his teeth / and walked quickly to the bus stop. / He waited for ten minutes. / No bus! / Then suddenly he remembered / . . . It was Sunday!

2) Tell the class that they should help you to tell a story. Write the opening words 'Yesterday morning Artur . . .' on the board. Mime the first action (*opening eyes*) and show the picture if you have one. Elicit the next few missing words from students. If they say 'open his eyes,' point at the word *yesterday* on the board and write up *'-ed'*. If that does not help them, then model the word *opened* yourself. Model the chunk yourself when appropriate and get students to repeat the line. Point out the use of *-ed* to make a past simple verb.

3) Go on to the next mime (*looked at the clock*) and reveal the next picture if you are using them. Elicit the next part of the story and get students to repeat it. Continue miming, revealing pictures and getting language from students until the story has been completed. Occasionally get students to repeat the whole story so far.

4) Ask students in pairs, to retell the whole story – then elicit it once more and write it up on the board.

Practice

You may find it difficult to find activities that restrict practice entirely to regular verbs. Many teachers choose to introduce and work with a few important irregular verbs alongside the regular ones: *went, saw, said*. Alternatively, select the most useful mix of regular and irregular verbs for introducing first.

Mixed up verbs

Prepare a story using regular past simple verbs (*Last year I visited my aunt. She lived in Australia then . . .*). Print out the text with the verbs mixed up (*Last year I printed my aunt. She washed in Australia then*). Set students the task of writing the story out correctly.

List to story

Give students a list of about ten regular past simple verbs. Working in pairs they should see if they can come up with a short story using at least six of them.

Incomplete timelines

Concept questions are a good way to check if students understand the meaning of a grammatical item. An interesting variation is to use partially-drawn timelines. To do this draw a blank timeline on the board.

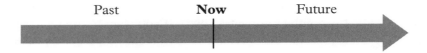

Past   **Now**   Future

Now, write a sentence on the board (*He walked to the town centre*) and invite a student to come up to the board and try placing it on the timeline. This is, of course, presuming that you have sometimes used timelines with students – so that they know what they are looking at! When the student has marked something on the timeline, don't immediately respond with your own evaluation. Instead, get other students in class to comment and maybe suggest alternatives. See if the class can achieve some consensus as to the best way to represent the time of the sentence.

Concept questions

- **He lived in Rome when he was a child.** Does he live in Rome now? (*Maybe – but probably not. We don't know*) Did he live in Rome in the past? (*Yes*) When? (*When he was a child*)

- **She worked at Ferrari for five years.** Did she work at Ferrari in the past? (*Yes*) Does she work at Ferrari now? (*No*) How many years did she work at Ferrari for? (*Five*)

When making good concept questions, it's usually best to avoid using the grammatical item that is being checked. However, there are some items where this is very hard to do, without making some rather odd questions – and this is definitely one!

Meaning and use

Core meaning: Events in the past

We use the past simple (NB examples include both regular and irregular verbs) . . .

1) to talk about single momentary past events.
   They bought the paintings in 1989.

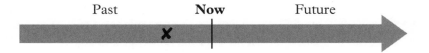

2) to narrate a sequence of actions to tell a story.
   The candle flared, then flickered and went out.

3) to talk about things that happened over a period of time in the past.
   We went to the same school when we were children.
   He studied theology in Vienna for three years.
   He lived most of his adult life in prison.

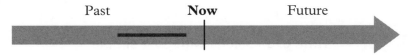

4) to talk about repeated past events, ie (non-continuous) things that happened a number of times in the past.
   I rang them first thing every morning.
   Monet painted 400 or so pictures at Giverny.
   We went to church every Sunday.

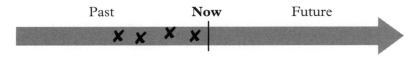

5) to talk about sudden events, in contrast to another ongoing background action. The event might have interrupted or stopped the earlier event.
He was vacuuming when I arrived. ('*was vacuuming*' is past progressive. '*arrived*' is past simple).
We were having breakfast when Birgit phoned ('*were having*' is past progressive. '*phoned*' is past simple).

→ **Unit 37 Past progressive 'interrupted actions'**

6) to talk about events happening at the same time (with *while* or *when*). Both verbs could be past simple – or one might be past progressive.
She watched me with interest while I ate.
The gun went off while he was cleaning it.

7) after *if*, to make the idea sound unlikely or impossible.
If Luke paid more attention in class, he would achieve better results.

→ **Unit 58 Second conditional**

Remoteness

Some writers have proposed that the key meaning of the past simple is 'remoteness' – whether in time (ie indicating the past), in hierarchy or relationship (ie *I wondered if you . . .*) or in likelihood (ie *If I went to the moon . . .*).

Time expressions with past simple

Ago

Ago tells us about the period of time between two times – now and an earlier time. We are looking back from the present and measuring how much time there was between now and the time in the past when something happened. It is used to say how far back in the past something happened.

I started my job two months ago.

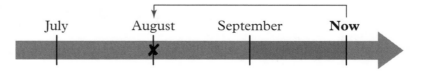

For

We use *for* to say how long a past event or state lasted.
He studied theology in Vienna for three years.

Until

We use *until* to state when an event or state finished.
She sat on the bottom step until she got cold.
We waited until he left.

Since

We don't usually use *since* with the past simple, but it is common with the present perfect or past perfect.

→ **Unit 42 Time words: *for* and *since***

The past simple is an absolutely crucial tense for students – not just to study for one week and then move on. The past simple is used all the time in speaking and writing and is essential for almost any kind of narrative or description. It is relatively straightforward to use – but students will make mistakes with irregular past forms, questions and negatives. You cannot 'teach' this once and then assume it's done. Of all language items, this is one to keep returning to. The initial 'presentation' doesn't count for much. Repeated practice does.

Pronunciation

The *-ed* ending can be pronounced in three different ways:

* /ɪd/ *wanted, waited, waded* (after /d/, /t/)

* /t/ *walked, coughed, flicked* (after /f/, /k/, /p/, /s/, /ʃ/, /tʃ/)

* /d/ *stirred, fired, signed* (after all other sounds)

Emphatic statements

It is possible to make past simple statements using *did* and the base form of the verb.
I did lock the door. I'm absolutely sure.
He did pass his final exam – but only just.

In these sentences, *did* will usually be stressed – sounding louder, longer and higher in pitch than the main verb. This form is only used to emphasise a statement – to say that something actually happened, probably in contradiction to what someone else has just said.
A: *You didn't walk to work. I bet you took the tram!*
B: *I did walk to work.*

Watch out for students who seem to think that this emphatic form is the normal way of making past simple statements.

Watch out for these problems . . .

- **Students use *was* with the base form as an 'easy' past form:** ✗ *I was go to the shops.* ✗ *She was listen to me.*

- **Students overuse the /ɪd/ pronunciation:** ✗ *I walked* /wɔːlkɪd/ *to school.* Some students use it for many verbs where it is inappropriate. Help by pointing out that a word like 'walked' has a /t/ ending and is actually one syllable, not two. Get them to try saying it as one syllable.

- **Students have wrong ideas about the past simple:** Depending on their first language students may have false assumptions about the limits of past simple use. They may wrongly think that it is only used for story narratives or only for single events. Watch out for the incorrect learner assumption that use of the past simple always means 'distant' past. Using the past simple does not indicate how far back in the past something happened; we can use the same tense whether it happened a few seconds ago or back in the Jurassic Age.

Teaching tip: gestures

Many teachers use a simple 'pointing backwards, over their shoulder' gesture to indicate 'past'. This is useful as a quick correction technique when a student forgets to use a past tense in a sentence. Instead of giving a spoken correction, simply use the gesture and see if the learner can correct themselves.

33 Past simple: irregular verbs

Form

Affirmative statements (irregular verbs)

Irregular past simple verbs have different and unpredictable forms. They need to be learnt individually.

run → ran, fly → flew, go → went

Some irregular past forms are spelt the same as the base form (though may be pronounced differently).

put → put (same pronunciation)

read → read (change of vowel sound)

Irregular past simple forms are made using the verb listed in the second column of a standard verb table:

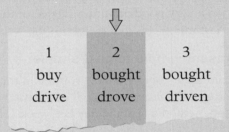

1	2	3
buy	bought	bought
drive	drove	driven

I went to London.
She ate supper.
He wrote a letter.
We read it.

Presentation

wake	→	woke
see	→	saw
eat	→	ate
go	→	went
run	→	ran
find	→	found
take	→	took
break	→	broke

Story seeds

1) Dictate a list of 15–20 past simple verbs (*woke, saw, ate, went, ran, found, took, broke*).

2) Check if students have written them down correctly. Work through the list and find out if students can guess which verbs they are the past form of. Build a table on the board listing infinitive and past form (*wake / woke, see / saw, eat / ate*).

3) Ask students to work in pairs to make a story using all the verbs in the order you dictated. They can make a story about anything they wish but they must use the given verbs in <u>exactly the order you dictated</u> (ie verb 1 must be in the story before verb 2).

4) Compare stories.

Practice

Chat about last night

The classic lesson warm-up when you chat with students as they arrive in class is often a very good, natural practice of the past simple. You can say 'What did you do last night?' or 'Tell me about the weekend'.

Present simple to past simple

Build up a story of a daily routine in the present simple (*Jonas usually gets a lift to school. He meets his friends at the gate*). Then build a contrasting picture of what happened on a specific day last week (*He walked to school. He met a teacher at the gate*).

I went out today

Write up the first ten letters of the alphabet on the board. Elicit or tell students past verb forms (regular or irregular) for each letter (*ate, bought, caught, dreamt, explained, fought, gave, heard, invited, jumped*). Write them up on the board. One player starts by saying 'I went out today and I . . .' They should then complete the sentence with the 'A' verb and an appropriate ending (*ate an apple*. NB: verb and noun both begin with A). The second player can then continue by repeating the first sentence and adding a second sentence with a new verb and noun, both starting with B (*I ate an apple and bought a book*). As the game continues through the alphabet students have to remember and repeat more and more. If students enjoy it, you could try extending it further into the alphabet (*kissed, left, met*).

Storytelling

Narratives of all kinds are at the heart of work on the past simple. Try telling your class anecdotes about your life or little stories and jokes you collect from different sources. In class you can try different techniques to keep the activities varied. Tell a story and then . . . (a) the class repeats it afterwards in pairs (b) you retell it with gaps for each verb which the class call out (c) you retell it with mistakes which the class should try to spot and correct.

A few common ideas and contexts for past simple practice

Holidays (*flew, stayed, visited, saw, bought, climbed, enjoyed*)

Shopping trips (*looked, asked, tried, chose, paid*)

Losing something (*went, lost, looked, asked, remembered, found*)

Concept questions

- **Carrie gave me a new clock.** Is Carrie giving me a clock now? (*No*) Will she give me a new clock tomorrow? (*No*) When did she give me the clock? (*In the past*) Recently? (*We don't know*) A long time ago? (*We don't know*)

- **I went to Auckland on holiday last year.** Am I in Auckland now? (*No*) Am I going to Auckland in the future? (*No*) When did I go to Auckland? (*Last year*)

Watch out for these problems . . .

- **Students use an incorrect past form:** (often creatively generating a regular ending for an irregular verb) ✗ *We goed to the beach.* ✗ *She flied with Etihad Airlines.*

- **Students avoid using a past form:** ✗ *After the pub Russell go to the bus station.* ✗ *Last year she work in an office.*

34 Past simple: questions and short answers

Form

Yes / No questions

Did / Didn't	+	I / you / he / she / it / we / they	+	base form verb

Did you visit the Great Wall when you were in China?

We make past simple questions using *did*. Regular and irregular verbs both have the same form.

As with negatives, the past form is not used. The auxiliary *did* shows the tense.

Wh- questions

Where / Why / Who / When / How long etc	+	did / didn't	+	I / you / he / she / it / we / they	+	base form verb

When did she pass her exams?
Why didn't you call me?

Negative questions

These are quite common. Use *didn't* instead of *did*.

Didn't you know?
Why didn't you tell me?

Rising intonation questions

A third way of making past simple questions is to say a statement with rising intonation. This is often used to show surprise or doubt – or to ask for confirmation of something.

You told Tony what I said?
He cheated?
We went to the same school?

Short answers
Regular and irregular past simple verbs have the same form.

Yes,	I / you / he / she / it / we / they	did.
No,	I / you / he / she / it / we / they	didn't.

These are fixed phrases – *Yes, I did* and *No, I didn't*. They are a common way of replying to past simple questions.

A: *Did they ever pay you?*   B: *Yes, they did.*
A: *You promised to come with me.*   B: *No, I didn't.*

Presentation

Prison chat

1) Draw a sketch of two cellmates in prison. Elicit or model questions they ask each other about their past lives. The prison context helps to keep the focus on the past. You can introduce *Yes / No* questions (*Did you like your work? Did you rob banks? Did you have a lot of friends?*) and / or *Wh-* questions (*Where did you live? What work did you do? How did they catch you?*) as you choose.

2) Practise asking and answering the questions in the whole class, imagining what the prisoners would say.

3) Get pairs to role play the conversation with questions and answers.

Practice

These are the answers — what are the questions?

Draw a picture of a job interview and make sure students are clear what the situation is. Write up a list of ten answers on the board (*2008. Prague. Yes – First Certificate*). Students work together to decide what the interviewer's questions were (*When did you leave university? Where did you study? Did you take any English exams?*).

Guess who?

Tell students 'I'm a famous person from history. Ask me some questions and find out who I am.' Students ask questions to work out who you are (*Did you work in politics? Where did you live?*). Let students play the game after they have guessed your demonstration.

Picture questions

Divide the class into two halves, A and B. Show group A a large picture showing a lot of things happening – and a different picture to group B. Tell students that their pictures show some things that happened yesterday. Students work in pairs or small groups to write ten questions about what happened yesterday in their picture (*What did the blonde woman buy? Where did the man put his gun?*). When they are ready, make new pairs of students (with an A and a B in each pair). The students in each pair swap pictures. They can look at the new picture for 20 seconds and then must put it face down on the table. Then they try to answer their partner's questions.

Red Riding Hood

Choose a familiar, famous story that all the class will know (*Red Riding Hood*). Help students to brainstorm and collect as many questions about the story as they can onto the board (*Where did she live? What did she wear? Who did she meet?*). There are a very large number of possible questions. However, answering with creative new answers could make a new story! Students don't need to answer the questions!

Pronunciation

Elision

The past simple question form often includes features of elision (= when sounds get lost) and assimilation (= when sounds change into others). *Did you go?* can be pronounced in any of the following ways:

- Full, strong pronunciation /dɪd juː gəʊ/

- Faster, more fluent pronunciations /dɪdjə gəʊ/; /dɪdʒuː gəʊ/; /dɪdʒə gəʊ/; /dʒə gəʊ/

Watch out for these problems . . .

- **Students use the past form (rather than the base form) in a past question:** ✗ *Did you went to the office?* ✗ *What did she lost?*

- **Students use a main verb instead of *did* to answer a question:** ✗ A: *Did you walk there?* B: *Yes, I walked.* ✗ A: *Did you buy it?* B: *Yes, I bought.* (NB Including the object (*there* or *it*) in the answers would make these possible – though less likely than the short answer *Yes, I did.*)

Teaching tip: teach first?

Some teachers choose to teach past simple questions and negatives along with short answers (*Yes, I did / No I didn't*) *before* introducing irregular affirmative forms. This is because question and negative forms do not make use of the past simple verb form – which means that students can start to practise talking about the past without learning lots of irregular verbs.

35 Past simple: negative

Form

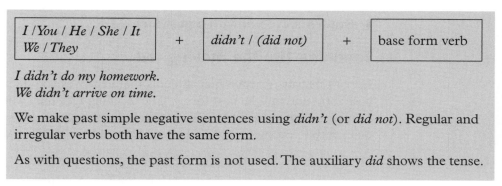

| I /You / He / She / It We / They | + | didn't / (did not) | + | base form verb |

I didn't do my homework.
We didn't arrive on time.

We make past simple negative sentences using *didn't* (or *did not*). Regular and irregular verbs both have the same form.

As with questions, the past form is not used. The auxiliary *did* shows the tense.

Presentation

Mime story

1) Use a familiar past simple story that students have already studied (such as the story about Artur from Unit 32). Rewrite the story so that this time he didn't do many of the things (*Artur opened his eyes / and looked at his clock. – '9.15!' / He didn't jump out of bed. / He didn't wash. / He didn't dress. / He didn't brush his teeth etc … He knew it was Sunday!*).

2) In class, use the pictures to elicit, model and get students to repeat the story as you build it.

Practice

Use ideas from the affirmative and questions section Units 32, 33 and 34 – but include negative sentences (*Tell me some things that didn't happen yesterday*).

Children's stories / folktales

The Little Red Hen (*planted, watered, cut, others didn't help, baked, ate, didn't give*)

Jack and the Beanstalk (*planted, grew, climbed, cried out, chopped down, fell*)
Peter and the Wolf (*felt bored, cried 'help', villagers came, wasn't a wolf, didn't come, killed*)

Pronunciation

did not

The uncontracted form *did not* is rarer than *didn't* and sounds more emphatic (as if the speaker is saying *I definitely didn't …*), and depending on context, perhaps more assertive or ruder. The word *not* is usually stressed.

I did <u>not</u> sign my name on that contract.

Watch out for these problems . . .

- **Students use *didn't* with a past form:** ✗ *She didn't went there.* ✗ *They didn't came in time.*

- **Students use *not* with a past form:** ✗ *She not made a cake.*

Teaching tip: the moving -ed

Here's one way of reminding students that negatives and questions use the verb base form and not the past form. (The teaching idea only works with regular *-ed* forms.) Use the board to show the *-ed* (indicating pastness) moving from the main verb to the auxiliary verb where it transforms a little and becomes *did:*

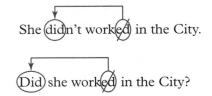

She didn't worked in the City.

Did she worked in the City?

The auxiliary verb now indicates 'pastness' so the main verb doesn't need to do this.

36 Past progressive: 'in progress'

Form

In many books the past progressive is called the past continuous.

We make the past progressive in a similar way to the present progressive – but with the past simple of *be* (*was* / *were*) instead of the present simple (*am* / *is* / *are*).

Affirmative

I / He / She / It	was	
You / We / They	were	watching TV.

We don't contract *was* or *were*.

Negative

I / He / She / It	wasn't (was not)	
You / We / They	weren't (were not)	watching TV.

Yes / No questions

Was / Wasn't	I / he / she / it	
Were / Weren't	you / we / they	walking in the right direction?

Wh- questions

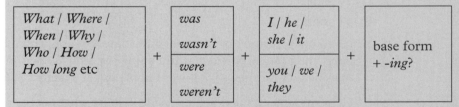

| What / Where / When / Why / Who / How / How long etc | + | was
wasn't
were
weren't | + | I / he / she / it
you / we / they | + | base form + -ing? |

Short answers

Yes,	I / he / she / it	was.		No,	I / he / she / it	wasn't.
	you / we / they	were.			you / we / they	weren't.

Negative questions

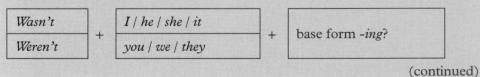

Wasn't	+	I / he / she / it	+	base form -ing?
Weren't		you / we / they		

(continued)

Although not often mentioned in many coursebooks, negative questions are actually quite frequently used in everyday communication – especially as a way of double-checking something, for example, when you thought you knew what would happen, but actual events seem to be going in a different way *Weren't the children coming with us?* (= I thought the children were coming – but they don't appear to be).

Presentation

Busy scene

1) Hand out a cartoon or photo of a bustling location with lots of things happening (an airport departure lounge or a busy open-plan office). Explain that the picture shows what was happening at exactly 12.00 midday yesterday.

2) Help students to make sentences describing what people were doing (*Some children were climbing on a pile of suitcases*).

3) Hide the picture, erase the sentences and close all student books. Write 'At 12.00 yesterday . . .' Ask students to work in pairs and see how much they can remember to complete that sentence in different ways.

Practice

Crime scene

Add a 'crime' to the idea above (something was stolen). Students make witness sentences for characters in the picture in answer to police questions (*What were you doing at 12 o'clock?*).

Interrogation

Tell students that you are a military policeman. You have caught someone that you think is a spy from another country. You believe that they stole some secrets from your government. Get a volunteer to play the spy. Interrogate them about what they were doing yesterday (*What were you doing at 10.00 yesterday morning? / What were you doing at 10.30? / 11.00?* etc). Each time the student should give a convincing answer (*I was drinking coffee in Starbucks®*). Once students have seen the demonstration, they can repeat the game in pairs.

Alibi

This popular teaching game is a variation on Interrogation (above). It doesn't only practise the past progressive, but is likely to include a lot of this tense.

- You need two capable volunteers (ie stronger students who have a creative imagination and reasonable language ability).

- Tell them that there was a bank robbery in town yesterday afternoon. The police suspect them. They have told the police that they couldn't have done the robbery because they were together for the whole time – away from the robbery's location.

- The two students must now go outside the room and prepare a detailed alibi (= a story about what they were doing) for the hours between 1 pm and 4 pm. It is vital that they both try to have exactly the same story.

- While they are out of the room, the class (playing the role of the police) think of some good questions they could ask them.

- When everyone is ready, one of the students is invited back in and questioned by the class (who keep notes of the answers).

- When that is over, the other student is asked in and asked the same questions.

- The aim for the suspects is to produce the same answers as each other. The aim for the police is to ask questions that the suspects answer differently.

- If more than three suspects' answers are significantly different – the police win and arrest the suspects – otherwise the suspects win.

Simultaneous actions

Get two students doing different things at the same time (cleaning the board and looking out of the window). After they have sat down again, challenge the class to make one sentence that includes both actions (*Sara was looking out the window while Bill was cleaning the board*). Don't get students to make the sentences while the actions are going on – or it will be a present situation rather than a past one.

Concept questions

- **Susan was working at Reception at 10 o'clock.** Where was Susan at 10 o'clock? (*At Reception*) Was she there before 10 o'clock? (*Yes*) Was she there after 10 o'clock? (*Yes*)

- **While Trey was cooking supper, Madalena was surfing the net.** Are these sentences about the past? (*Yes*) Did both actions – surfing and cooking – happen at the same time? (*Yes*) Did one action last longer than the other? (*Maybe – but we don't know*) Which action started first: surfing or cooking? (*We don't know*) Which thing ended first: surfing or cooking? (*We don't know*)

Meaning and use

Core meanings

Something in progress in the past – typically temporary rather than permanent.

Uses

We use the past progressive to talk about . . .

1) something in progress over a certain past period.
   This could be a continuous action or an action that happened repeatedly.
   We were making too much noise.
   I was doing the same old thing, week after week.

2) something in progress at a certain past moment / time – often using *at* or *on*. It started before the named time – and finished after the time (which could be a named time / date or an implied one – the time when something happened).
   City were leading 3–0 at half time.
   We were living in Edinburgh at the time.
   Why was Mark wandering around the streets at 2 o'clock on Sunday morning?

   Also for something in progress up to / after a time.
   I was working until the early hours of the morning.

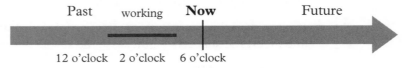

3) something in progress at the same time as something else was in progress (typically using *while*, *when* or *and*). The two events are simultaneous – though one may last longer than the other. We may use the past progressive for both events or the past progressive for one and the past simple for the other.
   I was working in the garden while you were having lunch!

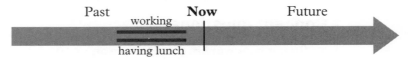

4) polite enquiries.

We use the past progressive to make a formal, very polite enquiry about the present.

I was wondering if I could use your phone? (= Can I use your phone?)
Were you leaving? (= Are you leaving?)

Interestingly, this can also be used with state verbs.
Were you wanting some help? (= Do you want some help?)

You may be wondering why a past tense is used when there is a present meaning in enquiries such as *Were you leaving?* It is arguable that the action of 'leaving' is partly in the past – but this answer doesn't feel satisfactory. In fact, using a past tense is a way of showing distance or remoteness from the present moment. Most commonly, this is a distance in time – but it can also be a distance that shows formality and politeness. So *Were you wanting some help?* sounds significantly more polite and formal than *Do you want some help?* – though, also nowadays, possibly sounds a little over-formal.

5) setting the background.

We often use the past progressive to set the 'background' for a story, before the actual narrative begins with past simple verbs.

The sun was setting over the forest. The last few tourists were wandering back to the hotels. Suddenly, a loud noise echoed round the hills.

As a shorthand guide for students, this simplified summary may help:
Background scene-setting: past progressive
Actions in the story: past simple

Pronunciation

Weak form pronunciation and spelling

In normal fluent speech *was* and *were* are weak forms. *Was* is pronounced /wəz/. *Were* is pronounced /wə/. Students may over-pronounce these words, using the strong forms /wɒz/ and /wɜː/. ✗ *I was working at midday.*

Watch out for these problems . . .

- **Students use the past simple instead of past progressive to describe background activities:** ✗ *We had lunch when the front door bell rang* (= *We were having lunch . . .*)

- **Students use past progressive with stative verbs:** ✗ *I was believing him.* ✗ *They were having a new car.*

- **Students get the wrong idea about the length of events:** Students sometimes think that the past progressive always indicates an action that lasts a long time while the past simple refers to shorter events. This is not a useful guideline. Compare the two tenses of *stand* in these sentences: *Everest stood for millions of years before man conquered it. Now Mike was standing on the summit.*

37 Past progressive: 'interrupted actions'

Form

past progressive	*when* or *and*	past simple

I was running for the train when I fell over a bag.

Presentation

Cooking

1) Draw a simple picture of a person cooking in a kitchen. Elicit that this shows Enrique at 7 pm yesterday. Elicit a sentence to describe what he was doing (*Enrique was cooking dinner at seven o'clock last night*).

2) Draw a phone and indicate a ringing noise (by making the noise or adding ✗✗ to the picture). Elicit a sentence in the past simple to describe this (*The phone rang*).

3) Ask students to put the two sentences together (*Enrique was cooking dinner when the phone rang*). Get students to practise saying this.

4) Draw some more simple situations for students to make sentences about (*Marie was playing golf when it started raining. The children were walking to school when Graca fell over*).

Practice

Mime

Set up similar situations to the presentation (above) live in class and get students to make sentences describing what happened (*The teacher was coming into the room when he tripped over Karl's bag. Marcia was texting her friend when the teacher asked her a question*).

Physical response

Get all the students to stand away from their desks in a clear space and do actions to follow your sequence of your instructions (*Touch your toes . . . pick up a pen . . . give the pen to your partner*). After a few instructions, do an 'interrupting' action (*dropping a book loudly onto the floor*). Get students to make a sentence describing what happened (*I was giving a pen to my partner when you dropped a book*). Continue with more instructions and more interruptions. After a while you could get a confident student to lead the actions.

Hotel robbery

Show a picture of a busy hotel scene (or shopping mall or restaurant) with lots of people. Explain that it shows the place at 7.59 yesterday evening. Ask each student to choose one of the people in the scene, imagine that they were that person and think about what they were doing at that time. Explain that at 8.00 all the electricity suddenly went off and it was pitch black. Many people were robbed! Explain that it is now the next morning and the police are questioning everyone. Make small groups. In each group one person should be the 'police officer' and ask questions to the others (*What were you doing when the lights went out? Who were you talking to?*). When they have noted the answers, the police can report back to the whole group.

Concept questions

- **Ewan was taking a shower when the postman knocked at the door.** Where was Ewan? (*In the shower*) Did he start to take his shower before the postman knocked at the door? (*Yes*) Where was he when the postman knocked? (*In the shower*) Did he finish his shower before the postman knocked? (*No*) What did he do when the postman knocked? (*We don't know – maybe he stopped showering to answer the door – or maybe he ignored the knocking*)

- **Rachel was still putting on her make-up when the taxi arrived.** When the taxi arrived was Rachel ready? (*No*) Why not? (*Her make-up wasn't finished*) When did Rachel start to do her make-up – before the taxi arrived or after? (*Before*) When did she stop doing her make-up – before the taxi arrived or after? (*After*) Did she stop putting on make-up when the taxi arrived? (*We don't know*)

Meaning and use

Something in progress in the past when something else happened often with *when, and* or *while.*

This meaning is often called the 'interrupted past progressive'. The interrupted action may be stopped by the interruption or it may continue after the interruption. The two clauses can come in either order.
I tripped up when I was running after the dog.
I cut myself while I was shaving.
She was still breathing when the ambulance arrived.

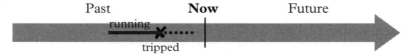

Watch out for these problems . . .

- **Students use two past progressive forms:** ✗ *I was standing just behind her when she was fainting.* ✗ *I was just closing my eyes when the phone was ringing.*

- **Students use two past simple forms:** ✗ *James caught malaria while he worked in West Africa.* ✗ *I found the letter while I tidied the drawers.*

In many cases, such sentences may still have a clear meaning and might sound fine in colloquial speech. Their meaning could be improved by correct use of tenses.

Teaching tip: revisiting the past progressive

Keep using the Mime idea (see Practice, on page 153) to create spontaneous little 'incidents' in class at unexpected moments in future lessons. For example, while writing on the board, fake a sneeze and deliberately drop your pen. Turn to the class and say 'While our teacher was . . .' and see if they can finish the sentence (*While our teacher was writing the homework answers on the board he sneezed and dropped his pen*). Once you have done one or two of these, it might even become a habit to describe amusing events in class life . . . and you may find students themselves initiating comments in this way.

→ **Unit 32 Past simple: regular verbs**

→ **Unit 33 Past simple: irregular verbs**

→ **Unit 36 Past progressive: 'in progress'**

38 Present perfect: *Have you ever . . .?*

Form

We make the present perfect with the auxiliary verb *have / has* + a past participle.

Question

Have	I / you / we / they		climbed	a mountain?
			seen	a blue whale?
		ever	eaten	snails?
Has	he / she / it		run	a marathan?
			been	to Kyrgyzstan?

Regular verbs end in *-ed*.
Irregular verbs have various forms.

Short answers

Yes,	I / you / we / they	have.
	he / she / it	has.

No,	I / you / we / they	haven't (have not).
	he / she / it	hasn't (has not).

Present perfect question and past simple answer

Many dialogue exchanges begin with a present perfect question (asking about an event at any time between the past and now) and then continue in the past simple.

A: *Have you ever been to the Middle East?*
B: *Yes, I visited Egypt last year.*

Presentation

Have you ever . . .?

1) Display some pictures of famous places on the board or write up some place or location names (ones that your students will know) on the board. Elicit some more from students.

2) Write up the question 'Have you ever been to . . . ?' and 'Yes, I have. / No, I haven't.' Start drilling questions (using locations from the list on the board) and answers (*Have you ever been to Egypt?*).

3) Once students have got the idea, get them to walk around asking each other (or asking people sitting near them). Encourage students to give true answers.

4) If you would like to go on to introduce more past participles: Sit students down again. Write up some films, makes of car, jobs, book titles, pop stars etc (*Macbeth, Fiat, Madonna, policeman*). Write the question 'Have you ever . . . ?' and elicit possible verbs that would go with some of the things you wrote (*Have you ever driven a Fiat? Have you ever read Macbeth? Have you ever kissed a policeman?*). Get students to repeat the new sentences. Practise as before.

Practice

Many teachers find that the question form *Have you ever . . .?* is a good way for learners to first meet the present perfect (because it's very useful and it's relatively easy to grasp the meaning and use).

Short Q & A dialogues

Write the following dialogue on the board and practise it:
'A: Have you ever been to Paris? B: Yes. I went there last year.'
Point out that the opening question is present perfect and the reply is a 'yes' that states when something happened. Ask students to think of more verbs that they could use in similar Q & A dialogues (*Have you ever eaten snake? Have you ever seen Coldplay in concert?*). Write all the new verbs on the board. With weaker classes, you could also write up some ideas for time expressions. Ask students to stand up or pair them if you don't want a mingle. Students should now meet others and have a short conversation (following the model) with each person.

Find someone who . . .

This classic game works very well here. Prepare 10 statements on a handout. Each starts with a . . . gap followed by 10 present perfect statements about people (*. . . has been to London. . . . has never seen Star Wars. . . . has eaten snails*). Don't worry that you haven't 'taught' the affirmative form yet – just focus on the questions for the moment. Students must stand up, mingle and ask them questions (*Have you ever eaten snails?*). If they get a *Yes, I have* answer they can write the person's name in the gap (*Paulo has eaten snails*). Students can try to see who can complete all 10 names first.

Variation

When they get a *yes* answer, students must ask a past simple follow-on question (*What did they taste like?*) and make a note of the answer for reporting back later.

Star interview

Draw a chat show TV studio (two chairs and a camera). Add two people: an interviewer and a 'star' (this could be a real local star). Check that students know what your picture shows! Explain that the interviewer is going to find out about the star's life. Elicit some questions about the star's experiences up to now. Help students make some likely questions (*Have you ever bought a Ferrari? Have you ever been to America?*) and the possible answers. For useful practice, students can repeat the interview lines one by one, write them down and / or role play the interview.

Concept questions

- **Have you ever been to Paris?** Am I asking about the future? (*No*) Am I asking about the past? (*Yes*) Am I asking about a specific time? (*No*) Am I asking about an experience in your life? (*Yes*) Are you in Paris now? (*No*) Are you planning to go to Paris? (*Maybe, we don't know*)

Meaning and use

Asking about a past experience in someone's life (for which the time is not known or not stated). *Ever* means 'at any time'.

Have you ever eaten octopus? means 'Have you – at any time in the past – eaten octopus?' The words *in my / your / his / her life* are often implied.
Have you ever been to Venice . . . (in your life)?

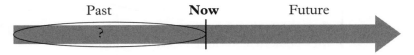

→ **Unit 39 Present perfect:** *just*

→ **Unit 40 Present perfect: 'up to now'**

→ **Unit 41 Time words:** *already, yet* **and** *always*

→ **Unit 42 Time words:** *for* **and** *since*

Watch out for these problems . . .

- **Learners avoid using the tense – typically using the past simple instead:** ✗ *Did you ever go to France?* If a learner makes this mistake, remind them by saying 'Have . . .' and see if they can finish the question with the correct past participle.

39 Present perfect: *just*

Form

I / You / We / They	've / have	just	been	to the shops.
			finished	the report.
He / She / It	's / has		left	the airport.

Regular past participles end in *-ed*.
Irregular past participles have various forms.

Presentation

Video still

1) Find and cue up a suitable clip on a DVD or downloaded from the Internet, showing an interesting still image just after a key event (perhaps with people who are jumping up and waving flags).

2) Ask students what they think has just happened. Help them to understand the meaning of *just* if they don't know it. Collect predictions and help learners to make correct sentences (*Italy has just scored a goal*).

3) After all the ideas, replay the clip to show the sequence prior to the still picture, and see if they were correct.

4) Show some new stills that show people's reactions. Get students to make sentences saying what has just happened in each case.

Variation

You can use magazine pictures instead of video clips – though of course you won't be able to rewind them to show what happened earlier!

Practice

Statues

Prepare a set of cue cards (*You've just won the lottery! You've just broken a vase. You've just run a marathon*). Put students into pairs. A is an artist. B is their statue. Hand a cue card to each pair. The artist must 'sculpt' B into a statue that expresses the idea on the card (*looking exhausted after a long marathon*). When students are ready, the whole class looks at each statue in turn and tries to guess what the image shows.

Classroom actions

Do a visible action (*open the window, drop a pen*). Then say 'Tell me what has just happened.' Elicit or model a good sentence (*You've just dropped your pen*). Get students to repeat the sentences. Repeat with new actions and then ask students to do actions themselves to prompt new sentences.

Truth or lie?

Prepare two cards before class, one with 'Tell the truth' on it, the other with 'Tell a lie' on it. In class choose three students and send student A out of the room into the corridor, out of sight of the class. Get students B and C to stand in the doorway where they can see both student A and the class. Hand B and C the cards so the rest of the class don't know who has which card. Student A now does an action in the corridor. Both students B and C report what she has just done (B: *She has just read a notice on the board.* C: *She has just sat down on the floor*). The class must guess whether B or C told the truth. Repeat with different people.

Concept questions

- **They've just come into the office.** Are they in the office now? (*Yes*) Were they in the office a few minutes ago? (*No*) Did they come into the room a very short time ago? (*Yes*)

Meaning and use

Things that happened in the very recent past – very close to 'now'.
They've just announced that our train will be delayed.
Their latest car has just gone into production.

This meaning of the present perfect is usually realised in American English by the past simple rather than the present perfect.
British English:
He's just gone out for a few minutes.
American English:
He just went out for a few minutes.

→ **Unit 41 Time words:** *already, yet* and *always*

Pronunciation

I've	/aɪv/	We've	/wiːv/	You've	/juːv/
They've	/ðeɪv/	He's	/hiːz/	haven't	/hævənt/
She's	/ʃiːz/	hasn't	/hæzənt/	It's	/ɪts/

Watch out for these problems . . .

- **Students omit the auxiliary verb *have / has*: ✗** *I just seen him.*

40 Present perfect: 'up to now'

Form

Affirmative

I / You / We / They	've / have	finished	the cake.
		flown	over the Sahara.
He / She / It	's / has	solved	the problem.

Regular past participles end in -ed.
Irregular past participles have various forms.

Negative

We make present perfect negatives with has / haven't or has / have not.

I / You / We / They	haven't ('ve not)	finished	the cake.
		flown	over the Sahara.
He / She / It	hasn't ('s not)	solved	the problem.

We can also make a negative meaning using *have / has* + *never* + past participle.
I've never tasted figs.

Yes / No questions

We make *yes / no* questions by reversing the auxiliary verb and the pronoun / noun.

Have	I / you / we / they	seen	the Grand Canyon	(before)?
Has	he / she / it	eaten	shell fish	

Wh- questions

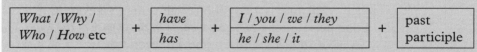

What / Why / Who / How etc	+	have / has	+	I / you / we / they / he / she / it	+	past participle

Short answers

Yes,	I / you / we / they	have.
	he / she / it	has.

No,	I / you / we / they	haven't (have not).
	he / she / it	hasn't (has not).

Presentation

Hard work

1) Show a 'before' picture of a derelict, untidy room. Elicit some simple descriptions (*The door is broken. The windows are dirty. There are newspapers all over the floor*).

2) Show a picture of Joanna and Al. Explain that Joanna is a cleaner and Al is a handyman and that they are going to make the room better.

3) Show a new picture of the same room, after Joanna and Al have done their work. Elicit new descriptions of the room (*Al's mended the door. Joanna's put the newspapers on the table. She's cleaned the windows*).

Practice

Before and after 'crime scene' pictures

This is a variation on the presentation idea above but with a crime scene. The 'before' picture is a tidy room with some money or jewellery lying on a table. Elicit descriptions (*There's a chair in the corner of the room. There's a small TV set. There's £100 on the table*). Show a second picture which shows the same room in a chaotic state after a burglary. Elicit sentences to describe the new scene using *someone* (*Someone has broken the window. Someone has taken the money*). Use *someone* so as not to accidentally introduce passive sentences.

Interpreting business statistics, diagrams and graphs

Students look at some detailed information and discuss it (*Fashionmark has lost a lot of money this year. Inflation has risen by 23%*).

Our room

Say to students 'Look at this room. What things have people done since we came in this morning?' (*Silvia has opened the window. Three people have left the room*).

Boasting party

Tell students to stand up. They are all guests at a party. When they meet someone, they should say a sentence about something they have done in their life. Their partner should reply by boasting that they have done something even more extraordinary. Encourage students to use exaggerated intonation. Demonstrate the task by writing up and drilling one or two model conversations:

A: *I've been to America.* B: *You've been to America? I've been to the Moon!*

B: *I've eaten octopus.* A: *You've eaten octopus? I've eaten camel!*

A: *I've met Janet Jackson.* B: *You've met Janet Jackson? I've met Beyoncé!*

Star interview (2)

Expand on the idea in Unit 38 Present perfect: *Have you ever . . . ?* to allow students to give longer answers and negative sentences. (Interviewer: *Tell me about your life. Have you ever been to America?* Star: *Yes, I have. I've been to so many interesting countries. I've been to Vietnam. I've been to Iran, but I haven't been to North Korea*). For useful practice, students can repeat the interview lines one by one, write them down and / or role play the interview.

Concept questions

- **Matt's gone to Paris.** Is Matt in Paris now? (*Probably, or he's on his way*) Did he go and come back? (*No*)

- **She's worked in Paris.** Did she work in Paris at some time in the past? (*Yes*) Do we know exactly when? (*No*) Is she working in Paris now? (*No*)

- **David's cooked supper.** Is supper ready now? (*Yes*) Who cooked it? (*David*) When did he cook it? (*Sometime before now*) Is he still cooking now? (*No*) Do we know exactly when he started cooking? (*No*) Do we know exactly when he finished cooking? (*No*)

Meaning and use

We use the present perfect to talk about events in the past – but it is a 'present' tense. How is that possible? The key idea with this tense is that it is about the past as it affects the present – ie there is always some link to now. All present perfect meanings connect the past to now in some way. This is a rather complex concept – and quite hard to convey to students.

I've been to four different countries in Africa (and the experience of visiting these countries is still live and important to me. It doesn't feel like a distant, dead event).

She's bought 20 copies of the book (and she still has them now).

He's eaten camel meat (and he is still a person who knows what that tastes like).

We use the present perfect for . . .

1) things that happened once or a number of times in an unfinished period of time that started in the past and continued up to now. In many cases the connection to now is not stated but we can still guess it.

We've been burgled! (and now we don't have a TV)
I've already spent this month's salary (and now I have none left).

They've already had two foreign holidays this year.
Natalya has vetoed every idea I've had.

2) changes over time – with verbs like *increase, grow, fall* in an unfinished period of time that started in the past and continued up to now etc.
Sales have shown a slight improvement this year.
I've put on two kilos in the last month.
The business has grown very fast.

3) states that started in the past and continued up to now (and may go on into the future).
My family has lived in this area for years.
Greece has been a republic since 1973.
Dr Watson has worked in the region for 40 years.

Sentences with this meaning typically incorporate the unspoken words '. . . and still do / does / is / are.'
I've lived here since 2007 . . . and I still do now.

Present perfect with specific time reference

One standard guideline is that you cannot use the present perfect with any mention of a specific time (*at 12.00; last Friday; at the weekend; in January; in 1998*). For example, learners may make incorrect sentences such as ✗ *I have been to Paris in 2006.* This guideline appears to be relaxing in contemporary English.

→ **Unit 42 Time words: *for* and *since***

Been and *gone*

When talking about movement to and from a place, *gone* refers to movement to a location and *been* refers to movement to a location and back again.
She's gone to the dentist's – suggests that she is still there.
She's been to the dentist's – suggests that she has finished there and returned.

Watch out for these problems . . .

- **Students assume that the present perfect is only for 'recent past':** This is an over-generalisation of the 'just' usage.

- **Students think the present perfect means 'incomplete action':** They think *I have read the book* means *and haven't finished it yet* when it actually means *I finished the book*. Compare *I've been reading the book* which is still incomplete.

- **Students completely fail to grasp the meanings and uses of the present perfect:** Some students may expect that every tense in their own mother tongue will map directly onto the set of English language tenses. The present perfect is often one that blows this theory apart. The form may exist in the students' mother tongue but with a different usage. As a result, students may go through some period of confusion and puzzlement.

Teaching tip: past simple or present perfect?

Many students find it hard to decide whether to use the present perfect or past simple.
He bought the whole company last year.
✗ *He's bought the whole company last year.*

Another important question is whether or not there is a connection to 'now'. If a past event has no obvious connection to 'now', we use the past simple. If it does have a connection to 'now', we can use the present perfect. Please note that this apparently simple guideline is actually quite hard to apply. Drawing two timelines – past simple and present perfect – may help students decide.

In many cases, a speaker has a choice whether to use the past simple or the present perfect to describe something. The present perfect is typically used to make something seem more 'live' and relevant. Compare (a) 'Kimanji's won the election' and (b) 'Kimanji won the election.' Both may be reporting something that happened yesterday. Sentence (a) sounds more like 'news' and is more likely to be used if the speaker wants to convey a sense that this is live news. The tone may suggest surprise, excitement, interest etc. Sentence (b) sounds more like a purely factual report.

Teaching tip: the present perfect problem

The present perfect often seems to be the tense that causes the most serious problems to learners. It's the meaning and use rather than the form that is problematic – not least because learners' own mother tongues often don't have a comparable meaning. Don't worry if your students take a long time to use the tense appropriately.

41 Time words: *already*, *yet* and *always*

Form

We use *already* and *yet* to say that something has or hasn't happened when we expected it to.

Already

already = 'before now' (or 'before a certain time in the past')
We've already finished the second unit.

Yet

yet in questions = 'before now'
Have you written to him yet?

yet in negatives = 'not before now'
I haven't been to Singapore yet.

In both cases there is an expectation that the event will happen / be true in the future.

Always

always = at all times in the past up to now

I've always lived in London.

Presentation

Yet or *already*?

1) Draw a picture of Helena and Julie in a room. It's 4 pm. A notice says 'Party 8 pm.' Write (or draw icons in thought bubbles) above Helena to show 'Buy present ✓ Cook food ✗ Buy drinks ✗ Decorate room ✗.'

2) Explain that Helena wants to throw a surprise birthday party for her friend Bob tomorrow. Helena is getting things ready now. She is checking what she has done and what she still needs to do – and is telling Julie.

3) Ask students to look at the list on the board. Write up the words 'yet' and 'already.' Ask if students can make Helena's sentences using these words.

4) Elicit answers and help students to make good present perfect sentences that Helena is saying (*I've already bought a present. I haven't cooked the food yet*).

5) Show the clock at 7 pm. Change the food and drinks crosses to ticks. Elicit new sentences that Helena is saying to Julie about what she's done and what still needs to be done (*I've already cooked the food*).

Practice

What people have and haven't done

Get a photo or draw a sketch of people working or preparing for something (a couple planning a wedding). Elicit what they have or haven't done (*They've already sent out the invitations. They haven't bought the flowers yet*). You could provide picture cues to help give ideas (invitation with tick; flowers with cross).

Concept questions

- **I haven't seen *Freedom Writers* yet.** Did I watch *Freedom Writers* in the past? (*No*) Will I watch it in the future? (*Probably*)

- **I've already seen *Freedom Writers*.** Did I watch *Freedom Writers* in the past? (*Yes*) Do you know when exactly? (*No*)

Meaning and use

Already + present perfect

We usually use *already* only in affirmative sentences with the present perfect and it means 'before now'. It is typically used to show that something was expected later, but happened before that (and perhaps surprisingly).
I've already paid for everything.
He's only 24, but he's already achieved worldwide fame.

In this time line for the sentence *I expected him at 12, but he's already arrived* the clock marks when I expected him to arrive. The cross shows when he actually arrived. So – at the moment now – he is *already* here.

Already + past simple

We use *already* with the past simple, to mean 'before a certain time in the past' and / or earlier than expected.

He already spoke Japanese fluently.
She was only three months pregnant but already had a slight bulge.

Present perfect + *yet*

We don't usually use *yet* in affirmative sentences in the present perfect. In negatives, we use *yet* to say that something has not happened before now (although we expect that it will happen in the future).
They haven't got here yet.
I haven't done my homework yet.

In this time line, the *not* words show that, up until now, something has not happened (although expected). In questions, we use *yet* to ask whether something that we're expecting to happen has happened before now or is still in the future.
Has she fallen asleep yet?
Has he called for his parcel yet?

Always

Always means 'all the time', 'at all times' or 'every time.'
She always loved Zoom ice lollies.
They always used to ring me and say what they were doing.
His mind was always buzzing with new and exciting ideas.
On winter evenings we'd always sit around the fire.

When we use *always* with the present or past progressive it often refers to repeated actions that are irritating.
He's always forgetting my name.

We use *always* with the present perfect to mean 'at all times in the past up to now'.
Entrance to the museums has always been free.

Watch out for these problems

• **Students confuse *already* and *yet*:** ✗ *I haven't been there already.*

• **Students mix up word order:** ✗ *She's finished already the homework.* ✗ *You haven't told him yet anything.*

42 Time words: *for* and *since*

Form

> **Since**
>
> *since* + when something began – the start time
>
> **For**
>
> *for* + the duration of something – how long it lasted

Presentation

Since and *for*

1) Draw a simple timeline on the board.

2) Point out that Since tells us when something Started.

3) Say some sentences with the word *since* or *for* missing (*I've lived in this town . . . 2009. The students have been in this room . . . 25 minutes*). Ask students to decide (using the timeline to help) if the missing word in each case should be *for* or *since*. Get them to repeat the correct answers.

4) For practice, try a very fast exercise that forces students to choose between the two options. Prepare a list of times like these examples:

1 ten minutes	5 last night	9 a lifetime
2 Christmas	6 three years	10 a week
3 1966	7 winter	11 last week
4 10 o'clock	8 August	12 a weekend

5) Dictate them to students who have to quickly decide if they need *for* or *since*. Students can call out answers individually or in teams. Alternatively they could write answers individually, in pairs or part of a team quiz. For a livelier version, you could label one corner of the room 'for' and the other 'since'. When you call out each time expression, students must go straight to the corner they think is correct.

Concept questions

- **Today is Thursday. Meera has been in Lima since Sunday morning.** When did Meera arrive in Lima? (*On Sunday morning*) What was her first day in Lima? (*Sunday*) What day is it today? (*Thursday*) How many days has Meera been in Lima? (*Four days*) Finish these sentences: 'Meera has been in Lima for . . .'(*four days*) Meera has been in Lima since . . .' (*Sunday*)

  You could substitute the current real day instead of *Thursday*, changing the other answers as appropriate.

- **Luis moved to Nepal in 2010.** What year did Luis start living in Nepal? (*2010*) What year is it now? (*Give the real current year*) Make a sentence with 'since'. (*Luis has been in Nepal since 2010*) Make a sentence with 'for'. (*Luis has lived in Nepal for X years. NB X = the real number of years since 2010*)

Meaning and use

For

We use *for* to describe duration, to say how long something lasted in a period of time that has a beginning and an end. After the word *for* we say the length of time (*for three years, for two months, for five minutes*). When we use *for* with the past simple, the end time is in the past. When we use *for* with the present perfect, the end time is now.

For with past simple

I worked there for three years.

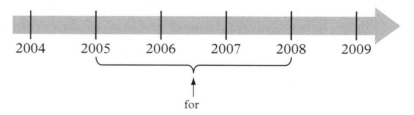

For with present perfect

I've worked there for three years.

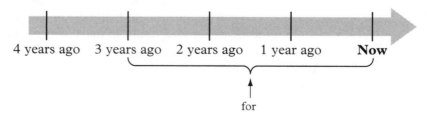

Since

We most commonly use *since* with the present perfect. It tells us when something began ie the start time. The period of time that starts with *since* ends with 'now'. We are looking back from the present moment 'now' to see the time that something began.

I've worked there since April.

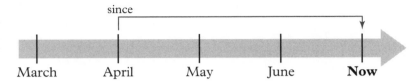

We can also use *since* with other perfect tenses, such as the past perfect. In this case both the start time and the end time are in the past.

He'd been studying German since he got married.

Pronunciation

For

In sentences where it describes the duration of something, the usual pronunciation of *for* is a weak form: /fə/. It would be very unusual to stress the word. If students insist on saying a strong for /fɔː/ – tell them to try saying the word as if it was just an 'f' before the following word (*I've lived here ftwo years. She's worked here fnine months*).

Watch out for these problems . . . .

- **Students mix durations and start points:** Even when they understand the difference between *for* and *since*, some students may still find it hard to recognise which times are 'start points' and which are 'durations'. This problem may arise because some start points are actually quite long. For example *since 2005* refers to a whole year but we are thinking of the year as a single start point; we are not imagining the year as an event with length. To help with this problem, try quick discrimination exercises (see the Presentation).

43 Present perfect progressive

Form

We make the present perfect progressive with *has / have* + *been* + verb + *-ing*.

The form is similar to the present perfect, but the past participle is always *been* and there is a main verb in the *-ing* form.

I / You / We / They	've / have	been	working
			living
			studying
He / She / It	's / has		waiting
			watching

We often use *for* and *since* with the present perfect progressive as well as the present perfect simple.
I've been driving for 15 years.
She has been acting since she was 17.

Questions

We make questions by inverting the pronoun and *has / have*.
Have you been waiting long?

Wh- questions are more common – especially with *How long . . .*
What have you been doing since I last saw you?
How long have you been renting this place?

Presentation

Unhappy girlfriend

1) Draw a picture of a cinema exterior. A woman is waiting, looking unhappy. Draw a clock showing 2.00. Ask students why they think the woman is unhappy. You could mime 'waiting' by tapping your foot and looking at your watch to help students if they are struggling. Establish that she is waiting for her boyfriend.

2) Change the clock to show 2.15. Establish that she is still waiting. Add in some rain starting to fall. Mime the girl looking at her watch. Ask students if they can guess what she is thinking (*Where is he? Oh no! Rain!*). Elicit or model 'I've been waiting since two o'clock. I've been waiting for 15 minutes!'

3) Repeat for 2.30. Show a noisy street musician starting to play his trumpet. Mime the girl looking at her watch. Ask students if they can guess what she is thinking (*Where is he? Oh no! A trumpet!*). Elicit or model 'I've been waiting since two o'clock. I've been waiting for 30 minutes! It's been raining for 15 minutes!'

4) Repeat for 2.45. Show her starting to cry at 2.45. Elicit or model 'I've been waiting since two o'clock. I've been waiting for 45 minutes!'

5) Draw the boyfriend arriving. You could mime running and panting. Mime the girl complaining at her boyfriend and pointing at her watch. Ask students if they can guess what she is saying (*Where have you been?*). Elicit or model *I've been waiting since two o'clock. I've been waiting for an hour! It's been raining since 2.15. He's been playing his trumpet since 2.30. I've been crying for 15 minutes.* Get students to repeat.

Practice

Role plays

Write a number of short role play situations on separate cards (Man has been painting kitchen all morning – then has a cup of tea. Wife comes home and says he is lazy. A businesswoman at airport has been travelling all day. She is at an airport information desk and now finds her next plane has been cancelled). Get students to prepare and perform very short dialogues including the present perfect progressive.

Visitor interview

Students prepare a set of questions to ask a tourist, immigrant or visitor who will be interviewed about their experiences in the country (or school, or workplace) including a number of present perfect simple and present perfect progressive questions (*How long have you been living in a hotel? How long have you been working at the kebab shop? How long have you been waiting to get a work visa?*). When ready, they can role play an interview for a TV show, immigration panel, promotion board.

Desert island

Draw a desert island with one lone long-bearded inhabitant. Add a rescue ship arriving and a rescuer jumping off to greet the Robinson Crusoe. Elicit some of their conversation (*How long have you been living here? I've been eating coconuts for ten years*). Challenge pairs to come up with three more present perfect progressive sentences.

Prison

As with the desert island, this context works well for the tense (*I've been working in the library for seven years*).

Concept questions

- **Michiko's been working at the bank since 2009.** When did Michiko start work at the bank? (*2009*) Does Michiko work at the bank now? (*Yes*) Did she work at the bank between 2009 and now? (*Yes*) Will she work for the bank in the future? (*We don't know, but probably*)

- **It's nearly dark! Yusuf's been playing on that computer all day!** Was Yusuf playing on the computer in the morning? (*Yes*) Was Yusuf playing on the computer in the afternoon? (*Yes*) Did Yusuf do any work today? (*No*) Has Yusuf finished playing on the computer? (*No – not yet!*) Will Yusuf continue playing on the computer after it gets dark? (*Possibly – but we don't know*)

Meaning and use

Although students often assume that a difference in tense indicates a difference in time, this isn't always the case. Present perfect simple and present perfect progressive can both refer to exactly the same time. Compare:
I've worked in the garden all day.
I've been working in the garden all day.
Both refer to the same period of time ie a time starting sometime earlier in the day and lasting up until now:

The progressive form, however, sees the action as ongoing, temporary and incomplete at the moment that it is talked about. It might continue into the future and that may be some visible evidence present.
The children have been making a cake (and the kitchen is a mess).
He's been mending his bike (and he has oil on his hands).

The progressive form may also be used by the speaker to emphasise the duration of the action. Someone saying *I've been working in the garden all day* may want to emphasise the length of their work. For this reason, the present perfect progressive can be used to complain, to whinge, to criticise etc.

I've been filling in this form all evening.
I've been waiting for over an hour.
I've been chasing round all day buying presents.
I've been calling him for weeks but I still haven't made contact.

Watch out for these problems

- **Students avoid using two auxiliary verbs:** ✗ *I been studying here a long time* (NB acceptable in some colloquial varieties of English).

- **Students use infinitive instead of *-ing* form:** ✗ *She has been work here for two months.*

Teaching tip: teach it as lexical items?

Whereas the present perfect simple is a very common, widely used tense, the present perfect progressive is relatively rare. It may not be worth spending too much time on. So . . . consider teaching the tense as a number of lexical items rather than as a grammatical one! There is a fairly limited set of verbs that tend to be used with the tense. The verbs below account for a large percentage of usage:

I've been . . .

working, living, doing, looking, going, trying, running, taking, waiting, using, talking, saying, thinking, making, getting, looking

Maybe it's enough for your students to learn, phrase-book like, a few useful chunks using these verbs *I've been waiting for ages, I've been living here for two months, I've been working there since April* and then let them use these as a base on which to construct the meanings they need which may only involve changing a time or date.

44 Past perfect simple

Form

We make the past perfect with *had* + past participle.

I / You / He / She / It / We / They	*'d / had*	*worked*	*in Spain . . .*
		been	*to Rome . . .*
		flown	*in a helicopter . . .*

Regular verbs end in *-ed*, irregular verbs have various forms.

Negative

We make past perfect negatives with *hadn't / had not*.

I / You / He / She / It / We / They	*hadn't (had not)*	*visited Rome . . .*

Yes / No questions

Had	*I / you / he / she / it / we / they*	*flown*	*in a helicopter?*

Although *yes / no* questions are grammatically possible, they are actually pretty rare – and you don't need to spend too much time on them in class.

Wh- questions

Wh- question word	*had*	*I / you / he / she / it / we / they*	past participle

What had you said?
Where had he gone?

Short answers

Yes,	*I / you / he / she / it / we / they*	*had.*
No,	*I / you / he / she / it / we / they*	*hadn't / had not.*

We often use the past perfect simple:
with *already*: *Joan had already checked out of the hotel.*
with *just*: *I'd just arrived at the conference.*
with *before*: *They'd checked it out on the web before they arrived.*
with verbs such as *realised, noticed, heard, discovered, saw*:
When I opened the book, I saw that several pages had been torn out.

after *said* or other reporting verbs in reported speech:
He said the cash machine had swallowed his card.

→ **Unit 63 Direct and reported speech**

Conditional

Past perfect is also taught as part of the third conditional structure and features in many sentences starting *I wish.*
If he'd studied more at school, he'd have passed his exams.
I wish you had told me earlier.

→ **Unit 59 Third conditional**

Presentation

Why were you so tired?

1) Tell a story about a business trip that went wrong (Jeff lost his passport, arrived late at the airport, missed his plane, dropped his phone in the toilet, missed the last bus from the airport, walked all the way to the hotel).

2) Explain that it's now the next morning. His boss wants to talk to him. Write up one of the boss's questions 'Why did you arrive late at the airport?' and elicit Jeff's answer (*Because I'd lost my passport*). Point out the use of *I'd* + past participle and make sure students are clear about the time references (*were late* = past; *I'd lost* = time earlier than that). Get students to repeat the question and answer orally in pairs.

3) Continue with more questions and answers (*Why did you miss the plane? Because I'd arrived late at the airport. Why didn't you phone me from the airport? Because I'd dropped my phone in the toilet. Why did you arrive so late at the hotel? Because I'd missed the last bus. Why were you so exhausted when you arrived? Because I'd walked all the way from the airport!*).

4) Show a picture of a new character – someone looking rather distressed or worn out. Explain that this was last Thursday. Ask students to think what had happened to them before this moment.

Practice

Hero and villain

Invent an adventure story involving a continuing pursuit or chase between hero and villain; the story should include lots of situations in which the hero repeatedly gets to places just after the villain has done something. Draw pictures to elicit the story, scene by scene (*By the time Karina reached the docks, Harry had already left on the cargo ship*).

Changing the 'story start point'

Prepare a short story in the past simple and display it for students. Ask them to choose a different story start point and rewrite / retell the story from this new perspective.

Why?

Write up a 'mystery' sentence on the board (*He bought five cans of pink paint*). Students speculate about what had happened earlier that led to this (*He had promised to decorate a toy castle in a children's playground. His wife had just given birth to a baby girl*). Other example mystery sentences include *He laughed very loudly on the bus. She shouted at the computer. They jumped into the river.*

Backwards story

Prepare a short story about Jen's day yesterday relating a chronological sequence of events up to a certain time (5 pm), using past simple verbs (*She drove into town. She chose some new socks in Primark® and then had a coffee in Mr Bean*). In class, tell the story and ask students to note all the verbs or hand out a list at the end. Write up 'Before 5 o'clock . . .' and encourage students to retell the story from this new start point, using past perfect verbs (*. . . she had driven into town, chosen some new socks in Primark®*).

Concept questions

- **The concert had just started when Ali's phone rang.** Which started first – the phone or the concert? (*The concert*)

- **By the time Aimée arrived at the meeting, Hamdi had left.** Who was in the room first, Aimée or Hamdi? (*Hamdi*) Were Aimée and Hamdi in the room at the same time? (*No*) What did Hamdi do before Aimée arrived? (*He left the meeting*)

Meaning and use

Core meaning

We use the past perfect to talk about the relationship between events in the past. The past perfect indicates that an event happened further back in the past than another event (typically in the past simple or past progressive).

We use the past perfect to describe . . .

1) one thing happened before another (often using *when* or *by the time*). The past perfect is often used in sentences along with the past simple, contrasting two times. The clauses can be in either order.
   I put my hand into my pocket and found I'd left my keys at home.
   By the time we arrived at the conference centre, the presentation had finished.
   It was midnight before I'd written the last sentence of my essay.
   John had already left for work when Susie called.

2) background events.
   The tense is used to narrate earlier background events that happened before the perceived main starting point of a story (or part of a story).
   George had always tried to lead a good life.
   In a sequence of past perfect verbs we only need to use *had* once.
   She'd opened the door, walked across the hall and taken the necklace (*opened*, *walked* and *taken* are all past perfect).

3) something expected, intended or planned didn't happen (or was unfinished) at a certain time or before something else happened.
   The deal was announced before Akira had agreed to it (Note: Akira possibly never agreed to the deal – we cannot tell from this sentence if he did or not).
   They decided to start before safety checks had been made.

4) superlative experiences.
   As with the present perfect, *ever* is commonly used, often in sentences beginning *It was the . . .* and including a superlative.
   It was the best meal I'd ever had.
   It was the most wonderful feeling she had ever experienced.

→ **Unit 15 Superlatives**

5) reported speech.
   When we report what someone's said using the past simple or present perfect, we often use the past perfect.
   'He broke the record' → *She said that he had broken the record.*
   'I've never met Mr Jones' → *He said that he had never met Mr Jones.*

→ **Unit 63 Direct and reported speech**

6) being very polite (especially with *wondered* and *hoped*).
I had wondered if you could record the show for me.

How long before?

There is nothing in the structure that tells us how much time passed between the past perfect event and the past simple event. The events could be seconds apart (*I'd just clicked the 'purchase' button when she shouted that she wanted a different title*) – or millions of years (*Dinosaurs had become extinct long before man first walked on the planet*).

Before

We use *before* with the past perfect to say how long prior to one event, another event happened.
The tribe had died out centuries before (ie before something else happened).

We cannot use *ago* with the past perfect ✗ *The tribe had died out centuries ago.*

Watch out for these problems . . .

- **Students think that the past perfect is used for events in the 'distant past' (as opposed to the past simple for the 'recent past'):** This can be a hard error to spot – but it may explain why *Although TV had been invented in England, there are still lots of bad programmes there* sounds wrong.

- **Students overuse past perfect when past simple would suffice:** Some keen students want to use the past perfect a lot once they have learnt it – but the past perfect is relatively rare and it can sound odd to hear it used a lot. It indicates a relationship between past events, so unless we are saying that one event happened before another, we use the past simple: ✗ *She had gone to the cinema last night.* ✗ *I'd caught a bus to come here.*

Teaching tip: tackling avoidance

Just as some students overuse this tense, others avoid it, using the past simple instead – and it is a rare enough tense that this avoidance may not be noticed by student or teacher. Encourage students to try adding the past perfect to their repertoire by asking that each student tries to say one past perfect sentence at some point in each lesson. Allow students to use a marker (a Cuisenaire rod, a tick on a poster, a sticky label etc) to indicate that they have fulfilled their goal. Occasionally discuss whether this challenge is hard or not.

Teaching tip: choosing your story start points

As with a lot of grammar, choosing when to use the past perfect isn't just a scientific decision – in fact, there is a lot of choice involved. The main choice for the speaker or writer is deciding when each new sequence of events in the story is perceived to begin.

Look at this short text:

We walked along the canal path and went under the bridge. We found a bench and ate our sandwiches silently. Midge's phone rang.

In that text, the 'main story' is seen as starting at *We walked* and the narrative proceeds from there. The ringing phone is placed as something that happens in the natural, linear flow of event after event.

Compare that with the following version:

We'd walked along the canal path, gone under the bridge, found a bench and eaten our sandwiches silently. Midge's phone rang.

In this version, the 'main story' is seen as starting with the phone ringing. All other events are set as 'background' to that event. The ringing phone takes on a greater significance here. Note that there is no difference in the sequence of events. A timeline for both texts would show the same events in the same order. The only difference is the writer's 'story start point'.

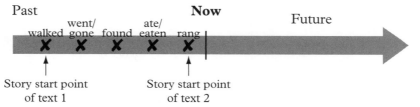

Everything that happens before the story start point is in the past perfect.

Notice what happens when we add a new sentence to the end of the first text:

We walked along the canal path and went under the bridge. We found a bench and ate our sandwiches silently. Midge's phone rang. Suddenly I realised that I had lost my wallet.

Had lost my wallet, because it is in the past perfect, is marked as (1) happening before the previous past simple verb (*rang*) and (2) probably (but not always) before the story start point.

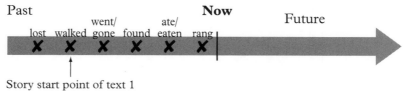

A story may have very many 'story start points'. An author can repeatedly 'restart' the story.

45 Past perfect progressive

Form

We make the past perfect progressive with *had + been* + verb + *-ing*.

I / You / He / She / It / We / They	'd / had been	expecting	it for a long time.

Negatives

We make past perfect progressive negatives with *hadn't / had not*.

I / You / He / She / It / We / They	hadn't / had not	been	travelling	for a long time.

Yes / No questions

Had	I / you / he / she / it / we / they	been	waiting	long?

Wh- questions

Wh- question word	had	I / you / he / she / it / we / they	been	verb + -ing

What had you been hoping for?
Where had you been working before you built the study?

Short answers
Yes, I had.
No, I hadn't → *had not.*

Presentation

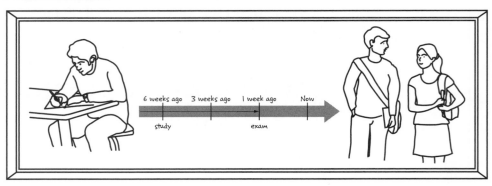

The exam

1) Draw a timeline across the whole board with points labelled 'six weeks ago,' 'three weeks ago,' 'one week ago' and 'now.' Add the word 'exam' under 'one week ago'.

2) Add Li, at the left of the time line, and an image to show him studying very hard six weeks ago. Establish that he worked very hard. Check 'Did he watch TV?' (*No*) 'Did he go out with friends?' (*No*) 'Did he do any sports?' (*No*) 'Why?' (*Because he was studying all the time*)

3) Add Li studying through the whole period from six weeks ago till yesterday.

4) Under 'one week ago' add 'FAIL' to the exam. Draw Li on the right of the time line, looking unhappy. Establish that he failed his exam.

5) Next draw his friend Sylvie asking him a question (*You failed the exam? Did you prepare for it?*). Write up four possible replies from Li.
   a) 'Yes. I'm studying for 6 weeks.'
   b) 'Yes. I was studying for 6 weeks.'
   c) 'Yes. I've been studying for 6 weeks.'
   d) 'Yes. I'd been studying for 6 weeks.'
   Ask students which they think are possible replies.

6) Discuss answers with the class. Agree that (a) is wrong (reference to present not past), (b) is colloquially possible and that (c) suggests the studying continued until now and (d) is best because it relates a past event (*he failed the exam*) to something that came before it (*he had been studying*). Use the timeline to help clarify this relationship. Elicit if there are any other past perfect progressive sentences Li could say (*I'd been expecting a good result. I'd been looking forward to celebrating after the exam*).

Practice

Meanings and situations

Write this sentence on the board 'I'd been working so hard, I felt I hadn't seen daylight for weeks.' Ask students to think of possible situations in which it might be said. Give an example answer if they are puzzled. (You are talking with friends about a project you finished last week. You worked very hard and never went out with your friends until it was over.) When a good solution has been agreed, write up two more sentences 'He'd been lying from the start. He found out she'd been robbing him for months.' Students can work in pairs to find good contexts. Check answers in the whole class, then ask each pair to invent two new contexts and past perfect progressive sentences. They can then meet up with other pairs, read out the sentences and let the others guess the contexts.

Cartoon problems

Draw a simple cartoon sequence showing a stick-figure comic character (a cat) undergoing various difficulties. Tell students that each sentence can be described using the past perfect progressive. Do the first one together, then let them work out the rest.

Possible sequence:
Felix the cat had been sleeping all morning. He'd been dreaming of a large piece of fried fish. The fish had been running away from him. He'd been trying to catch it with a fishing net. The fish had been calling for help. Some mice had been throwing buckets of water at him. When Felix woke up, he found that it had been raining – and he was soaking wet!

Concept questions

- **We'd been painting the bedroom all morning when Michaela called us for lunch.** When did they start painting? (*Early in the morning*) Did they work all morning? (*Yes*) Until lunchtime? (*Yes*) Had they finished painting at lunchtime? (*We don't know, but probably not. Maybe they continued in the afternoon*)

- **On Thursday some officers broke down the front door and arrested two men. The police had been watching the house since Monday night.** Did the police watch the house over a period of time? (*Yes*) When did they start watching the house? (*Monday night*) What happened on Thursday? (*Police broke down the door* etc) Did they continue to watch the house after Thursday? (*We don't know – but it is possible*)

Meaning and use

We use the past perfect progressive . . .

1) for a past event that was in progress up to a certain point in the past. This event could be temporary or unfinished.
We had been driving for three hours when we saw lights in the sky.
I had been living with a host family up to then.

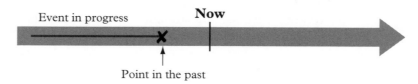

The past perfect progressive does not have to refer to a single continuous action.
Neda's father found out that she'd been skipping lessons.

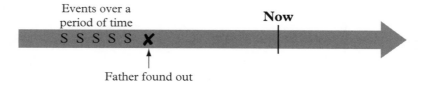

In this timeline the S letters represent the times Neda skipped lessons; they are separate events over a period of time. The 'skipping lessons' happened in an earlier period of time before Neda's father 'found out'.

2) to emphasise the duration of something, perhaps to make a point of the time, work, stress, commitment, inconvenience etc involved.
   She'd been waiting at the airport for five hours.
   I'd been staying up late every night to finish that report.

3) to explain a reason for something in the past.
   They'd been marching all morning so they were very hungry.
   We failed the test because we'd been studying the wrong book.

The past perfect progressive compared with the past perfect simple

a) *We had been driving for three hours . . .*
b) *We had driven for three hours.*

When we use the past perfect progressive there is a focus on the length of the action or a suggestion that the action wasn't finished whereas when we use the past perfect simple the focus is more on the action itself or a suggestion that the action is complete.

This is something which students may find difficult to grasp as it is quite a subtle difference in meaning.

The past perfect progressive compared with the present perfect progressive

The present perfect progressive and the past perfect progressive both show the same sort of relationship in time between events – that one thing happened earlier than another. The present perfect progressive relates the earlier events to *now* whereas the past perfect progressive relates the earlier events to *a past time.*

Watch out for these problems . . .

- **Students mismatch tenses:** ✗ *They missed the bus because they have been chatting in the café.*

Teaching tip: unrealistic expectations

Don't have unrealistic expectations about how much students should use this tense. Even native speakers tend to avoid it in spoken English. The natural inclination to simplify and avoid complex grammar means that many speakers will convey the meaning using the past progressive (*I had been waiting for hours before the flight showed on the departures board → I was waiting for hours . . .*). It makes sense to mainly practise in written rather than oral work, for example in formal narratives (*The share price had been falling all week until the rescue plan was made public*).

46 *Will*

Form

Will is a modal verb and so it doesn't change form to show tense or person. There are also no infinitive or participle forms. The negative of *will* is *won't / will not* and we make questions and question tags without *do*.

→ **Unit 55 Modal verbs: an overview**

Affirmative

I'll enjoy the party.
The verb is usually contracted both in written and spoken English. If we use the verb in its full form, the meaning is much more emphatic.
I will ask my boss tomorrow.

Negative

We make negatives by using *won't*.
They won't find the treasure.

If we don't contract, the meaning is again much more emphatic.

Yes / No questions

Will he arrive before lunch?
Will you get me a glass of water?

Negative questions

Won't you have another piece of cake?

Short answers

Yes, we will.
No, I won't.

Wh- questions

When will they arrive?
How will you travel?
Who will come to the party?

In speech, *will* is often contracted after *wh-* questions, and after names and nouns.

Presentation

Predictions: What will happen?

1) Ask students to help you list some things that they think will definitely happen over the coming week. Start with some answers of your own (*School will end at 3.30 today. School will be closed on Sunday. The sun will rise tomorrow morning*). Once they are clear how to form sentences, get more ideas from the class.

2) After that, ask students to list some things that they think are very likely to happen. If they aren't 100% sure, they should say 'I think' or '. . . probably' (*The weather will be cold tonight. Marv will come late to class tomorrow. The teacher will give us homework*).

Making decisions

→ Unit 48 *Will* contrasted with *going to*

Offers and promises

1) Display a picture on the board of a businessman sitting at his desk and introduce him as Mr Svensson. Also introduce his personal assistant Ms Gomez. Explain that Ms Gomez really wants to be promoted and so is keen to impress her boss.

2) Write up the words 'conference call' and tell students that she is offering to set up today's conference call. Elicit what she might say (*I'll set up the conference call if you like*).

3) Use prompts or pictures to elicit other offers that she might make (*I'll email the Hong Kong office. I'll call the suppliers for you*).

Variation

King talking to knights who want to marry his daughter, elicit from students the offers and promises the knights make.

Practice

Prediction

2099

Write '2099' on the board. Ask students to imagine what the world will be like then. Offer some predictions of your own (*People will live on Mars. Robots will do all the work. The seas will be dead*) then get them to make predictions themselves. Help with sentence starters (*All children will . . .*) or key vocabulary (*extinct*) where needed.

Fortune telling

Hand out a list of possible personal predictions (*You will meet a tall dark stranger. You will win a lot of money*) and check that students understand them. Make pairs – A is a fortune teller and B a visitor. A tells B his fortune, using ideas from the list and adding to them where possible.

Horoscopes

Select some magazine horoscopes that have appropriate use of *will* and read them with students. Students work in groups to write a horoscope for one star sign. Collect them together as a full horoscope.

Making decisions

Making spontaneous travel plans

Ask students to tell you a number of steps to make some journeys (*How will you travel from here to the top of the Eiffel Tower? How will you get to the cinema?*). They should not prepare what they are going to say, but speak as they think of the steps (*I'll walk out of this room. I'll catch a number 59 trolleybus to the station. I will take the train to Bangkok. I'll buy a ticket to Paris*). If students have a wider vocabulary, you could extend the challenge to include other non-journey tasks (*How will you tidy this room? How will you prepare to pass your exam next month?*).

NB if students prepared their plan, they would need to use *going to*.

Secret Santa

Write down the names of all the students on separate pieces of paper. Tell them that they are going to a Christmas (or some other kind of) party and will have to choose and buy a present for one person. Go round the class. Each student randomly picks a piece of paper with a name and immediately thinks of a suitable present they will buy for that person (*Mmmm – Philip – I'll buy him a new lunch box*). If you are worried that students might choose unsuitable or unkind presents, do the same task with famous people as recipients (President of the USA, famous pop stars etc).

Offers and promises

Negotiation

Before you start this, warn the student to say 'no' to your questions. Walk over to a student and pretend to admire their pen or something else on their table. Say 'I really want that pen' and then make an offer or a promise (*I'll give you a hundred pounds*). When the student says 'No' make more offers and promises (*I'll return it in two weeks' time. I'll help you with your homework. I'll buy you a new one*) until you either persuade him or give up! Once the class have the idea, get other students to make similar attempts to get objects from other students.

Concept questions

Simple future

- **The conference will be on the first Wednesday of June.** Is the conference in the past or the future? (*The future*) Is it a definite plan? (*Yes*) Is it 100% certain that the conference is on that date? (*Well – there could be some problems – but it is almost certain*)

Prediction

- **Katya said to James 'You'll pass the exam next month.'** Is the exam in the past or the future? (*The future*) James passing the exam – is that 100% definite? (*No*) Is it a fact or a prediction? (*A prediction*) Is it likely to happen? (*We don't know – but Katya thinks it is very likely or she wants to encourage him*)

Making decisions

→ Unit 48 *Will* contrasted with *going to*

Offers and promises

- **Jin said to Klara 'I'll help you mend your computer.'** Does Jin want to help Klara? (*Yes*) Is he offering to help her? (*Yes*)

Meaning and use

Will is sometimes called the 'simple future' but in fact, it has a large number of different functional uses related to future actions. In some ways, if students want an all-purpose future, they might do better with *going to*.

→ Unit 47 *Going to*

Will for future

We use *will* for . . .

1) 'certain' future events.
   Interviews will be held on 2 December.
   Marc will be in charge in my absence.

The band will release their third album in May.
The celebrations will include fireworks and dancing.

2) making predictions about the future.
When you're my age, you'll understand.
This time next week we'll be in Ibiza.
It'll be another 45 minutes before our flight is called.

The line between certainty and prediction is slippery. In reality, all statements about the future are to some degree predictions – even when saying *The sun will rise tomorrow!*

3) announcing decisions about the future as they are made.
I'll sing and you can do the actions.
We'll give the plan an airing at the next meeting.
I'll send my luggage on ahead.

In these examples, the decision to do something is made only moments before it is stated. This is in contrast to the use of *going to* or other futures for decisions made earlier.

→ **Unit 47** *Going to*

Other functional uses of *will*

4) promises.
I'll give you a definite answer tomorrow.
Simply order from our website and we'll deliver the goods to your door within 24 hours.

5) confirming intentions, decisions, arrangements, agreements.
So, you cook the lunch, and I'll look after the children.
I'll book a table for 8 o'clock then.
OK, I'll settle my account in the morning.

6) requests.
Will you get me a glass of water?
Will you pick me up after the party?
Will you be able to set up my PC?

7) indirect requests.
I'll need your name and address.
You'll have to tell me again – I wasn't listening.

8) shows of willingness and offers.
I'll take you to the station in the car.
Sit down and I'll get you lunch.
Will you have a cup of tea?

9) invitations and suggestions.
> *Won't you stay for lunch?*
> *Won't you have another drink before you go?*
> *Will you have dinner with me this evening?*
> *Will you come with me?*
> *Call me and we'll do lunch.*

10) accepting offers.
> *I'll just have some water, thanks.*
> A: *All I've got to offer you is instant coffee.* B: *That'll do me.*

11) advice.
> *You'll have to install a new Ethernet card.*
> *Take a couple of aspirin – you'll soon feel better.*

12) warnings and threats.
> *Don't have any more chocolate – it'll spoil your appetite.*
> *We must leave now or else we'll miss our train.*
> *Wear a hat or you'll fry.*
> *Stop or I'll shoot.*

13) giving directions.
> *A little further ahead, you'll come to a crossroads.*

14) asking or ordering someone to do something.
> *Will you hurry up? I haven't got all day!*
> *Will you scratch my back for me?*

Shall

We use *shall* to suggest doing something, offer help, ask for agreement or permission.
Shall I call you a cab?
Shall I put the kettle on for a cup of tea?
Gentlemen, shall we begin?

Beyond this, we sometimes use *shall* as an alternative to *will*. It suggests more certainty, emphasis, forcefulness or determination, perhaps indicating an element of inevitability or personal control over events. It is also a slightly old-fashioned use and might be one which students do not encounter regularly.
I shall collect your books in at the end of the lesson.
We shall never see his like again.
We shall have to make some fundamental changes in the way we do business.
I shall treat that remark with the contempt it deserves.

In all these examples, we could use *will* with minimal change of meaning.

Pronunciation

The contraction *'ll* is more common than the full form of *will*. It can be a problem for many learners to say it well. The sound of *'ll* is known as 'dark l' and is pronounced like /ʊl/.

1) Help students to hear it by pointing out the sound's occurrence in words like *bottle, steal* etc.

2) Help them to say it by first separating the sound out and letting them hear it on its own – then by putting it together with *we* to make a two syllable 'we . . . ll'.

3) After this encourage them to say it faster and with less distinction into two separate syllables.

We use the uncontracted form of *will* to emphasise a strong intention that something is going to happen or be done, often as a promise or threat:
I WILL call you tomorrow.
I WILL be there, I promise you.
I WILL tell him the truth.

Watch out for these problems . . .

* **Students at low level overuse *will* as an 'all-purpose future' to the avoidance of all other ways of talking about the future:** ✗ *It will to rain.* This is because it is met early on, quickly learnt and then it is easy to place the single word into any sentence where they wish to convey a future meaning. Even if grammatically incorrect it may often be a sufficiently successful piece of communication to encourage students to use it again and again.

* **Students use present simple instead of *will* for instant decisions:** ✗ *I check the dates.* ✗ *I think I colour my hair.*

47 Going to

Form

We make the structure with *be* (in the correct form) + *going to* + base form.
Whether affirmative, negative or question form, the words *going to* never alter.

Affirmative

I	'm (am)		leave	soon.
You / We / They	're (are)	going to	catch	the last train.
He / She / It	's (is)		buy	her a present.

Negative

I	'm not (am not)		leave	soon.
You / We / They	're not (aren't / are not)	going to	catch	the last train.
He / She / It	's not (isn't / is not)		buy	her a present.

Yes / No questions

Am	I		leave	soon?
Are	you / we / they	going to	catch	the last train?
Is	he / she / it		buy	her a present?

Short answers

Yes,	I	am.
	you / we / they	are.
	he / she / it	is.

No,	I	'm not (am not).
	you / we / they	're not (aren't / are not).
	he / she / it	's not (isn't / is not).

Wh- questions

Who is / Who's going to look after the baby?
What is / What's the government going to do about the Health Service?
How are we ever going to catch up?

Presentation

Tonight

1) Draw Yun Ju smiling and thought bubbles over his head. In the bubbles, write some notes about things he is going to do later (walk into town, buy present for Marie, McDonalds®, Marie's birthday party, night club, taxi home).

2) Ask students why Yun Ju is smiling. Establish that he is thinking about this afternoon and tonight – and looking forward to it. Ask students if they can say what he is thinking. Elicit or model Yun Ju's sentences (*I'm going to walk into town. I'm going to buy a present for Marie. I'm going to have a snack in McDonald's*). Get students to practise these.

3) Ask students to tell you what they are going to do tonight – and to guess what you are going to do.

Practice

Arrangements already made

Diary

Prepare a diary page showing interesting events that an (anonymous) famous living person (the UN Secretary General) will do next week. First, get students to guess whose diary it is. After that, ask them to tell you what he / she is going to do (*He's going to meet the Malian President*) and what they think is going to happen at those events (*They're going to talk about the food problem*).

Present evidence and predictions

Pictures

Draw two standing people. One of them is pointing at a dark cloud in the sky. Elicit what she is saying (*It's going to rain*). Add a plane coming in to land in the fields behind (*It's going to land*). Add a dog and a ball in the person's hand (*You're going to throw it. He's going to catch it*). Add a bull (*It's going to attack!*) etc.

Story – the journey

Bring along some simple props to represent a car, a road and a few locations and items along the way. As you tell a story about a journey using present tenses, occasionally pause and ask students to predict what is going to happen next based on the story so far (*Anna and Rajiv are driving from their home in Bigville. A few kilometres outside town they see a large box lying in the middle of the road. What do you think Anna and Rajiv are going to do?*).

Mime

Prepare a set of cards with actions written on them (*You're going to drive a car. You're going to swim across a lake. You're going to run a marathon*). Make pairs and give one card to each student, warning them to keep them secret. Tell students that their task is to mime someone who is going to do the thing on their card. Their partner must guess what they are going to do. Emphasise that they must only mime the things a person would do **before** doing the action on the card. Elicit some examples (*someone who is going to drive a car will open the door, get in, adjust the mirror*). After pairs have guessed their actions, redistribute the cards for more practice.

Paused film

Show a short video clip of a dramatic action scene and then pause at a suitable moment just before a character does something. Students predict what they are going to do (*He's going to rob a bank*). You can also use photos for this activity.

Objects

Bring in a selection of unusual objects. Ask students to imagine that an inventor is going to use the objects. Collect predictions (*She's going to make a time machine*).

Plans

Say 'Tell me your plans for tonight / the weekend / the holidays' or 'What are you going to do this evening / next week / in the holidays / at Christmas?'

→ Unit 48 *Will* contrasted with *going to*

Concept questions

Arrangement

- **Diana's going to meet Chris tonight.** Was the meeting in the past? (*No*) Is the meeting in the future? (*Yes*) Have they already decided to meet? (*Yes*) When did they decide about this meeting? (*Sometime in the past*)

Present evidence

- **Look at those clouds – it's going to rain.** Is it raining now? (*No*) Does the speaker think it will rain in the future? (*Yes*) Does he think this because of something he can see? (*Yes*) What? (*Dark clouds in the sky*) Will it definitely rain in the future? (*No*) Is it possible that it will rain? (*Yes*) Is it probable that it will rain? (*Yes – according to the speaker*)

Meaning and use

Core meaning

Future events that have previously been thought about, mentioned, planned or arranged and imminent events based on evidence in the present.

We use *going to* for . . .

1) an all-purpose future.

   Going to is a pretty all-purpose way of talking about the future. It's suitable for most (but not all) sentences that have a future meaning. In this respect, it is a more natural option for students who always use *will* for everything futureish.
   The images aren't going to look as good in print as they do on screen.
   It's going to be an all-American final.

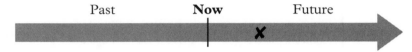

2) events initiated before now.

   Going to is particularly likely when talking about future events that have been thought about, mentioned, decided, planned or arranged before now.
   I'm going to see him tonight.
   She's going to buy that Ferrari.

→ **Unit 48 *Will* contrasted with *going to***

3) present evidence.

   Talking about imminent events based on evidence in the present (something you can see, hear, smell or feel).
   It's going to rain. (You can see the clouds or feel the temperature change.)
   I'm going to be sick! (You feel nauseous.)

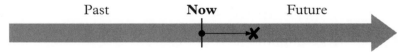

4) predictions.

   Going to is commonly used in predictions – not just the fortune-telling kind, but any statement about what is expected to happen in the future. This meaning seems closely linked to meaning (3) except that the supposed 'evidence' for the prediction may only be in our thoughts inside our heads.
   They're going to win the election.
   It looks as if the negotiations are going to fail.

5) emphatic intentions.

   To state a strong decision to do something.

No, you can't persuade me. I AM going to tell him the truth.
I AM going to take that shirt back.

Pronunciation

What is the correct pronunciation?

Going to is an item whose pronunciation often surprises students. By looking at the spelling they will probably expect that it is pronounced /ɡəʊɪŋ tuː/ or /ɡəʊɪŋ tə/ – and while this is entirely acceptable, if this is the only way of saying it that they know, it won't prepare students for hearing and understanding native speakers using the item. The most common fluent native speaker pronunciation of 'going to' is /ɡənə/ – a fact recognised in the often-used spelling 'gonna'. Another very common pronunciation is /ɡəntə/.

A surprisingly large number of people believe that it is wrong or lazy to say /ɡənə/ or /ɡəntə/. In my time as a trainer I have occasionally been lectured by native speakers who considered that I was not far off committing a criminal act in suggesting that /ɡənə/ was an acceptable form that might be worth teaching to students. My response has usually been to suggest that we just go with the evidence – and I tell them that I strongly suspect that they themselves regularly use this pronunciation (which they of course deny vehemently). At this point, I let the argument rest. It's usually not more than five minutes later that I can point out to the person that they have just said /ɡənə/ themselves.

Should I teach it to my students? I would say a resounding 'yes' – because that's what I say myself. Should you teach it to your students? You have to decide – but read the Teaching tip TWYS but KWYS on the next page before you decide!

Pronouncing the pronoun

A less important pronunciation point – though also one that students need to know for listening and recognition purposes, even if they don't use it themselves – is that an initial pronoun may often be spoken very weakly.

/mɡənə duːwɪt/ rather than /aɪm ɡənə duːwɪt/ (I'm going to do it)

/jəɡənə duːwɪt/ rather than /jɔː ɡənə duːwɪt/ (You're going to do it)

/zɡənə duːwɪt/ rather than /hiːz ɡənə duːwɪt/ (He's going to do it)

This may make it hard for students to recognise what is being said – and is the reason why it's vital to teach realistic pronunciation rather than imagined 'perfect' versions. If a learner is expecting to hear /ðeɪ ɑː ɡəʊɪŋ tuː duːwɪt/, it may be impossible for them to interpret /ðəɡənə duːwɪt/.

Watch out for these problems . . .

- **Students avoid *going to*:** Students often find it difficult to select an appropriate future form. Lower level students often plump for one form (typically *will*) and use it for all sentences that refer to the future. Thus, a major problem with *going to* is simply that students don't use it when it would be appropriate.

- **Students omit the main verb after *going to*:** ✗ *I'm going to football.* ✗ *Sarah's going to shopping.*

- **Students use different forms (possibly also omitting *be*):** ✗ *He's go to leave now.* ✗ *He goes to play tennis next week.*

Teaching tip: pronunciation – TWYS but KWYS!

TWYS = (Teach What You Say)

My own rule of thumb in teaching pronunciation is basically to teach what I say myself. Where this is different from what a coursebook or other resource offers, I draw attention to the differences as interesting examples of different ways of saying something (*The coursebook recording says it like that and I say it like this*). This approach saves me from trying to mimic an accent I don't have.

KWYS = (Know What You Say)

The problem with TWYS is that it is surprisingly hard to get an accurate, clear idea as to how you yourself actually say something. It's a really odd thing that most people believe they say one thing but actually say something quite different. For example, many non-ELT-trained native speakers will be amazed, shocked and probably disbelieving to be informed that their normal pronunciation of *for* is /fə/ or that their normal pronunciation of *was* is /wəz/.

For an English teacher, it's quite important to find out what we actually say. I've heard quite a few teachers in class (a) carefully modelling an artificial pronunciation of an item (b) getting students to copy it (c) repeating it themselves with their normal, quite different pronunciation (d) telling students off when they copy that normal pronunciation – and all without any idea what the problem was or why their students looked so confused.

How can we know what we say? The problem is that as soon as we say a sentence so that we can listen to ourselves, it tends to become too careful, over-pronounced and artificial-sounding. So what's the answer? Well, recording ourselves is obviously one way – but in day-to-day work, it's not really practical. Better to learn to 'catch yourself' saying something naturally. I find that embedding the thing I want to know about within a longer piece of talk helps a lot. For example, if you want to know how you pronounce *going to* – don't just say *going to* to yourself. Instead, improvise a whole mini-conversation and surprise yourself by slipping in a *going to* at some point, as naturally as you can. Practise this technique a few times – and it starts to become quicker and easier to do – and very useful!

48 *Will* contrasted with *going to*

Form

→ **Unit 46** *Will*

→ **Unit 47** *Going to*

Presentation

Class party

1) Draw a picture of some students. Explain that they have just decided to have a class party. They are thinking about who will do what. Draw an icon of a cake above one student. Elicit that he is offering to make a cake, and see if students can think what he is saying (*I'll make a cake!*).

2) Continue to elicit more offers of help (*I'll tidy the room. I'll buy the drinks. We'll make some games*).

3) Add the students' teacher to the picture and establish that it is a few hours later. The students are telling their teacher about their plans. Elicit what they are saying (*I'm going to tidy the room. I'm going to buy the drinks. We're going to make some games*). Check with students that they have noticed the changed tense. Establish that they said *will* at the moment that they made their decision to help and *going to* later on when the decision was already in the past.

4) Working in small groups, get the students to role play the activity of planning a party for their own class. Do it in two stages; first the students make spontaneous offers of help, then, later, they tell you what they have agreed to do.

Practice

Unexpected visit

Tell students that the CEO of their company is going to make a surprise visit in three hours' time. Build a dialogue between different people saying what they will do to get ready (*I'll print the reports. I'll hide the dirty plates. I'll book the board room*). At the end a manager must sum up what everyone is going to do (*Harvey is going to print the reports, Billa is going to hide . . .* etc).

My 'To Do' list

Show students a 'To Do' list with two items on it (buy eggs, post letter). Demonstrate a monologue to the students. Say 'I'm going to buy some eggs. I'm going to post a letter'. Then pretend to remember some more things. Say 'Bread. I forgot bread. I'll buy some bread as well. Oh – and I'll visit Sunita this afternoon. Oh – I nearly forgot Rob – I'll email him this evening'. Add each item to your list. Now ask students 'What am I going to do today?' and get them to summarise your new 'To Do' list (*You're going to buy eggs and bread. You're going to visit Sunita. You're going to email Rob* etc).

Staged role play: in a restaurant

Set up groups of three for a role play. Explain that A is a customer who is waiting for their friend B and that C is a waiter. Students will role play each part of the story as you instruct, stage by stage. Only give the instructions for the next stage when students have all completed the previous one.

Stage 1: B is late and so A orders food from the waiter (*I'll have the soup and then a steak with salad*).

Stage 2: When the waiter has gone, B arrives and A tells B what he / she has ordered (*I'm going to have the soup and then a steak with salad*). B decides what to have when he / she listens to A (*OK – then I'll have the steak as well*).

Stage 3: A goes to the bathroom. The waiter comes over and B orders. The waiter recommends something different to B. B changes his / her mind and orders (*Good idea. I'll have the risotto*).

Stage 4: A comes back and B tells A what he / she has ordered (*I changed my mind. I'm going to have the risotto*).

Surprise day out

Make fours – each group is a 'family'. Hand one person in each family an idea for a 'day out' (*We're going to go to the seaside tomorrow*). Explain that this person has arranged a surprise day out for everyone tomorrow. He / she should read out the idea to the others – who will add their own reactions, comments and suggestions (*I think I'll stay in the sea all day. I'll take my surfboard. I'll phone my friend and meet her there. I'll make a picnic. I'll pack some beach games*). You may want to allow students some preparation time to think of ideas and prepare their dialogue before they act it out.

Will you please . . .

Get students to practise some order / response exchanges such as:

A: *Will you please tidy your bedroom?* B: *All right! I'm going to!*

A: *Will you please tell me her phone number?* B: *I'm never going to tell you!*

A: *Please will you finish the report?* B: *I'm going to do it tomorrow.*

Of course, this is nothing more than a simple drill . . . but it has potential for laughter and fun as there is lots of scope for overacting and exaggerated intonation!

Concept questions

- **A: I'm going to meet Nadif on Wednesday. B: Oh good. I'll come along too.** Will they both meet Nadif on Wednesday? (*Yes*) Did A decide to meet him now or sometime before now? (*Sometime before now*) Did B decide to meet him now or sometime before now? (*Now*)

Meaning and use

Will and *going to* are often contrasted: *'ll* / *will* for spontaneous decisions, plans, offers of help etc (*I'll do it*) and *going to* for reporting such decisions after they were made (*I've decided that I'm going to do it*).

Two people have been invited to a party. They are discussing what food they could take.

A: *I'm going to take a fruit salad.*

B: *What shall I take? Ah! I know. I'll bake a cake!*

(Person C joins them)

C: *Hi. What are you taking to the party? I can't decide!*

B: *I'm going to bake a cake.*

C: *OK – then I'll take some chocolates!*

People who spontaneously make a decision use *'ll* at the moment they make their decision. People who have already made a decision about what to take (even if only one second earlier) use *going to* to talk about their decision . . . and as a result . . . B's decision about what to take is initially introduced with *'ll* but later B uses *going to* to tell C what he / she has already decided to do.

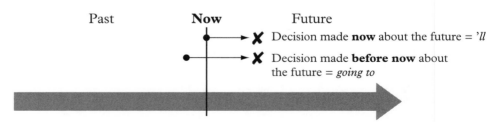

The distinction is also clear in order / response exchanges:

A: *Will you please tidy your bedroom?*

B: *All right! I'm going to!*

Remember that for many other uses, such as prediction, we can use either verb form.

It's going to rain soon.
It will rain at the weekend.

Watch out for these problems . . .

- **Students use *going to* for spontaneous decisions:** ✗ (doorbell rings) *I'm going to get it!*

- **Students use *will* for things already decided:** ✗ *Hey Frida – did you know? I will have a party next Saturday!*

→ **Unit 46 *Will***

→ **Unit 47 *Going to***

Teaching tip: dialogue acting

Dialogues such as the one in Meaning and use are often fun to read (or act) out loud – or can be good for little acted scenes. They can also form a model for getting students to create their own similar dialogues. Tell students to replace all the items (fruit salad, cake etc) with new ones. In this way they can have some creative input without having to write a whole text from scratch. Stronger students could be asked to change more elements.

49 Present progressive: 'future arrangements'

Form

→ **Unit 28 Present progressive: affirmative ('now' meaning)**

→ **Unit 29 Present progressive: negative and questions**

Presentation

> Would you like to come to the cinema tomorrow evening? I'd love to, but I'm playing tennis with Renate then.
>
> Can you join us for lunch today? I'm sorry, I'm meeting the boss then.

Excuses

1) Elicit some examples of social and work invitations (*Would you like to come to the cinema tomorrow evening? Can you join us for lunch today?*). Collect these on the board.

2) Elicit or model some convincing (or amusing) excuses involving a previous arrangement you have (*I'm sorry. I'm meeting the boss then. I'd love to, but I'm playing tennis with Renate then. Oh dear. I'm washing my hair tonight*). Get students to repeat them and practise saying them in response to invitations.

3) Say some new invitations and get students to try new excuses.

4) Get students to play the game themselves in pairs or groups.

Practice

My week

Ask students to note down two or three definite arrangements they have for the next seven days (eg *cinema Tuesday evening*). When ready, get students to stand up and meet another person. They should tell their partner about their arrangements (*I'm watching a DVD with Carole on Tuesday evening*). Students then move on to meet a new person. They report to this new person about the previous partner they met (*Krista is watching a DVD with Carole on Tuesday evening*).

Filling the diary

Prepare a blank diary page for Saturday or any other appropriate day with times marked from 9.00 to 20.00 and blank spaces for appointments. Copy and hand out one page to each student. Write up a list of possible things they might arrange to do that day (play a game of tennis; play football; go to the shops with friends; have a meal at a café; go to the gym; go to the cinema). Make small groups of approximately six people. Students should now 'pencil in' three possible things they'd like to do (with question marks) at different times – and the names of people in their group they might be able to do them with. After this, they should stand up, mingle, meet people and see if they can make the arrangements they planned – while agreeing to or turning down other people's suggestions – or rearranging things when necessary. Once they have placed an appointment or two, it will become harder to arrange other things as times may clash. Encourage use of the present progressive (*Sorry, I can't come to the cinema with you; I'm having supper with Beth then*).

Famous diaries

As a variation on the diary activity above, allocate each person a role-play character (President of the USA, famous pop star).

Concept questions

- **Robbie's meeting the boss tomorrow.** Is Robbie with the boss now? (*No*) Will Robbie meet the boss in the future? (*Yes*) When? (*Tomorrow*) Does Robbie have an arrangement to meet the boss? (*Yes*)

Meaning and use

Students usually learn the 'now or around now' meaning first, but the future meaning of the present progressive is also very common. We use the present progressive to talk about events in the future that (in the speaker's view) have already been arranged.
They are having another of their parties.
We're meeting to discuss the matter next week.
He's bringing his new girlfriend over to our house tonight.

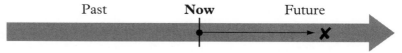

When we use the present progressive with a future meaning, there is often one or more of the following . . .

a) a specific time reference.
 I'm leaving soon.
 We're going there tomorrow.
 Sheila's heading off at 10.25.

b) an implied time reference through mention of an event that suggests a time.
We're having the meeting before lunch.
I'm leaving when he tells me I can.

c) a reference to a location (*at the department store* or *in London*).
I'm flying out from Heathrow.

d) something earlier in the conversation that clarifies that it is the future not the present that is referred to.

But future reference is also possible without any of these. The context will give the clue as to what time is meant. For example:
(Two people chatting at a party)
A: *Are you sure it's OK for you to stay? The last bus leaves in five minutes.*
B: *Sure, my dad's picking me up!*
In this example, B seems to suggest that there has been a prior arrangement for her dad to collect her from the party, allowing B to stay without worrying about how she will get home. The situation (ie she's at a party right now, not in a car) and the previous question both clarify that the reference is to the future rather than the present.

Pronunciation

→ **Unit 28 Present progressive: affirmative ('now' meaning)**

→ **Unit 30 Present progressive contrasted with present simple**

50 Future progressive and future perfect

Form

Future progressive

We form the future progressive with *'ll / will* + *be* + present participle (*-ing* form). We can also (more rarely) form the future progressive with *be* + *going to* + *be* + present participle (*-ing* form).

We'll be arriving about 6 o'clock.
We're going to be working to a very tight schedule.

We often use the future progressive with

- a time phrase (next January, all winter etc).

We'll be working in Barcelona next year.

- *at* + time (at midday, at 2.30 etc).

He'll be arriving at 2.30.

- *when* + event (when he arrives, when the boss is ready).

She'll be working when he arrives.

- *while* + event (while I sign in, while the machine is moving).

I'll be slaving away at work next month, while you're lying on the beach!

Future perfect

We form the future perfect with *'ll / will* + *have* + past participle (+ *by* + time phrase).
I'll have finished by midnight.
The building project will have been completed by this time next year.

We often use the future perfect with *by* and a time (*by 6.30*) or mention of an event.
He'll have finished cooking by the time you arrive.

Presentation

- arrive
- hotel
- problem

I'll be waiting (future progressive)

1) Draw a picture of Chiara talking with her friend Felice in Pisa. Explain that they are going to have a holiday in Britain – but Felice is flying a day before Chiara – and Chiara is very nervous about the visit.

2) Use picture cues, key words or mime to elicit her questions and Felice's answers – for example:
   C: *What do I have to do when I arrive?* F: *Don't worry. I'll be waiting in the airport!*
   C: *How can I get to the hotel in London?* F: *Don't worry! I'll be coming with you!*
   C: *What can I do if I have a problem?* F: *Don't worry! I'll be staying in the same hotel!*

3) Get students to practise the dialogue in pairs.

Building plans (future perfect)

School plan		Builders' plan
Sunday		Finish electrical wiring and check
Monday	Show Governors round school	
Tuesday		Tidy away any dangerous leftover materials
Wednesday		Do final safety check before handover
Thursday	Important parents' meeting	
Friday	New school opens to pupils	

1) Explain that a brand new school has been built. It is due to open very soon – but the building work has overrun. The Head teacher is meeting the Building Team leader. The Head wants to have reassurance that everything will be ready.

2) Tell the class what the Head says – and elicit possible reassuring (or worrying) responses from the Builder. For example:
   H: *The Governors are visiting on Monday.*
   B: *That's fine. We'll have finished all the electrical wiring by then.*
   H: *Will the building be safe?*
   B: *Well . . . we won't have tidied away all the leftover materials . . .*
   H: *Goodness! On Wednesday we have a very important parents' meeting.*
   B: *Don't worry! By then we'll have done a final safety check on everything.*

Practice

Future progressive

Diary

Hand each student a diary page with spaces for writing events at different times of day (9.00, 10.00, 11.00). Ask them to fill in imaginary events at five or six of the times (*write essay, play tennis*). Students should then meet up with others and try to agree times to meet for a coffee. They will need to give explanations (*Sorry. I can't come at 10.00. I'll be playing tennis with Robert then*).

Receptionist excuses

Make pairs. Explain that A is a receptionist for a rather dodgy business. Their boss has told them that if anyone phones and asks to speak to him / her, they must make a good excuse. B is an angry customer who really wants to speak to the boss! B phones A and tries to make an appointment (A: *He's busy right now.* B: *OK – then I'll call back in an hour.* A: *I'm sorry, he'll be having a meeting with a supplier then*).

Future perfect

My life

Tell students a future date (about 20 years in the future). Ask students to write down three things they will have done by then and something they won't have done yet. Students can then meet up and compare predictions.

Today

Same idea as My life (above) – but keep the focus to today or this week. Ask students to write down things they will have done by the end of the day or the week.

How will the world have changed?

Ask students to come up with a list of ways in which the world will have changed in 100 years' time (*Pandas will have become extinct. Scientists will have found a way to make us all invisible*).

Concept questions

- **James 'Can I call you at three o'clock tomorrow afternoon?' Holly 'Yes, sure. I'll be painting at home all day tomorrow.'** Where will Holly be tomorrow? (*At home*) What does she plan to do? (*Painting*) Where will Holly be at three o'clock tomorrow? (*At home*) How long will she paint for? (*All day*) Will she start painting before three o'clock? (*Yes*) Will she finish painting after three o'clock? (*Yes*)

- **She'll have finished by midnight.** Will she work after midnight? (*No*) Will she finish her work at midnight? (*No*) What time will she finish her work? (*Before midnight*)

Meaning and use

Future progressive

We use the future progressive for . . .

1) a planned action that will be in progress at a certain time in the future or when something else happens.
   They'll be tidying the office when she calls.
   I'll be waiting in the foyer at seven o'clock.

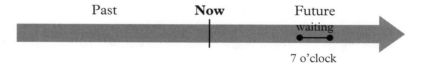

2) a planned action in progress over a certain period of time in the future.
   I'll be working there all next month.

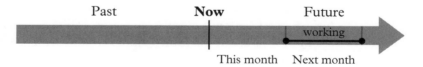

In both cases, we think of the action as lasting for some time – it isn't a momentary action. For example, in the sentence *She'll be waiting at Reception when you finish work* the *waiting* is in the future. Her waiting will have started before you finish work – so it will be in progress when you finish.

We often use the future progressive to explain what someone will be doing at a certain time – as an explanation or an excuse or in answer to a question.
What'll you be doing at seven o'clock?
We'll be waiting for you when you get off the train.
We'll be going over to Sydney for live coverage in just a couple of minutes.

Future perfect

The future perfect is quite complex! It involves three key concepts:

a) looking into the future to a certain time (midnight).
b) looking backwards from that future time towards the present.
c) noticing what actions will be done (and possibly completed) in the period between that future time and the present.

I'll have finished work by midnight.

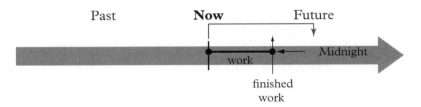

Teaching tip: equal weighting

It is important for your students to notice that some future forms are much less used than others. While it's important to know forms such as the future perfect or future progressive, we use them significantly less frequently than *going to*, *will*, and the present simple. When studying the language in neatly divided chunks it can often mean that each point is covered in about the amount of detail, so it may seem as if something relatively unimportant we don't use very often (such as the future perfect) has equal importance to something of high frequency and usefulness (such as *going to*).

Teaching tip: lexical time words / phrases

Lexical time words / phrases are very important in indicating that a sentence refers to the future. Compare *I'm going there* and *I'm going there tomorrow*. If we hear the first sentence out of context, we can't immediately tell if it's a sentence about now or about the future. In the second sentence, it is the word *tomorrow* (rather than the grammar) that unequivocally sets the sentence in the future.

51 Requests, orders, offers, permission: *can, could, will, would, may, might*

Form

Can, could, will, would, may and *might* are modal verbs. They do not change form, they have no infinitive or participle forms, and don't add an *-s* for the third person singular. For modal verbs, we make negatives, questions and question tags without *do*.

Requests and orders

We use *can / could / will / would* + *you* + bare infinitive to make requests or orders.
Can you explain again?
Could you bring me a plate from the kitchen?
Will you please tidy your bedroom?
While the band is setting up, would you check on the food?

Offers

We use a modal verb *Can* + *I* + bare infinitive to offer to do things.
Can I get you a sandwich or anything?
I'm driving into town – can I drop you somewhere?

Permission

We use *can / could / may / might* + *I* (or other pronoun / noun) to request permission.
May I see your ticket, please?
Could I use your phone?
Can I have a try?

We use negative modals to make a request sound stronger.
Can't we open a window?

Presentation

Requests

1) Prepare some pictures to introduce a scene in which one person repeatedly asks another for things (boyfriend and girlfriend; two students; worker and boss; customer and shop assistant).

2) In class elicit or model conversations in which one demanding person repeatedly asks for different things:

   A: *Could I borrow some paper, please?*   B: *Sure. Here you are.*
   A: *Could I borrow a dictionary, please?*   B: *Sure. Here you are.*
   A: *Could I borrow your jacket, please?*   B: *Er . . . well . . . OK*
   A: *Could I borrow your car, please?*   B: *NO!*

3) Get students to practise saying the dialogue. Encourage them to play around with different levels of politeness.

4) With stronger classes, you could introduce more exponents (A: *Excuse me. I wonder if I might use your telephone?* B: *Yes, of course.* A: *Could I sit here?* B: *Yes, sure.* A: *Can I have one of these biscuits?* B: *Er, yes. Please do.* A: *Do you think you could lend me £200?* B: *Certainly not!*).

Offers

1) With a volunteer student, model a conversation 'A: Can I get you a drink?' 'B: No, thank you.'

2) Check that students understand the meaning (offering). Use the board to analyse how the offer is formed (*Can I . . .*). Elicit some more ideas for

offers from class (*Can I bring you a dictionary? Can I help you?*). As the ideas come out, draw little icon sketches on the board to reflect each idea (*a book, a helping hand*).

3) Invite pairs to come up front and try to make a dialogue. They won't know which one they have to say until you point at the icon of your choice.

Permission

1) Prepare a chain of five or six requests for permission that you could ask to students in class (*Can I come through here? Could I check your book? Can I open the window? May I look in your bag?*).

2) Ask students to listen to what you say. Act out the chain of requests one after the other (*walking up to a narrow space and asking 'Can I come through here?' Then going to another student and asking to borrow a book* etc).

3) At the end, see if students can recall the sequence of requests. Write them on the board if necessary – but erase them before the next stage.

4) See if a student can act the sequence as you did. Then make pairs, As and Bs. Get As to do the sequence – then swap so that Bs do it.

Practice

Requests

Picture offers

Prepare a set of picture cards for each pair with images that suggest possible requests (a cup of tea, a closed window, a heavy box). Student A picks one card and makes a request to B (*Could you make me a cup of tea, please?*) who invents a response. Student B can then pick a new card and make a new request . . . and so on till all the cards have been used.

Offers

The annoying waiter

Make pairs. A is a customer in a cafe. B is a waiter. A just wants to have a cup of coffee and read the newspaper. B must keep offering more and more things . . . until the customer gets angry. Before students begin, elicit or suggest some ideas (*Can I bring you another coffee? Can I bring you some cake? Can I get you a bigger cup? Can I clean your table for you?*).

Permission

The customs officer

Put students into pairs. Explain that A has just arrived at the airport after a holiday. B is a customs officer who has stopped A and wants to ask some questions. Elicit possible ideas and then get pairs to role play the scene.

(Could I stop you for a minute, Sir? Can I ask you a few questions? Can I open your bag, Sir? Can I ask you where you have been? Can I see your wallet, please?).

Meaning and use

Requests and orders

Formality and politeness			
++ more			——less
could	*can*	*would*	*will*

Permission

Formality and politeness		
++ more		——less
may / might	*could*	*can*

If we want to refuse or deny permission, it is common to give a reason.
Could you pick Helena up from the station tomorrow?
I'm sorry, I'm going to visit my parents.

Watch out for these problems . . .

- **Students use imperatives instead of modal verbs for requests and sound rude and / or impatient:** ✗ *Give me some paper.*

- **Students use the wrong register for the situation:** you could try presenting the verbs on a scale to show their varying levels of formality.

52 Ability: *can, can't, could, couldn't, be able to*

Form

Can, can't, could and couldn't are modal verbs.

We use can, can't, could, couldn't and be able to to talk about ability.

	Past	**Present**	**Future**
Affirmative	could was able to / used to be able to	can am / is / are able to	will be able to
Negative	couldn't wasn't / weren't able to / didn't use to be able to	can't am not / isn't / aren't able to	won't be able to

For ability in the present we use *can*.
I can count up to ten in German.
Neda can dance really well.
I can't open the window.
They can't swim.

For ability in the past we use *could* or *was able to* or *used to be able to*.
Ingrid could play the violin by the time she was six.
Fortunately for Liverpool, he was able to play.
The pilot was able to land the plane safely.
The governors used to be able to control the recruitment process directly.

For ability in the future we use *will be able to*.
The party will not be able to govern alone.
The baby will soon be able to stand up all by itself.
Thabo will be able to come too.
Will you be able to set up my PC?

Yes / No questions

Past	*Could you ski last January?* *Weren't they able to find a hotel?*
Present	*Can you swim?* *Are they able to climb the stairs?*
Future	*Will we be able to visit the museum when we're in Madrid?*

(continued)

> **Wh- questions**
>
> *When could you ski?*
> *Where were they able to stay?*
> *How fast can you run?*
> *When will you be able to visit the museum?*

→ **Unit 51 Requests, orders, offers, permission:** *can, could, will, would, may, might*

Presentation

Questionnaire: Can you . . .?

1) Prepare a simple questionnaire with about 10–15 questions about abilities (*Can you play a musical instrument? Can you ski? Can you ride a horse?*).

2) In class, use pictures and mimes of people doing different things to introduce the idea of ability (a picture of two people and a horse). Introduce the question form first (*Can you ride a horse?*) and short answers (*Yes, I can* and *No, I can't*). Establish that Micah can ride a horse but Michiko can't. You might want to try a few more before students move on (*Can you swim / play the piano / speak Spanish / design a web page?*).

3) Hand out the questionnaire and get students to interview each other and collect answers.

4) Work with the class to write up a short report at the end (*Soon-Yi can ride a horse, but she can't swim*).

5) Get students to prepare some new questions of their own which they can later ask each other.

Variation

To focus on talking about the past, change the questions to *When you were ten could you / were you able to . . .?* or similar.

Practice

Medical check up

Prepare 10 or so questions about simple physical actions (*Can you hop on one leg? Can you bend your elbow? Can you clap your hands? Can you touch your toes?*). Students work in pairs. Explain that one is a doctor and the other is a person who had a sports accident. The doctor needs to check how well the patient is by asking the questions. The patient should role play trying to do the actions and then saying 'Yes, I can' or 'No, I can't'. To practise talking about the past, change the questions to 'After your accident, could you / were you able to . . . '

Health patterns

With some changes, the task above can also provide practice for past or future. In either case, explain that a TV programme is looking at changing health patterns in different generations. An interviewer is speaking to members of the public to collect views and information (Past: *When you were ten years old, could you run a kilometre / swim ten lengths / climb a rope?* etc. Future: *Do you think that children in the future will be able to run a kilometre / swim ten lengths / climb a rope?* etc).

Meaning and use

When talking about ability in the present *can* is more common than *be able to*. When talking about ability in the past we normally use *was able to* (not *could*) when talking about a specific situation.
Fortunately for Liverpool, he was able to play (on that particular day).
The pilot was able to land the plane safely (on that occasion).
I could design a web page when I was still a kid (general ability at any time in that period).

Pronunciation

Can is usually pronounced with a weak form /kən/ and with stress on the main verb following.
I can SWIM.
When *can* is a strong stressed form it is often to emphasise a point, for example to contradict someone:
A: *Of course, Jeanne doesn't know how to swim.*
Jeanne: *Excuse me! I CAN swim!*

53 Obligation and compulsion: *must, have to, should, ought*

Form

Obligation

We can use modal verbs (or non-modal alternatives like *have to*) *must* and *should* to talk about obligation.

For obligation in the present we use *must, have (got) to, should* or *ought to*.

For obligation in the past we use *had to* or *should've*.

For obligation in the future we use *will have to, should* or *must*.

Must and *have to*

	Past	Present	Future
Affirmative	*had to*	*must / have / has (got) to*	*must / will have to*
Negative	*didn't have to*	*mustn't / don't have to / doesn't have to*	*won't have to / will not have to*

Must has two 'opposites' with quite different meanings:

Mustn't means that something isn't allowed, is not permitted.

You mustn't use this door.

Don't have to indicates a lack of obligation.

You don't have to use this door. (= you can use it if you want to – but there is no requirement to use it)

Have to is interchangeable with *have got to*. *Have got to* is more common in spoken British English.

Questions

We often use questions with *must* or *have to* to show someone that what they are doing annoys us.

Must you rush around without looking where you're going?

Do you have to make so much noise?

Wh- questions are quite common:

What must we do?

When have you got to be home?

Should

	Past	Present	Future
Affirmative	*should have*	*should*	*(should)*
Negative	*shouldn't have*	*shouldn't*	*(should)*

Questions

What should I say?
Should I have spoken earlier?
What should we have done?
Shouldn't you cancel the meeting next week?

Ought to / oughtn't to / ought not to

Ought is different to standard modals in that it takes a *to* infinitive rather than a bare infinitive.

I suppose we ought to tip the waiter.
He ought to lose weight.

It has no past tense and we make the negative with *not*.
Teachers ought not to swear in front of the children.
I know I ought not to have taken the money.

Presentation

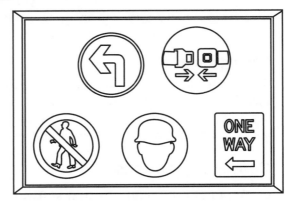

Road signs and notices

Draw some familiar road signs and notices, one by one, on the board (or show flash cards or illustrations). Elicit from students what they mean, helping them to make the correct sentences and focussing on the different uses of modals as appropriate (turn left sign = *You must turn left here*, seat belt sign = *You must wear a seat belt*, No entry sign = *You mustn't enter this street*).

Practice

Design the sign

Ask students to design a new notice for placing somewhere in the school / premises where they are studying. Most notices / signs contain implied modality (No running = *You must not run*) rather than explicit ones. Get students to think of a notice where they might need to spell out detailed rules saying what must / mustn't be done (rules for use of the photocopier = *You mustn't leave the lid open when copying. You should phone reception if there is a paper jam*).

Improvements

Suggest some life problems that people often have (getting into debt, being unfit). Get students to decide some improvements they would like to make in their own life. Give some examples and then see what true ones students can offer about themselves (*I must lose some weight. I ought to be more polite to my parents. I must go to bed earlier*).

Rules for the new place

Tell students that they are going to be the first people to start working or living a new life as part of a new communal flat / community / school / country / island / political party etc. They need to agree a set of basic rules for their group (*Everyone must help to look after the children*).

Routines and rules

Use pictures to establish the daily routine of someone in a place where the rules are set by others (a prisoner, a schoolchild, a mother at home looking after a young baby). Draw a magazine / TV reporter interviewing the person. Elicit how the person would describe their day (*I usually have to get up at 4 am when the baby wakes. I have to bath her every evening*).

Getting ready

Set the situation that a group is preparing to go on an expedition to the South Pole. They are discussing what they must do before they leave. Get students to talk and fill in endings for some written sentences (*We have to take . . . The ship must . . . We ought to tell . . . We mustn't forget to . . . We will have to go . . .*).

Concept questions

- **You ought to install the new software on your computer.** Is it important for me to install the new program? (*Yes*) Do I have a choice about whether to install it or not? (*Yes*) Is it a good idea for me to do it? (*Yes*)

- **Henry's parents said that he has to be home before 11.30.** Can Henry leave before 11.30? (Yes) Can he go home later than 11.30? (*No*) What will happen if he goes home later? (*He will be in trouble with his parents*) Does Henry have a choice about what time he goes home? (*No*)

- **You don't have to take your shoes off in our house.** When you come to our house is it essential that you take your shoes off? (*No*) Can you take them off if you want to? (*Yes*) Is there a problem if you don't take them off? (*No, it's up to you*)

Meaning and use

We use *must, have to, ought to* and *should* for . . .

1) strong obligation.
   We use *must* and *have (got) to* to indicate a strong obligation to do something – such as following the laws of a country or the rules of an organisation.
   In the UK you must drive on the left.
   You have to finish all your assignments before the end of the month.

2) weak obligation.
   We use *should* to give advice and opinions. *Should* indicates much weaker obligation than *must* or *have to*. There is more implication of a personal opinion being given. The speaker who says 'you should . . .' to someone implies that they know something that the listener doesn't and has a better knowledge than they do of the right thing for them to do.
   If it still feels bad, you should see the doctor today. (= In my opinion, it is important or necessary for you to see the doctor)

   Ought to has a very similar meaning to *should*. We use *ought to* to say what we consider to be the sensible, necessary or correct thing to do.
   You ought to tell him.

   We can also use *ought to* when we have strong reasons for believing that something will happen.
   The French team ought to win.

3) advice, suggestions and recommendations.
   In everyday speech, we often use *must, should* and *ought to* to give a strong suggestion, strong advice, encouragement or even an implied request.
   You should see the exhibition.
   He must get these wonderful pictures framed.
   You ought to go home now.

In these cases, some obligation is still there, but not meant seriously. For example, when someone says 'You must give me the recipe' the person being spoken to might feel that they will try to remember to give the recipe but would probably not feel under a strong obligation to do so.

Teaching tip: what's the difference between *must* and *have to*?

It's quite tricky to determine exactly what the difference is between *must* and *have to*. A standard explanation given in many grammar books and coursebooks is that: *must* shows obligation created by the person speaking while *have to* shows obligation imposed from outside the speaker by rules or circumstances.

For example, if you say 'I have to go' it suggests that there is some external reason that requires you to go (there is a timetabled train to catch soon) whereas if you say 'I must go' it suggests that you feel the need to go yourself.

Similarly:

a) *I must bake a cake for Marta's party!*

b) *I can't come now. Mum said I have to fill in this form before I can go to Marta's party.*

Personally, I've never managed to make much sense of this – and have found it rather problematic as a guideline to give to students. It's quite a complex concept to make use of in communication and, anyway, I can never remember which way round it's supposed to work.

With my students, I prefer to suggest five basic but realistic and usable guidelines. I know they are incomplete and a simplification – but they do offer some manageable starting points:

1) If you are talking about laws or rules or requirements, use *have to*.
   You have to get a fishing licence.

2) Use *must* after *I*.
   I must try to lose some weight.

3) But . . . use *have to* if you are talking about something a person doesn't really want to do.
   I have to eat less chocolate.

4) Use *have to* with adverbs of frequency.
   I usually have to finish my homework before I can watch TV.

5) If you are giving friendly suggestions or advice about what someone could do, use *must*.
   You really must try the fish.

54 Possibility and certainty: *may, might, could, must, must have, can't, can't have*

Form

Possibility

We can use *may, might, could, must, must have, can't* and *can't have* to talk about the possibility of something being true.

	Past	Present	Future
Affirmative	*may have* + past participle *might have* + past participle	*may / might / could*	*may / might / could*
Negative	*may not have* + past participle *might not have* + past participle *can't have* + past participle	*may not / might not / can't*	*may not / might not / can't*

Presentation

223

Present – what might happen?

1) Find a picture of a street scene with various imminent potential actions.

2) Show the picture to the class and ask 'What might happen in the next two minutes?' Help students to make good predictions (*The dog might walk into the street. The car could hit the ladder. It might rain. The lady may drop her bags*).

Variation

Use a DVD / Internet video still. When students have made their predictions, show the next section of the video to check if they are correct. Comic excerpts work well here, especially ones where funny and unexpected things happen.

Past – Ugg

1) Display a picture of a caveman on the board and tell the students it is Ugg, who lived many years ago.

2) Add extra icons to the picture and elicit sentences (*He can't have worn sunglasses. He might have worn shoes. He might have lived in a cave*).

3) Add a dinosaur into the picture and ask students how Ugg felt about them (*He must have felt scared*). Ask students how sure they are and make sure the modal verb they use reflects this.

4) Add in other prompts so that students can make other sentences about what Ugg might have / must have / could have done.

Practice

Present

What's in the box?

Bring in a box or shopping bag full of unusual, interesting (and noisy) items. Explain that a mystery person came into school yesterday and left this box behind. You need to find out some information about this person. Let a student put a hand into the bag and tell the class what they can feel (*I think it may be a bag of crisps*). Move on to other students and repeat this so that more objects are described. When students know a number of things from the bag they can speculate about the person (*He may be rich. He could be an inspector. He might be a foreigner. He could be a new teacher. He might be a thief*).

The missing person

Show a picture of a business meeting (if possible with an empty chair). Tell students that the chairwoman hasn't come and is now 20 minutes late. Tell students that the others are talking about her. Ask students to think of reasons why she is not there (*She could be ill. She may be in another meeting. She might be shopping*). Include past forms if students have met them (*She might have forgotten. She may have missed her bus.*).

Guessing jobs

Find some good large pictures of people who clearly have specific jobs, especially pictures where there are a number of tools, typical items etc (a doctor with perhaps a stethoscope, a bag, medicines, bandages). Cut up the picture into a number of pieces, like a jigsaw, so that the items are separate. Tell the class that you will show them a part of the picture and they must guess what job the person does. Show a piece that does not immediately identify the specific job with certainty (a book). Collect student guesses. Go on to show more pieces, one by one, until someone feels sure that they are certain what the job is and can say a *must be* sentence (*She must be a doctor*). This person should be able to state their logical reasons (*She has a doctor's bag. She has lots of medicines*).

NB if you don't have suitable pictures, the game works well with words / descriptions alone (*She has a large black bag with medicines inside*).

Where do they come from?

A simpler version of the game above involves guessing people's nationalities from some typical or stereotyped possessions (a football shirt, a jar of marmalade, a newspaper – *He must be English!*).

Past

Crime scene

Write a description of an unusual crime scene (*The windows are closed. The door is locked. There is a fireplace and chimney*). Students must discuss and draw logical conclusions about what the crime was and how it was done (*He can't have come through the door. He must have climbed down the chimney*).

Who was it?

Get students to prepare three short single sentences to describe a famous person that they pretend they saw yesterday. Write up this dialogue starter: 'A: You'll never guess who I saw yesterday! B: No – Who? A: I'll give you a clue . . . ' After this, A reads out the first of their sentences (*He is an actor in the Indiana Jones films*). B can then guess the person (*It must have been Harrison Ford*) if they are sure of the solution. If they can't guess yet, the speaker says another of their sentences.

Pronunciation

The /t/ sound in *must* is often not heard: *He must be home by now* /mʌs/.

'Have' in perfect infinitives is usually unstressed: *She must have been late* /mʌstəv/.

Concept questions

- **Michelle can't have stolen the money.** Am I talking about the past or the present? (*Past*) Is it possible that Michelle was the thief? (*Yes*) Do I think that she took the money? (*No*) Am I 100% sure? (*Not quite*) How certain am I that she didn't do it? (*Very*)

- **Juanita must have a well-paid job – she's just bought another new car.** Do I think Juanita is rich? (*Yes*) Do I know? (*No*) Am I sure about this? (*No*) Do I think it is very likely? (*Yes*) Why do I think this? (*Because she's just bought another car*)

- **The car is making a funny noise – there might be a problem with the battery.** Is there a problem with the car? (*Yes, it's making a strange noise*) Do I have an idea what the cause is? (*Yes*) Do I know for sure what is causing this? (*No*) Is it possible that the battery is a problem? (*Yes*) Am I sure it's the battery? (*No*)

Meaning and use

Possibility

There is no significant difference in meaning between *may* and *might*. *May* is arguably a little more formal and is perhaps more common in written English. *Might* is more common in spoken English but both have very similar meanings. For hypothetical / unreal situations, we use *might* not *may*. *May* isn't used with past reference.
If we have much more rain, the game might be called off.
I was frightened that he might see us.

We add *well* after the modal verb to say that we think something is very likely to happen.
We might well have to wait six months before we know the answers.

If the postal workers go out on strike, other sectors may well join them.
It might well be too late to stop sea levels rising.

Certainly true

When we reach a logical conclusion that something seems certainly true, we can use:

must

(typically with *be*) for a logical conclusion in the present.
He must be nearly 50.
This must be your sister.
He must be seriously rich.

The conclusion is the result of examining the evidence, which seems to leave no other possible solution. Sometimes, the evidence or logic that led to this inevitable conclusion is explicitly stated.

My keys must be in the desk – I've searched everywhere else.
The light keeps flickering – there must be a loose connection.
You must be tired after your long journey.

must have + past participle

for a logical conclusion about something that happened in the past.
The letter must have got lost in the mail.
They must have walked for at least three miles.
You must have picked up a bug on holiday.

As with *must* the logical evidence that helps lead to the conclusion may be stated.
I haven't seen our neighbours around – they must have gone away somewhere.

Certainly untrue

When we reach a logical conclusion that something seems certainly untrue or not possible, we can use:

can't

(often with *be*) to talk about the present.
The hotel can't be far from here.
Wait a minute – that can't be right.
The boy can't be more than 16 or 17.
He's getting married? Surely you can't be serious!

can't have (+ past participle) / couldn't have (+ past participle)

to talk about the past.
It can't have been as bad as that!
He can't have forgotten about the wedding!
He couldn't have planned the whole thing by himself.

55 Modal verbs: an overview

Form

I / You / He / She / It / We / They	*can*	*sing in the concert.*
	can't	
	won't	
	might	
	may not	
	etc	

Modal verbs include

can / can't / cannot	*would / wouldn't / would not*
could / couldn't / could not	*may / may not*
will / won't / will not	*might / mightn't / might not*
shall / shan't / shall not	*must / mustn't / must not*
should / shouldn't / should not	

Semi-modals (which do not all follow the grammatical rules for other modals):

have (got) to / don't have to	*had better / had better not*
need / needn't / need not	*must have / can't have*
dare / daren't / dare not	*must be / can't be*
used to / didn't use to	*be able to*
ought to / oughtn't to / ought not to	

Presentation

> Modal verbs are followed by a main verb base form (= infinitive without "to").
> They have no s in the third person singular.
> They have no infinitive.
> They have an -ing form.
> They have no past participle.
> Questions can be made by placing the modal verb before the subject.
> Negatives are always made using n't / not.

This presentation introduces a focus on the grammar of modals. Use it alongside other work on functional uses – see previous units.

1) Write up this gapped sentence on the board 'She . . . do her homework.'

2) Ask students to think of as many single words that could fill the gap as possible. Collect possible answers on the board (*She can / will / might do her homework*). Don't write up any non-modals (*did, didn't, does, doesn't*). If students do not know any possible answers, offer *must, can* and *might* yourself. Check if students have an idea of the different meanings they make.

3) Ask students what all the words have in common. Establish that they are modal auxiliary verbs and have an effect on the meaning of the main verb.

4) Write up the 'rules' above and ask students (whole class or in pairs) to decide which ones are true and which are false.

Answers: all are true except (4).
Illustrative examples: (1) *He can dance. They mustn't go.* (2) *She can play the drums.* ✗ *She cans play the drums.* (3) ✗ *to shall* (4) ✗ *coulding* (5) ✗ *musted* (6) *May I come in?* (7) Note: this is true even in tenses that don't usually make negatives this way (Present Simple & Past Simple) eg *He couldn't find the tap.*

Go through the answers when they have finished.

Practice

Modal cut-ups

Prepare a number of different short sentences on cut up cards – one word to a card (*Roscoe may go to Munich tomorrow. Sylvie should buy the new guidebook*). Shuffle the cards and then start picking them up one at a time and writing each word on the board. Pairs try to see how soon they can arrange some of the words to make a good sentence (that must contain a modal verb). Write good answers on the board. You could award points if you wish. NB some good new sentences you have not expected may turn up!

When a number of sentences have been written, write up *not / n't*. Ask students to change all of the sentences to make them negative (*Sylvie shouldn't buy the new guidebook*). Next, ask students to make them all into questions (*Should Sylvie buy the new guidebook?*).

Meaning and use

Modal verbs are auxiliary verbs. All auxiliary verbs except *be, do* and *have* can be considered modals. They are never main verbs. When they are used on their own, there is always an implied main verb *I can* (*play the guitar / fly a plane*).

They are 'modal' because they change the 'mood' of the main verb. *Mood* is a linguistic term that refers to ways that we can modify a meaning to indicate subjective, non-factual elements of possibility, necessity, obligation, desirability etc. If the main verb tense tells us about the 'facts' of an action, the modal verb tells us about a non-factual interpretation of the action.

Modals have many uses. A few of the more important ones are listed here:

- Ability in the present, past and future   *can / can't / could / couldn't / will be able / won't be able*

- Certainty   *will / won't*

- Probability   *will / won't / can / can't / may / may not / might / might not*

- Possibility   *can / can't may / may not / might / might not*

- Prediction   *will / won't*

- Promise   *will / won't*

- Obligation   *must / have to / should / shouldn't / need to*

- Lack of obligation   *don't need to / needn't*

- Conditional *would / wouldn't*

- Necessity   *must / should / have to*

- Deduction   *must be / must have / can't be / can't have*

- Habit in the past   *would / used to*

Watch out for these problems

- **Students use modals with infinitive with *to*: ✗** *I must to go.*

- **Students make questions using *does* or *did*:.** ✗ *Do you can read Russian?*

Teaching tip

It's usually best to teach modals by looking at different ways of expressing a functional meaning rather than by focussing on a single form and the range of meanings it may express. For example, it may be better to teach 'ways of requesting' rather than 'all the uses of *must*.'

→ **Unit 51 Requests, orders, offers, permission:** *can, could, will, would, may, might*

→ **Unit 52 Ability:** *can, can't couldn't, be able to*

→ **Unit 53 Obligation and compulsion:** *must, have to, should, ought*

→ **Unit 54 Possibility and certainty:** *may, might, could, must, must have, can't, can't have*

56 Zero conditional

Form

The zero conditional is made using two clauses, each with a present tense, typically the present simple. The *if* clause may come first or second.
The machine works better if you change the oil regularly.
If prices are too high, demand is choked off.

If clause			Main clause	
If	noun / pronoun	present tense	noun / pronoun	present tense

If something happens   . . .   something else happens
(or with the clauses reversed)

Presentation

If you heat ice,	you get wet.
If you heat water to 100°,	it melts.
If you drop a glass,	burglars can get in.
If you don't lock your door,	it boils.
If it rains,	it often breaks.

Beginnings and endings

1) Prepare a list of scientific and real-world truths as above and print the clauses on separate sets of cards.

2) Place about half the pairs of cards higgledy-piggledy on the board – separating beginnings and endings.

3) Ask the class to suggest pairs, matching beginnings and endings so that the meaning is plausible. Make sure students are clear about the structure.

4) Place the remaining cards on the board – some sentence starters and some endings from different sentences. Get students to work out what the missing parts of each sentence are.

Practice

School truths

Ask students to prepare a list of things that are invariably true about their school (and, perhaps, their town). Do one or two examples together (*If you arrive late, they write your name in the green book. If you feel ill, the nurse checks you. If you kick the drinks machine, you never get any free drinks!*). Afterwards, let pairs work to their own to find more.

Concept questions

- **If you spend all your money, you can't pay your rent.** Is it possible that you could spend all your money? (*Yes*) If you do this, can you also pay your rent? (*No*) How definite is this? (*100%*)

- **If you fall in the river, you get wet.** Is it possible that you could fall in? (*Yes*) Will you definitely get wet if you fall in? (*Yes*) Is there a chance that you won't get wet if you fall in? (*No*)

Meaning and use

The zero conditional is used to state things that seem generally or always true such as rules, inevitable outcomes and consequences, mechanical workings, scientific and economic laws, political truths, religious doctrines, guidelines.
The solution clouds if you shake it.

It is often used to state unavoidable negative outcomes if something else happens, perhaps with one of the clauses in the negative: breakdowns, fines, punishments, state changes etc.
There is a charge of £50 if you are over a week late with your payment.
The phone doesn't work if it isn't charged up.
An error message is displayed if invalid information is entered.
They face certain death if they are sent back to their home country.

Watch out for these problems . . .

- **Students think there is an element of chance and confuse the structure with the first conditional.**

Teaching tip: classifying conditionals

There are two rather different ways of analysing conditional sentences.

Real / Unreal

Grammar books tend to distinguish between *real conditionals* and *unreal conditionals*.

Real conditionals are made using exactly the verb tenses you would expect for the time they refer to.

If the children are playing in the garden, tell them to come in.
If you are going to fly to Paris, you'll need a new passport.
If you came late, what did you expect?

Unreal conditionals refer to unreal situations ie when you are imagining impossible or unlikely futures or alternative possibilities for the past. These conditionals are made using special verb forms to indicate that they are unreal:

Past simple = unlikely or impossible present or future
If humans lived on Mars, do you think they'd get bored with the colour red?
The sentence is about a possible but unlikely present or future. *Lived* is a past form. The speaker uses a past form to indicate (in his / her view) the unlikeliness or the remoteness of this idea ever becoming true.

Past perfect = an alternative past
If Kennedy had survived, the US would be very different now.
The sentence is about something that didn't happen in the past. The speaker is imagining an alternative reality. The past perfect form is used to indicate that the event never happened.

First, Second, Third, Zero

Coursebooks, teachers and students often prefer a classification into *First conditional, Second conditional, Third conditional* and *Zero conditional* (also known as *Conditional Type 1, Type 2, Type 3* and *Type 0*).

These are just two different ways of dividing up and looking at the same cake. You'll have to decide which one is most suitable for you and your students. The first way is arguably more accurate and encompasses the wide variety of conditionals used in the real world. The other way is favoured by many teachers because it allows for a more sequenced way of presenting and practising a number of common types of conditional sentence.

57 First conditional

Form

If clause			Main clause		
If	noun / pronoun	present simple	noun / pronoun	*'ll / will* *can* *might* *may* *should* *must* *have to*	verb base form

There are two clauses in a first conditional sentence. We use the present simple in the *if* clause and *will* (or another modal) in the main clause. The clauses can come in either order. When the *if* clause comes first, we use a comma.
If I see him, I'll pass on your message or *I'll pass on your message if I see him.*
If they change their minds, he might give them a refund or *He might give them a refund if they change their minds.*
The present progressive can be used instead of the present simple.
If Laura is coming to the party, Marco will be really happy.

Presentation

Chain story

1) Draw Magda on the board, looking miserable. Elicit from students why she's unhappy and after a few suggestions tell them she is unhappy because she thinks she is going to lose her job.

2) Elicit or model what she's thinking about what's going to happen. You might want to show a picture to help students here (*If I lose my job, I'll move to the countryside*). Drill this with students.

3) Follow this up with further links in the story (*If I move to the countryside, I'll buy a pet dog. If I have a dog, we'll go for a walk every day. If I go for a walk every day, I'll get fit. If I get fit, I could get a new job as a sports teacher*). To focus on meaning, the events in the story should all seem likely or possible.

4) Give students lots of practice repeating all the sentences. See if they can memorise the whole chain.

5) Start again, with a new story. Give a starter line (Pierre is thinking about his exam: *If I pass my exam . . .*). Get students to continue building the chain from there – either as a whole class or in pairs.

Practice

Weather

Get students to say what they will do at the weekend if the weather is good or bad (*If it's nice weather, I'll go to the beach. If it rains, I'll meet my friends at the shops*).

Holidays

Tell students that they are all going on holiday to a foreign country. Ask them to think about what they will do in different places. Give an example or two first (*If I go to Brazil, I'll dance in a carnival. If I go to London, I'll visit the British Museum*) then write up some new sentence starters for them to discuss and complete (*If I go to Russia . . . / Italy . . . / Spain . . . / Thailand . . . / India . . .*).

Big decision

Set students a situation in which someone has to make a big decision (leaving school, changing job). Write up the beginnings of some sentences (*If I move to Australia . . ., If I pass my exams . . .*) and get students to finish them.

Superstitions

See how many superstitions your class can describe using the first conditional (*If you walk under a ladder, you'll have seven years bad luck. If you see a black cat, you'll meet a stranger*). Then get them to invent a few brand new superstitions.

Bank robbery

Tell the students to plan a bank robbery! Give them a map of the town centre with banks marked. They should make some appropriate *if* sentences (*If we go at night, there will be fewer people. If the bank has lots of money, we'll need a large van. It will be better if we go in the back door. If someone tells the police, we'll get caught. If we escape, we'll be rich*). You could provide sentence starters to help them, if you wish.

Host family

Get students to think of warnings or advice that one student might give when a new student moves into the same host family (*If you touch the dog, it'll bite you. If you stay out late, she'll be angry. If you have any problems, I'll help you. If you go to

London, you'll love it). Extend by getting students to think of some advice, offers and warnings for another situation (a new student arriving in your class, a family taking a holiday in your town).

Concept questions

- **If Franz sees Gabi, he'll tell her.** Will Franz see Gabi? (*Maybe*) Will he definitely see her? (*No*) Is there a chance that he will see her? (*Yes*) Is it very likely that he will see her? (*We don't know but there is probably a good chance*)

- **If we don't go now, we'll be late for the meeting.** Are we going to the meeting? (*Yes*) Are we going to be late? (*Maybe*) Are we definitely going to be late? (*No*) What can we do to avoid being late? (*Leave now*)

Meaning and use

The first conditional is used to talk about things that are normal, possible and quite likely to happen. It is typically used to . . .

- give warnings and advice.
  If you pick it up when it's hot, you'll burn your fingers.

- make predictions; speculate about future events.
  If it works, we'll make a lot of money.

- threaten.
  If you don't leave right now, I'll . . .

- make offers, promises; barter.
  If you lend me the football, I'll lend you my Scrabble® set.

- discuss hypotheses; offer theories.
  If the lever moves clockwise, I think the gate will open.

- draw conclusions from evidence.
  If they are all here, then there is nobody at Reception.

- state instructions.
  If you press button C, the machine will switch off.

Teaching tip: conditional percentages

Teachers sometimes like to offer students a guideline for the meaning of the first conditional as '50% chance of happening', there is about an equal chance that the condition will or won't be fulfilled. This is a useful teaching shorthand, though not really accurate as the first conditional can also be used for conditions with very little chance of happening or 60% or 99% – or whatever.

However, the guideline does help clarify the contrast with the second conditional which is sometimes said to have a 0–1% chance of happening.

58 Second conditional

Form

If clause			Main clause		
If	noun / pronoun	past simple	noun / pronoun	*'d / would*	verb base form

If I went to Moscow, I'd buy you some caviar or *I'd buy you some caviar if I went to Moscow.*
If she believed you, she'd cancel the booking right now or *She'd cancel the booking right now if she believed you.*
If aliens visited us tomorrow, it'd prove your theory or *It'd prove your theory if aliens visited us tomorrow.*

Presentation

Changing lives

1) Show a picture of a seated woman waiting outside a door labelled 'interviews'. Explain that she is applying for a very exciting job as Personal Assistant to the director of a big international company.

2) Establish that she has few qualifications and little experience. She thinks that she has a very small chance of getting the job.

3) Draw a thought bubble over her head. Ask students what she is imagining. Elicit ideas. Elicit or model some sentences – you could give a first half and get students to suggest endings (*If I got the job, I'd be amazed! If I worked for this company, I'd earn a lot more money! If I were the director's personal assistant, I'd travel round the world*).

4) Draw a new situation: a miserable-looking man in prison daydreaming. Establish that he has very little chance of getting out. Draw a thought-bubble and elicit what he is thinking (*If the guard fell asleep, I could get the key! If I crept across the hall, I could climb out of the window. If I escaped, I'd go straight to France. If I lived in Paris, I'd eat croissants every day. If I were a free man, I could get up at midday!*).

5) Ask students to think of something unlikely that might happen to change their own lives for the better. They should write three sentences – then tell their partner.

Practice

Many practice activities can be used for both first and second conditionals. The key difference is in the likelihood of the events happening.

What would you do if . . .?

Draw a sketch of two people talking in a pub or cafe. One is asking the other 'What would you do if . . .?' Elicit some possible endings for the question (. . . *if you had a million dollars? . . . if you were President? . . . if you passed all your exams with top grades?*). When you have a number of questions, go back and elicit possible answers the person might give. Put students in pairs and get them to ask each other and give their own answers. This could also be done as a questionnaire.

Chain story

Tell a chain story (see ideas in First conditional unit) about a boy called Tom who dreams of being an astronaut (*If I were grown-up, I'd become an astronaut. If I were an astronaut, I'd go to Mars. If I went to Mars, I think I'd meet some aliens. If I met them, we'd become good friends*).

Desert island

Ask students to imagine what life would be like if they were marooned on a desert island. They should write some endings to the sentence (*If I were on a desert island, I'd . . .*).

Problems

Describe a 'relationship problem' situation to students (*Bruce has a girlfriend, Macy, but another girl he likes, Mayumi, keeps showing interest in him*). Get students to role play Bruce and a friend who will try and help him – including lots of conditionals on both sides (*If I went out with Mayumi, Macy would find out. If I told her to leave me alone, she'd be very upset. If Macy found out, you'd be in big trouble*).

Variation: business problems

Someone has offered your company some confidential information about a rival. What would happen if you used it?

Science dilemma

Put together a list of science dilemmas to put to students (*How would life be different if we all lived to be 200 years old? What would happen if the sun didn't set tomorrow? What would we do if winter lasted for nine months?*).

Concept questions

- **If I went to moon, I'd bring you back some cheese.** Is it possible to go to the moon? (*Yes, just!*) Is it likely that I could go to the moon? (*No*) Am I really going to the moon? (*No*) So . . . it is possible . . .? (*Yes*) . . . but very unlikely? (*Yes*) Will I bring you some cheese? (*No*) Why not? (*Because you are not going to the moon!*)

- **If Nanami went to London, she'd meet Jin.** Will Nanami go to London? (*We don't know but probably not*) Is it likely that she will go to London? (*No*) Will she meet Jin? (*No, probably not*) Why not? (*Because she probably won't go to London*) Which word tells us that it is unlikely? (*went*)

- **June has a boyfriend, Robert. Mary is talking to June about Robert and says 'If I were you, I'd leave him.'** Is Robert Mary's boyfriend? (*No*) Who is Robert's girlfriend? (*June*) Will Mary leave Robert? (*No*) Why not? (*He is not her boyfriend!*) So . . . why does Mary say she would leave him? (*She is imagining what she would do if Robert was her boyfriend*) Is she giving advice to June? (*Yes*)

Meaning and use

The second conditional is used to talk about things that are impossible or just possible – but unlikely to happen or nearly impossible. Many second conditional sentences could be continued with '– but I'm not . . .' (or similar endings).
If I went to Moscow, I'd buy you some caviar (– but I'm pretty sure I'm not going, so tough!)
If she believed you, she'd cancel the booking right now (– but she doesn't, so she won't).

The difference in meaning between the first and second conditionals is a matter of individual view – not fact. The same situation could be stated using either first or second conditional depending on how likely you felt it to be. Hence a pessimistic person might say 'If I won the lottery . . .' – but an optimist might say 'If I win the lottery . . .'
Teachers sometimes characterise the meaning of the second conditional as 0%–1% chance of happening ie it is either impossible or possible but improbable.

If I were you, I'd . . .

This means that the speaker is imagining what it would be like to be the other person and what they would do in his / her shoes. It is often used to give advice.
If I were you, I'd dump him.

59 Third conditional

Form

This is sometimes called the past conditional.

If clause				Main clause		
If	noun / pronoun	*'d had hadn't*	past participle	noun / pronoun	*'d have would've could've might've might have must've must have*	past participle

If I'd gone to Moscow, I could have bought you some caviar or *I could have bought you some caviar if I'd gone to Moscow.*
If you'd eaten all that breakfast, you wouldn't have been able to climb this hill or *You wouldn't have been able to climb this hill if you'd eaten all that breakfast.*
If John had told me, I'd have prepared for the meeting or *I'd have prepared for the meeting if John had told me.*

If only I'd ...

If only I 'd heard in time, I could have helped.

I wish I'd ...

I wish I'd never come.

Both of these are used to say how you wish a past situation had been different.

Presentation

If I hadn't done that . . .

1) Use board pictures to build a situation of two friends, Jo and Tony, who can't decide what to do. There is a party tonight and a good programme on TV. Establish that Jo decides to go to the party while Tony chooses to stay at home.

2) It is two hours later. Draw Jo looking miserable at the party – and Tony looking miserable watching TV. Check that students are clear what they chose and that they regret their choices. Elicit what they are feeling and thinking (*If I'd stayed at home, I could have watched Spacecops. If I'd gone to the party, I could have met some nice girls*).

3) You could extend the situation to make more sentences if you wish (*If I hadn't been so tired, I would have had a better time*).

Practice

Chain story

I've suggested chain stories for the first and second conditionals – so you might not be surprised to see that they work here too! For example, establish a miserable-looking man standing on the docks and a boat sailing off into the distance without him! A thought bubble over his head can help you to establish that he is thinking back on all the things that went wrong with his day (*If my alarm clock had rung, I'd have woken up early. If I'd woken up early, I'd have caught my train. If I hadn't missed my train, I'd have got to my girlfriend's house in time. If I'd got to her house in time, we wouldn't have argued. If we hadn't argued, she would have driven me to the docks*).

Variation

Other useful regret situations: man in prison, family standing outside a burnt-down house, soldier in middle of battle, old man sleeping on the street.

Stories forwards and backwards

Find a suitable story in which lots of things go wrong (Romeo and Juliet). Tell the story as normal and then, when you have finished, look back from the end of the story and make some third conditional sentences (*If Romeo had checked more carefully, he would have seen that she was alive. If she hadn't taken the poison, they could have got married*).

Rewriting history

Ask students to think of some historical situations that might have changed the world if they had been different. You could offer the sentence starters and get students to suggest endings (*If electricity had never been discovered . . . If dinosaurs hadn't died out . . . If Obama hadn't been elected President . . . If Columbus had never discovered America . . .*). Include local events to make it more relevant.

If I'd been . . .

Ask students to think of a famous dead person that they would like to have been and ask them to complete the sentence to say what they would have done (*If I had been Martin Luther King, I would have . . .*).

If I'd lived . . .

Similarly, ask students to imagine life in different ages (*If I had lived in the Middle Ages, I'd have . . .*).

Concept questions

- **If George had gone to the meeting, he'd have met Hiro.** Did George go to the meeting? (*No*) Did Hiro go to the meeting? (*Yes*) Did George meet Hiro? (*No*) Why not? (*George didn't go to the meeting*)

- **If only I'd bought that dress . . . !** Did I buy that dress? (*No*) Why not? (*We don't know*) Do I regret it now? (*Yes*) A little or very much? (*Very much*)

- **I wish I'd been at the concert!** Was I at the concert? (*No*) Do I regret it now? (*Yes*) Would I go to the concert if I had another chance? (*Yes, probably*)

Meaning and use

The third conditional is used to talk about events in the past that cannot be changed. The speaker using a third conditional is speculating about how things might be altered if something had or hadn't happened in a different way. As a result the third conditional is especially associated with the function of regret. *If I hadn't eaten so much at dinner, I wouldn't feel so sick now!* . . .

Teachers sometimes characterise the meaning of the third conditional as 0% chance of happening ie we cannot change the past.

I wish and If only

These are often used to say how we wish a past situation was different. There is often a strong element of regret. *If only* is frequently used without a second clause. *If only we could afford to buy a place of our own.*

60 Passives

Form

For all tenses, the form of the passive can be summarised as *be* (in the correct number and tense) + past participle. The tables show a comparison of active and passive forms.

	Present	
	Active	**Passive**
simple	*she drives*	*the car is driven*
progressive	*she is driving*	*the car is being driven*
perfect	*she has driven*	*the car has been driven*
perfect progressive	*she has been driving*	*the car has been being driven*

	Past	
	Active	**Passive**
simple	*she drove*	*the car was driven*
progressive	*she was driving*	*the car was being driven*
perfect	*she had driven*	*the car had been driven*
perfect progressive	*she had been driving*	*the car had been being driven*

	Future	
	Active	**Passive**
simple	*she will drive*	*the car will be driven*
progressive	*she will be driving*	*the car will be being driven*
perfect	*she will have driven*	*the car will have been driven*
perfect progressive	*she will have been driving*	*the car will have been being driven*

Some (especially the greyed-out ones) are quite unlikely in normal conversation.

Subjects and objects

The object of an active sentence becomes the new subject of a passive sentence. In these two sentences, the subject is underlined:
Active: <u>*The Burnham Brothers*</u> *made the film on location in India.*
Passive: <u>*The film*</u> *was made on location in India.*

Mentioning the doer using *by*

To include the doer in a passive sentence we use *by*.
A peace accord was signed by both leaders.

Presentation

Hamlet was written by . . .	Leonardo da Vinci
The moons of Jupiter were discovered by . . .	1896
The Internet was invented by . . .	James Cameron
Avatar and Titanic were directed by . . .	Tim Berners-Lee
The Mona Lisa was painted by . . .	Galileo
The first Modern Olympics were held in . . .	Shakespeare

Quiz (Past simple passive)

1) Prepare a short quiz using passives (*Hamlet was written by . . . The moons of Jupiter were discovered by . . . The Internet was invented by . . .*). Write up the questions and answers separately in a list on either side of the board. Let students tell you the answers. Draw lines to connect beginnings and endings of sentences.

2) Erase all the verbs and the lines (*Hamlet . . . by Shakespeare*). Let students work in pairs to see if they can write the sentences and replace the verbs.

3) Focus on the structure. Ask students to make some new questions themselves about other well-known facts.

4) See if you and the students can answer other students' questions.

Practice

Finding more questions

As a follow-on from the Presentation idea, get students to research on the Internet, looking for interesting facts that could be turned into new questions. You may want to direct them towards specific topic areas eg exploration, famous buildings, world sporting records, space travel etc.

Describing processes (Present simple passive)

Find a sequential diagram of a manufacturing or creative process (making chocolate). Work through the first steps of the sequence and help students to describe it (*Cacao beans are harvested → The beans are dried → The beans are sold → The beans are cleaned → The beans are roasted*). Get students to write a description of the remaining parts of the process using the diagrams (and perhaps some key nouns and verbs to help them).

The robbery (Present perfect passive)

Show a picture of a room after a robbery. Add a police inspector. Explain that he must make a report of what he sees. Elicit one or two example passive sentences (*All the drawers have been opened. The computer has been smashed. The door has been broken*) then see if students can produce more. Encourage them to imagine more things that they can't see.

Are we really ready? (Present perfect passive: questions)

Show a picture of a room ready for an important event (*a banquet, a conference meeting, a party, a ball*). Ask the students to imagine that they are responsible for making sure everything is OK. They should think of questions to ask the staff to check that everything has been done (*Have all the invitations been sent? Have the flowers been watered? Have the plates been washed?*). When students have collected a good set of questions, get them to role play the scene with one questioner asking two or three helpers.

Green worries (Present progressive passive)

Collect some pictures of contemporary environmental problems. Get students to write (or complete) sentences about the problems (*The air is being polluted by chemicals. The rainforests are being cut down. The climate is being affected. The ozone layer is being destroyed*).

Concept questions

- **This phone was made in China.** Which country does the phone come from? (*China*) Do we know who made it? (*No*) Why don't I say 'Someone made this phone in China'? (*Because we're interested in the phone and not the person who made it*)

- **Three men were arrested for the bank robbery.** Who arrested them? (*The police – probably*) Do I know who arrested them? (*Yes*) Why don't I say 'Three men were arrested by the police for the bank robbery'? (*Because it's obvious and unnecessary – the verb 'arrest' is usually only done by the police*) Will most people who hear the sentence know that it was the police? (*Yes – so there is no need to say it*)

- **My bike's been stolen!** Do I know who took my bike? (*No*) Could I say 'Someone has stolen my bike'? (*Yes*) Which sentence is about my bike more than about the criminal? (*My bike's been stolen*)

Meaning and use

The passive and active give two different windows onto the same event but they are not simply identically-meaning alternatives. When we choose to use the passive it is because we have a specific reason to do so.

Not mentioning the agent

We use the passive if we want to talk about what was done, perhaps without even mentioning the agent. This may be because . . .

- we want to follow an impersonal, academic or scientific style in which the action is important but the doer isn't relevant or of interest.
  The magazine is produced using a desktop publishing system.

- we don't know the doer.
  A page had been torn out of the back of the book.

- we don't want to name the doer for some reason.
  Not much has been done towards improving safety.

- we want to distance ourselves or avoid personal responsibility or we want to sound more formal.
  Latecomers will not be admitted until the interval.
  The minutes were approved.

- there is no specific or obvious doer.
  Almost everything was destroyed in the fire.

- there is no specific doer other than 'someone' or 'people'.
  He has been widely criticized for his ideas about shorter prison sentences.

- there is no need to mention the doer because it is clear who it is.
  Scientists believe a cure for the disease will be discovered soon. (ie by scientists!)

- we want to focus on what is done.
  The milk is specially formulated for babies.

A little counter-intuitively, because new information comes at the end of the sentence we also use the passive if we really do want to focus attention on who does the action by putting this information at the end of the sentence. We use *by* + noun / pronoun.
The new deal has been brokered by the UN.

Passives with *get*

Get is commonly used instead of *be* but only with non-stative verbs that have a meaning similar to 'became'. It is more informal than *be* and is much more common in colloquial speech than in writing.

My new trousers got chewed up in my bike chain.

Get is used for events where you wish to emphasise your out-of-controlness!
We got completely drenched by the rain.

Pronunciation

Passives can sometimes be hard for students to recognise when listening because the verb *be* may be pronounced with weak forms eg /wəz/ or /wə/. This is a good reason to make sure that students get practice saying these themselves when they learn to use the passive.

Watch out for these problems

- **Students do not recognise passives as passives, perhaps mishearing them as normal past sentences:** They hear *The prawns were all eaten* as *The prawns were all eating.*

- **Students make an active sentence when they want a passive meaning:** ✗ *The houses built on the hill. The car repaired last week.*

- **Students are not clear who did the action:** In the sentence *The child was annoyed by John* they may think that the child was annoying John.

Teaching tip: drawing attention

The structure of the passive is surprisingly straightforward. When teaching the form, draw attention to the way that the pattern is exactly the same across all tenses. Learners should be able to work out tenses that you haven't yet shown them.

The problems for students tend to come mainly with usage – and avoidance. Unless students are given lots of practice in using passives for particular reasons (eg in academic writing), they tend to avoid them, preferring what seems to be a simpler active alternative.

In your students' own languages the passive may be used in different ways or with different purposes, or there may not be a 'passive' or anything similar to it. To help students, draw attention to passives whenever they meet them on notices, in texts etc and ask 'Why do you think the writer used a passive here?'

61 Causatives

Form

We make causatives with subject + *get / have* + object + past participle.

Jean	got / had	her hair cut	at the beauty parlour downstairs.
↑	↑	↑	

Presentation

House restoration

1) Show a picture of a ramshackle and rundown house and introduce Pablo, who bought it.

2) Explain that Pablo works full time and has no time to work on the house himself.

3) Show a new picture of the same house, fully restored. Ask students to tell you what he got other people to do (*He had glass put in the windows. He had the roof mended. He had the door painted*).

Variations

Car repairs, cosmetic surgery, school improvement, etc.

Practice

Wedding plans

Write up a list of verbs connected with things that need to be done before a wedding (cut, printed, decorated). Tell students that they got married last month!

Make pairs. Each student tells their friend about all the things they had done before their wedding, using as many of the verbs as they can (*I had my hair cut. I had 60 invitations printed. I had the room decorated*).

Exclusive hotels

Students are checking into an exclusive hotel and role play a conversation about the services the hotel provides (*Can I have some champagne brought to my room? Can I have my nails done?*).

Celebrity lifestyles

Ask students to imagine all the things they could have done for them if they were a millionaire celebrity (*I'd have my dog walked. I'd have all my meals cooked*).

Concept questions

• **Maria had her car repaired last week.** Did Maria fix the car herself? (*No*) Who fixed the car? (*Probably a mechanic at a garage*) Did Maria ask the garage to organise this repair? (*Yes, probably*)

• **Stefano had fitted some new windows in his house before he had the rooms painted.** Are there new windows in the house? (*Yes*) Who put them there? (*Stefano*) Have the rooms been painted? (*Yes*) Who painted them? (*Someone else*) Not Stefano? (*No*) Did Stefano ask the other person to paint the rooms? (*Yes, probably*)

Meaning and use

The term *causative* refers to structures where you cause something to happen or be done. In this sentence Jean did not cut her hair herself – but she did something (made a request) that caused the action to happen.
Jean had her hair cut at the beauty parlour downstairs.

The form is often used to talk about medical and beauty treatment and about repairs and improvements.
The place is looking much better since they had it redecorated.

Pronunciation

In this structure, *had* cannot be contracted to *'d* in either pronunciation or spelling. (✗ *She'd her television repaired.*)

Watch out for these problems . . .

• **Students don't recognise it:** The causative can be quite hard for students to spot. It can look identical to other *had* + object + past participle constructions that are not causative.
Monga had his passport withdrawn, and was placed under house arrest.

62 Multi-word verbs

Form

A multi-word verb is made up of a main verb plus one or more *particles* (= prepositions or adverbs).
This meat smells as if it's gone off.

Some common particles
off, on, out, in, over, through, with, around, away, back, down, up, about, to, at, for, into, round, together

Some common verbs
come, get, go, look, make, put, take

A multi-word verb can be:
Transitive (ie it takes an object).
How do we get through so much milk?
I ran into Jed this morning.

Intransitive (ie it doesn't need an object).
A police officer grabbed him, but he got away.
Their water gave out two days ago.

Many verbs can be used both transitively and intransitively.
I'll ring up the theatre and see when the show finishes.
She rang up yesterday to make an appointment.

Word order with transitive verbs

Normally, the particle will come either before or after the direct object.
Lack of parking space was putting off potential customers.
Lack of parking space was putting potential customers off.

If the object is a pronoun, it must come in front of the particle.
Lack of parking space was putting them off.
✗ *Lack of parking space was putting off them.*

Inseparable transitive verbs

Some verbs (known as prepositional verbs) are inseparable ie the direct object cannot come between main verb and particle.
I came across a word I'd never seen before.
✗ *I came a word across I'd never seen before.*

Don's pretty upset, but he'll get over it.
✗ *Don's pretty upset, but he'll get it over.*

Three-word verbs

Verbs made up of a main verb with both an adverb and a preposition are known as phrasal-prepositional verbs.
I decided I must face up to the truth.
I will not put up with your bad behaviour any longer!

Not all verb + small word combinations are multi-word verbs. In the following examples, the underlined single word verb is complete in its own right. The word that follows it tells us something extra about the direction or nature of the action, but is not a core part of the verb structure.
He <u>walked</u> through a wooden gate into the field.
I <u>turned</u> over and went back to sleep.
I opened my eyes and <u>looked</u> around me.

Presentation

Text 1

At the meeting Kamal <u>brought up</u> the fact that we had a new competitor. Sam <u>pointed out</u> that in fact we knew almost nothing about them! The CEO said that we needed to <u>find out</u> a lot more – and quickly. So I said I would <u>ask around</u>. Mary promised to <u>look up</u> references on the Internet. We decided to <u>put off</u> our product launch until later in the month in case some important new information <u>turned up</u>.

Text 2

At the meeting Kamal <u>mentioned</u> the fact that we had a new competitor. Sam <u>explained</u> that in fact we knew almost nothing about them! The CEO said that we needed to <u>discover</u> a lot more – and quickly. So I said I would <u>ask questions in different places</u>. Mary promised to <u>try to find information from</u> references on the Internet. We decided to <u>postpone</u> our product launch until later in the month in case some important new information <u>unexpectedly appeared</u>.

1) Prepare a short text with between six and ten phrasal verbs in it (*We decided to <u>put off</u> our product launch*).

2) Rewrite the text replacing each phrasal verb with a different underlined verb or phrase (*We decided to <u>postpone</u> our product launch*).

3) In class, write up or show a copy of Text 2 to students. On the board, write these words: *find put bring turn look ask point* and underneath them write: *out off around up*.

4) Work through the text with students. For each underlined verb or phrase, ask if students can suggest a two-word combination that could replace it (replace <u>explained</u> with <u>pointed out</u>). In each case they will need to combine one main verb and one particle. They will also need to make sure that the tense is adjusted where necessary. Elicit ideas from the class, give them feedback and help them create a version of Text 1.

Variation

Do the same task in the other direction ie from phrasal verbs to other ways of saying the ideas.

Practice

Call my bluff

Make small groups. Hand out 4 or 5 sentences with a phrasal verb (*The milk has gone off. Can you put me up tonight?*) to each group and ask them to keep them secret from other groups. For each phrasal verb, the groups should prepare three definitions – two of which are untrue and one of which is true ('gone off' = (1) been spilled (2) become bad (3) been stolen by someone). When students are ready, groups read out their sentence and each of their definitions. Students vote for which one they think is the correct definition. The group wins one point for every student who votes for one of the wrong definitions.

Finding interesting collocations

Choose an interesting set of suitable phrasal verbs (*give up, get over, look up, blow up*). Ask students to think of a funny or unexpected collocation for use each one (*give up mountaineering*) and then use it in an amusing sentence (*My 80-year-old grandma finally gave up mountaineering last summer*).

Pelmanism

Prepare one set of cards for each group. Half the cards have sentences with phrasal verbs on them (*The oven blew up*) and half have synonyms that don't repeat nouns from the original sentence (*It exploded*). Students sit in groups with the cards laid face down on the table. One player turns over two cards and sees if they make a match (phrasal verb and correct synonym). If they do, they can keep the cards. If they don't, they should replace the cards face down (but everyone will try to remember where they are). The next student then tries to find two cards that match. The winner is the person who has the most cards at the end of the game.

Phrasal verb story

Dictate a list of about ten phrasal verbs (*get up, put on, turn on, drop in, give back*). Ask students to work together to create a story using as many of the verbs as they can. To make it harder, you could ask them to use the verbs in exactly the order dictated.

Noughts and crosses

Select nine phrasal verbs that all have the same particle (*give up, look up, take up, clean up*). Divide the class in two – X and O. Draw a large 3 × 3 grid on the board and write a phrasal verb in each of the nine squares. Teams take turns to try to make a good sentence using one of the phrasal verbs. If you agree that it is a good, grammatically accurate sentence, they 'win' the square and write their symbol. The winning team is the one that makes a line of three symbols.

Literal and idiomatic

Make a list with pairs of sentences where Sentence A has a literal meaning and Sentence B has a harder-to-guess idiomatic meaning (a) *He took off his dirty shoes before going in to the house* (b) *The plane took off*. Leave the first two sentences as examples but, after that, delete one sentence in each pair. Pairs see if they can think of sentences to replace the missing ones. At the end, compare with your original list.

Meaning and use

A multi-word verb expresses a complete meaning. The main verb on its own would not express the whole meaning. The meaning will often not be guessable from the sum of its parts. For example, a learner might understand the separate meanings of *gave* and *up* – but still not be able to work out the meaning of *He gave up his job*.

Multi-word verbs are normal everyday language. Generally speaking they are not slang, colloquial or lazy English (though a few verbs such as *shut up* are!).

In many cases an equivalent single word verb may sound over-formal when compared to the normal phrasal verb.
They put out the fire.
They extinguished the fire.

Watch out for these problems . . .

- **Students choose the wrong particle:** ✗ *I turned out his invitation* (= turned down)

- **Students put a pronoun after a particle:** ✗ *They looked up it in the library.* It's useful to ask form-related questions when working with multi-word verbs (*Can I put the pronoun here?*) to focus students on the different rules.

- **Students use a transitive verb without an object:** ✗ *We were looking forward to the party but they decided to put off till next week.*

Teaching tip: how to teach phrasal verbs?

It's often useful to introduce a set of related multi-word verbs. Different teachers might argue for different ways of grouping:

- **by particle** – teaching groups of verbs that have the same particle (verbs with 'off': *break off, turn off, set off*) – especially if there is some recognisable similarity of meaning given by the particle.

- **by main verb** – teaching groups of verbs that have the same main verb (*go away, go back, go on*).

- **by usage** – teaching groups of verbs that have a common context or function (a set of phrasal verbs used in the kitchen: *chop up, turn on, stir in*).

The last option perhaps offers the most interesting teaching opportunities. For example, if we wanted to teach eight verbs associated with driving we could fairly easily create an interesting story containing them – which we could then tell, work with, retell, base exercises on etc. Don't try to teach too many new multi-word verbs at once – they quickly become overwhelming! One of the most useful things you can do with multi-word verbs is to simply raise students' awareness that they exist and are really used. Draw students' attention to them in any authentic texts you use.

63 Direct and reported speech

Form

Direct speech		Reported speech (one step backwards)	
Present simple	*'I come to Dubai every year.'*	**Past simple**	*He said (that) he came to Dubai every year.*
Present progressive	*'I'm coming to Dubai.'*	**Past progressive**	*He said (that) he was coming to Dubai.*
Present perfect	*'I've been to Dubai.'*	**Past perfect**	*He said (that) he had been to Dubai.*
Past simple	*'I went to Dubai.'*	**Past perfect**	*He said (that) he had been to Dubai.*
Past progressive	*'I was going to Dubai.'*	**Past perfect progressive**	*He said (that) he had been going to Dubai.*
Past perfect	*'I had been to Dubai.'*	**Past perfect**	*He said (that) he had been to Dubai.*
going to	*'I'm going to go to Dubai.'*	***was going to***	*He said (that) he was going to go to Dubai.*
will	*'I will go to Dubai.'*	***would***	*He said (that) he would go to Dubai.*
can	*'I can go to Dubai.'*	***could***	*He said (that) he could go to Dubai.*
may	*'I may go to Dubai.'*	***might***	*He said (that) he might go to Dubai.*
must	*'I must go to Dubai.'*	***had to***	*He said (that) he had to go to Dubai.*

Reporting verbs

The most important verbs for reporting speech are, obviously, *said* and *asked*. However there are many others, some of which add extra meaning. For example *demand* means ask in a forceful way.

(continued)

Here are a few:

replied, told, complained, confessed, reported, demanded, suggested, claimed, answered, denied, confirmed, shouted, added, persuaded, yelled, announced, screamed, agreed, recommended, vowed, began, called, commented, explained, mentioned, ordered, requested, whispered, boasted, mumbled

Presentation

A: Mmm. My food is delicious. I really like fresh fish.

He said that . . .

B: Oh, I don't like fish. I prefer meat.

In a restaurant

1) Tell the class they are going to hear a restaurant conversation. Ask the class to take notes. Get a volunteer student to help you read a short script 'A: Mmm. My food is delicious. I really like fresh fish. 'B: Oh, I don't like fish. I prefer meat.'

2) When you have finished, see if students can recall the exact words of the dialogue. Write them up on the left-hand side of the board. Read the conversation again if necessary to help them get it correct.

3) On the right-hand side of the board, write 'He said that . . .' – and ask if students can finish the sentence. Elicit or model the correct sentence (*He said that his food was delicious*). Check that students understand the idea of direct and reported speech and have noticed the changes in verb tense and pronouns.

4) Get students to convert the remaining sentences into reported speech (*He said that he really liked fresh fish. She said that she didn't like fish. She said that she preferred meat*).

5) Repeat the activity with some new short dialogues, including questions with *asked* (A: *Where do you work?* → *He asked her where she worked*. B: *I'm a hotel receptionist*. → *She said that she was a hotel receptionist*).

6) After a few dialogues, omit the direct speech stage and go straight for the reported speech.

Practice

Improvised chat

Bring a student to the front and either improvise a short dialogue with them or read aloud a short prepared script. Ask students to write or say a report of the conversations.

Class survey

As a class, decide on a topic that you are interested in (cars, space, money, music). Each student then writes two or three questions based on the topic (*How important is money to you? What's the most expensive thing you've ever bought?*). Students then mingle so that they ask all the students in the class. They can then report their findings to a partner.

Video clip relay

Play a short video clip for students. Choose one which contains a lot of dialogue. When the clip has finished, students work in pairs to report exactly what was said in the clip. Add a competitive element by awarding points for things that are recalled exactly and that are grammatically correct.

Meaning and use

Reported or indirect speech is used to relay what one person says to another. *He said that he was coming to the party.*

In everyday speech, the word *that* can be omitted, especially after the verb *said*. *He said he'd resigned.*

One step backwards

A common guideline is: 'The tense in the reported part moves one step backwards in time (but you can't go further back than the past perfect)'.

So, for example, a sentence that was spoken using the present progressive would be reported using the past progressive.

However, despite this pleasing regularity, it isn't always true. If a situation is still true in the present, we can choose whether to use a present form or a 'one step backwards' one. For example

Direct: *I live in Paris*
Reported: *She said she lives in Paris* or *She said she lived in Paris.*

Reported questions

To report a *yes / no* question, use *whether* or *if*.
Are you married? → *They asked us whether we were married.*
Can I extend my holiday? → *I asked if I could extend my holiday.*

To report a *wh-* question include the *wh-* question word but don't invert the subject and the verb.

Why are you late? → *He asked me why I was late.*

✗ *He asked me why was I late?*

How do you know about it? → *She asked me how I knew about it.*

Reported thoughts

Reported thoughts, ideas, beliefs, decisions etc follow the same patterns as reported speech.

I thought we'd go for a ride.

Simplifying

In colloquial speech, there is a tendency to avoid the past perfect simple or progressive when reporting (unless really essential for clarifying exact sequences of events), substituting past tenses instead. For example:

Direct speech	'Correct' reported speech	Colloquial alternative
I went to London	He said he had been to London	He said he went to London
I've bought the tickets	She said she had bought the tickets	She said she bought the tickets
I was laughing all evening	She said she'd been laughing all evening	She said she was laughing all evening

Other reporting changes

It's not only the verbs that change when reporting the past – though, as with the verb tenses, you only need to use whatever language is normal and natural to describe the situation.

- **Pronouns:** we will often need to change the use of *I* / *my* / *me* / *we* etc in direct speech to *he* / *she* / *him* / *her* / *his* / *they* etc in reported speech.

- **Time and place:** When reporting, there is typically a shift of perspective from the 'here now' of a live conversation to the 'there then' of the same conversation being recalled and talked about later. So for example, someone who says 'We're leaving now' could be reported as
  He said they were leaving then.

Remember, though, that some perspectives may not change. If a conversation is reported in the same room where it originally took place, then it will still be natural to use 'here' words rather than 'there' words.

Direct speech and register

When we are telling a story we may want to include the exact words someone said. We can do this as direct speech (or quoted speech or quote structures).
'Don't worry,' he said.
'I did it,' she said in a clear voice.

Some relatively recent but already very widespread colloquial kinds of direct speech involve the use of noun / pronoun + *was like* or the verb *goes / went*.

Well, she was like 'I'm not going there' and he was like 'Oh, but I really want to.'
(= She said 'I'm not going there' and he said 'Oh, but I really want to')

She went 'Give it to me now' and he went 'No way.'

Watch out for these problems . . .

- **Students find the 'one step backwards' guideline confusing:** They may prefer this alternative. Ask them to consider the question: 'What is the natural tense to use in this sentence?' In other words if a sentence is true now, use a present tense, if a sentence is about the past, use a past tense and if a sentence is about something that happened before the thing being described, use the past perfect. Let's look at an example of the natural tense guideline at work: Imagine that yesterday Peri was sitting in a cafe looking at a menu and said the following words: *'I'm having the cheese and tomato pizza.'* When you report this the next day it would be odd to say *She said she's having the cheese and tomato pizza* because the meal is over and the pizza decision is no longer in the present. It is much more logical to report the event in the past – because that's when it happened: *She said she was having the pizza.* The fact that this 'natural tense' guideline works, only serves to show that reported speech isn't actually a special grammatical feature at all. It simply follows the normal grammar of English!

64 Used to

Form

I		drink green tea.
You		play tennis.
He	used to	work for the government.
She		call him 'Tiny'.
We		have a toaster.
They		vote Labour.

The negative is made with *didn't use to.*
I *didn't use to like him, but now we're good friends.*

The question form is *Did you use to . . .*

Used to is a fixed structure that doesn't change for person or tense. *Used to* always refers to the past. There is no present or future tense.

Presentation

1) Draw pictures on the board to show Evgeny's life now. Elicit sentences in the present simple (*He's poor. He sleeps on the street. He only drinks water. He eats food from dustbins*).

2) In a different part of the board, draw pictures showing Evgeny's past. Establish that students realise that these things were true in the past – but not now. Elicit or model sentences (*He used to be rich. He used to live in a big house. He used to eat caviar. He used to drive a Ferrari*). Also introduce *didn't use to* if you wish (*He didn't use to have a beard*). Add a 'punchline' if you'd like a happy ending (*He used to be miserable – but now . . . he's very happy!*).

3) Get students to think of some more sentences about Evgeny – then about things that were true of themselves in the past (*I used to play with LEGO®*).

Practice

Lottery winners

Tell half of the students in the class that they won the lottery a year ago. The other half are reporters. Reporters prepare questions to ask the winners about how their lives have changed since winning while the winners think of possible answers. Pairs then conduct an interview (which could be followed up by writing a report together).

When I was a child

Students write sentences about how their lives were different when they were children. Compare with a partner and make notes of things in common to report to the class (*We both used to climb trees*).

Past habits questionnaire

Students prepare a list of questions to ask the other members of their group about their past habits (*Did you use to like onions?*).

Meaning and use

Used to is used to talk about things that happened (regularly or repeatedly) in the past but which are no longer true in the present. After each *used to* we can imagine the words (. . . *but not now*).
We used to argue over who should drive (. . . *but we don't now*).

Used to has the same meaning as *would* in sentences such as I *would write a letter home every week.* NB *would* can only be used with actions. We cannot use it with stative verbs ✗ *I would love my friends' birthday parties* but we can say *I used to love my friends' birthday parties*.

Used to is pronounced /juːstə/.

Students often confuse the forms, meanings, uses and pronunciation of a number of similar verb forms:

Main verb *use*

Use has many meanings including *to do something with the help of a tool, method or ability.*
The electric drill can also be used as a screwdriver.
It is pronounced /juːz/.
Be careful, in some sentences the words *used to* are actually an example of main verb *use*.
The button is used to /juːzd tə/ *switch the machines on.*

Noun *use*

Use is pronounced /juːs/.

Structure: *get used to* something

This structure is typically studied in higher level classes than *used to*. *To get used to something* means to become familiar with something over a period of time.
It is pronounced /get juːstə/.

Structure: *be used to* something

This structure is typically studied in higher level classes than *used to*. *To be used to something* means to be familiar with something (after a period of time when you got used to it!).
It is pronounced /bɪ juːstə/.

Concept questions

- **Yu Jin used to study in Cambridge.** Does Yu Jin study in Cambridge at the moment? (*No*) Did Yu Jin study in Cambridge in the past? (*Yes*)

- **Sam didn't use to like olives but he does now.** Does Sam like olives now? (*Yes*) Did he like them in the past? (*No*)

- **They used to swim in the sea.** Do they swim in the sea now? (*Probably not, though it's possible*) How many times did they swim in the sea? (*Many times*)

Watch out for these problems . . .

- **Students add a final *d* to the negative form.**

- **Students confuse *used to* with the verb *use* as a main verb.**

- **Students use *used to* when they are not contrasting the past and the present:** Compare: (a) I smoked when I was at college and (b) I used to smoke when I was at college. These both refer to the same time period – but (b) also suggests that now I do not smoke. In sentence (a) we cannot tell if the speaker still smokes or not.

65 Question tags

Form

Question tags are made with an auxiliary verb (*be, have, do, will, shall, would* or other modal auxiliaries) and a pronoun. The most common tags are: *is it? isn't it? do / did you? does / did he / she / it?*

If there is an auxiliary verb in the statement – or main verb *be*, use that verb in the tag.
Your name's John, isn't it?
She'll do it for us, won't she?
They can't make it on the seventh, can they?

If there is not, use the dummy auxiliary *do / does / did*.
You never really talk to your parents, do you?

If a statement is affirmative, use a negative tag.
You do go on, don't you?

If it is negative, use an affirmative tag.
I can't really trust you, can I?

For commands, suggestions, requests etc use auxiliary *will* and ignore the affirmative / negative guideline above.
Pick that up, will you?

After *let's* use *shall we.*
Let's go, shall we?

Use *aren't I?* with *I am.* (But use *am I?* with *I'm not.*)
I'm on the list, aren't I? (*I'm not on the list, am I?*)

After *used to,* use tag *did / didn't.*
He used to live here, didn't he?

After the main verb *have / has* you can use *do / does* in the tag.
She has a new car, doesn't she?

Presentation

Party

1) Draw a picture of a party – with a number of people standing up and chatting. Above each person, write a word or short phrase that says some information about them (*Canadian, teacher, just married, got 7 cats, twin, lives in New York, 3 children, been in submarine*).

2) Tell the students that they are guests at the party. The other guests are strangers – but they have heard some stories or information about them. Ask them what they could say to get into a good conversation with each person. Students may suggest talking about the weather, complimenting on clothes etc. Acknowledge all good answers.

3) Model an example yourself using a question tag (*You're Canadian, aren't you? You've been in a submarine, haven't you?*).

4) Get students to practise in open pairs, taking care to distinguish between 'checking' intonation and 'real question' intonation. Point out how the tag is formed.

5) Elicit similar questions for all the other people at the party – and get students to practise. At the end they could stand up and hold a 'party'.

Practice

Beginnings and endings

Straightforward matching games work well here. You can write up separate sentence starts and tags on the board (*You're angry . . . aren't you? You like cricket . . . don't you?*). Alternatively, prepare cards and stick them on the board then get students to match them up – or, better, prepare a set of cards for each pair and see if they can pair up beginnings and endings themselves.

Interview

Students write a number of sentences about a partner which they think are true (eg *Raoul doesn't watch TV at the weekend*). They then work in pairs to check if they are right, 'Raoul, you don't watch TV at the weekend, do you?' They can use intonation to show how certain they are.

Meaning and use

Checking for confirmation

The main use of question tags is to seek confirmation of what the speaker believes to be true – to check that the person you are speaking to agrees that your understanding is correct.
Your name's John, isn't it?
Nice party, isn't it?

Such question tags help to bring the listener into the flow of conversation. They typically expect an agreeing answer – or no answer at all. The speaker might be a little surprised if the listener came back with a denial or disagreement.

The intonation of the tag ending *falls* (ie your voice goes down).

Asking real questions

Question tags can also be used to ask genuine questions. They function in exactly the same way as other ways of asking questions and listeners will typically respond with a genuine answer. You can turn a 'checking' tag question into a 'real question' by changing the intonation. For example:

Your name's John, isn't it? can be changed into a real question, expecting a real answer, simply by using a rising intonation (ie your voice goes up).

When written down, we cannot tell if a tag question is 'checking' or 'asking a real question' other than by interpreting the nature of the question, the context and the response. Many tag questions could be either type, depending on how they are pronounced.
You're in love with Rita, aren't you?
You don't buy into all this nonsense, do you?

Other uses: requesting, suggesting, directing, commanding, complaining, exclaiming

Question tags with *will you, won't you, would you* and *wouldn't you* can be used to make an imperative sound friendlier or less aggressive. Notice that in these tags the affirmative / negative balance guidelines are not followed.
Scratch my back for me, will you?
Chuck me the ball, would you?

Shall we is used after a request starting with *let's*.
Let's drop the subject, shall we?

We can also use question tags to complain or show anger or annoyance . . .
You just never let up, do you? (= you never stop!)
You haven't invited her husband, have you?

. . . and to exclaim.
It's a fantastic view from up here, isn't it!

Other tags

Innit?

Some British English native speakers, especially in London and other urban areas, use a single all-purpose question tag *innit,* a contraction from *isn't it.*
Suzie's coming to the party tonight, innit?
We're British. Innit? (*Book title*)
The use of *innit* is likely to be considered ungrammatical or uneducated.

Eh? OK? right? Yes? No? etc

These can be used in a question tag-like way.
Pretty good, eh?
I'll see you on Monday evening, OK?
You told everyone about tomorrow's meeting, right?

Pronunciation

For checking question tags the intonation of the tag ending *falls* (ie your voice goes down).

You've never been to Tokyo, have you?

You can turn a 'checking' tag question into a 'real question' by changing the intonation. Simply use a rising intonation.

You've never been to Tokyo, have you?

Watch out for these problems . . .

- **Students get locked into a single question tag:** Many languages have a single word or construction that works in a similar way to the English question tag. This accounts for the way that some students get the basic idea of question tags quickly, but then get locked into always using a single tag for all sentence types. ✗ *I'll see you tomorrow, isn't it?* ✗ *He's beautiful, isn't it?*

- **Students don't understand (and / or avoid) dummy auxiliary *do*:** *They cooked a meal, wasn't they?*

- **Students mismatch verbs:** ✗ *She was lying, didn't she?* You can draw students' attention to this by writing their sentence on the board and drawing an arrow from the auxiliary verb to the verb in the tag. Point at the two verbs and shake your head or look puzzled, indicating that they don't match.

66 Relative pronouns and relative clauses

Form

Relative clauses

I've got a friend <u>who works at the BBC</u>.

Relative pronouns

Relative pronoun	Used for
who, whom, whose	people (and sometimes other living creatures, pets)
which	non-living things (but can sometimes refer to living things such as groups of humans *the class which*)
that	living and non-living things. *That* can substitute for *which* or *who*. The following two sentences are both correct and mean exactly the same: *There's a woman who wants to talk to you.* *There's a woman that wants to talk to you.*
when	times
where	locations
why	reasons
what	= *the things that*

Omitting relative pronouns

You can leave out *that*, *who* or *which* when they are the object (ie when the person or thing they refer to is <u>not</u> doing the action of the verb).
Pam's the only person (that) I can trust.
It's a story (which) every child will enjoy.

If the relative pronoun is the subject of its clause, it can't be left out.
We had a Chinese meal, which made a nice change.

Presentation

Who?

1) Bring in about 6 or 7 photos of different men (or women). The people should look reasonably similar but with different hats, bags, features etc. Put them on the board and write a number above each.

2) Tell the class that you are thinking of one of the people. Say a sentence (*He's the man who's got a beard* or *He's the man who's bald*). Students must tell you which numbered picture you are describing.

3) Write up the sentence you used and point out the relative pronoun and relative clause.

4) Repeat the activity with a few more different examples. You can stay with *who* or introduce more relative pronouns if you wish (*He's the man that's talking on the phone. He's the man whose arm is broken*). If you want to expand the presentation to focus on other relative pronouns, you will need to also have some pictures of objects and places (*It's a place where people buy fruit and vegetables. It's something that you can travel in*).

5) Ask if students can make sentences about one of the pictures themselves starting *He's the man who . . .* Write up the sentences. Elicit more with other beginnings.

Practice

Guess who

(as a follow-on from the presentation) Find a picture that shows a large number of cartoon characters (a 'Where's Wally / Waldo / Walter' picture). Students work individually to (secretly) choose two people and write sentences about each to clearly identify which ones they chose. For example: *He's the man that's cleaning some steps. She's the person who's wearing a blue uniform.* Working in pairs, students read their sentences to another student who must identify the person in the picture.

Guess what

Same game as *Guess who* – but with sentences about objects rather than people – for example: *It's the book that's lying on the bottom shelf.*

NB the task works best if there are a number of examples of each item in the picture ie lots of different books in different places.

Quiz

Prepare a few descriptions using relative clauses that could be used as a general knowledge quiz (*It's the place where the Queen of England lives. He's the man who won the last US presidential election*). Make pairs. Read the questions to students who write answers. After these have been checked, students can prepare descriptions of their own to use in a second quiz.

Life changing moments

Write sentence starters with relative pronouns on the board for students to fill in and discuss (*A day when my life changed was . . . The person who influenced me when I was growing up was . . . The time when I felt happiest was . . .*).

Improving texts

Prepare a text that includes a number of sentence pairs that could be combined using a relative clause (*He met a girl. The girl loved Elvis Presley*). Get students to read the text and identify where possible improvements could be made – then get them to write the shorter sentences (*He met a girl who loved Elvis Presley*).

Meaning and use

In the sentence *I've got a friend who works at the BBC*, the relative clause identifies and tells us more about the friend. In this respect, a relative clause is quite adjective-like in meaning. It's a bit like saying ✗ *I've got a work-at-the-BBC friend.* In some languages this is how the meaning would be conveyed.

Relative pronouns

Relative pronouns typically have a linking function, joining two separate clauses into one sentence. For example:
The story is about a man + The man was a friend of mine = The story is about a man who was a friend of mine.

The team contained ten players. Their ages ranged between 10 and 16. = The team contained ten players whose ages ranged between 10 and 16.

Relative clauses can refer to various kinds of noun and noun phrase:

- **Single nouns** *We hold <u>meetings</u> where residents' problems can be aired.*

- **Determiner and noun** *It's <u>a show</u> that appeals to young and old alike.*

- **A longer noun phrase** <u>*The aging nuclear reactors*</u>*, which were regarded as dangerously out of date, were replaced.*

The pronoun *which* can also refer to:

- **The situation in a whole clause or sentence** <u>*He was called away unexpectedly today*</u>*, which is why I came to meet you instead.* <u>*We cancelled the trip*</u>*, which was just as well, because it rained.* <u>*She said I looked nice*</u>*, which made my day.*

Who

Who is used about people (and sometimes animals).
We only employ people who already have computer skills.
When *who* is the object of a clause, you can leave it out.
You are free to marry the man (who / whom) you love.

Whom

This can be used when the relative pronoun *who* would be the object of a clause.
He wrote a letter naming the people whom he suspected.
However, in current usage, *whom* is rarely used. Instead we might completely miss out the pronoun or use *who* instead.
He wrote a letter naming the people (who) he suspected.
You are more likely to use *whom* if there is a preceding preposition, but this quite formal.
To whom did you speak?

Whose

Whose is used about people (and occasionally animals) to show a relationship or possession.
Jones is a director whose television credits include NYPD Blue.
It is used in place *of his, her, our, their, Mike's, the teacher's* etc. It is often used for companies, groups or organisations containing people.
They were a shadowy secret society, whose activities were shrouded in mystery.
Although mainly used for people, *whose* can be used for things, in which case it means *of which*.
They live in a house whose roof could collapse at any time. (= the roof of which)

That

That (or *which*) is used about things.
We have built a structure that (which) should last for hundreds of years.
That can be used instead of *who* in defining relative clauses *We haven't met the people that live next door* but not in non-defining clauses.

→ **Unit 67 Defining and non-defining relative clauses**

When

When is used for times.
I'm trying to put off the moment when I have to leave.
In defining relative clauses *when* is normally only used after a word or phrase that refers to a time (*the moment when, the time when, the year when, the period of my life when* etc).

Where

Where is used for places.
Jeremy is now at Dartmouth College, where his father also studied.
In defining relative clauses *where* is typically only used after a word or phrase that refers to a place (*the mall where, the road where, the country where* etc) though some words that imply places may be used.
I like the kind of holiday where I can sit on the beach for a week and do nothing.

Why

Why can normally only be used after the noun *reason*.
He finally told me the reason why he was so upset.

Teaching tip: missing out the relative pronoun

If you or your students find it tricky to decide whether or not they can omit the relative pronoun, here are a few ideas on how to clarify this for them.
Write up these two sentences and ask students to compare them:
a) *Finally, Jed found the person that he was looking for.*
b) *Finally, Jed found the person that had the keys.*

Elicit or explain that . . .

- in (a) we <u>can</u> omit *that* because *Jed* is the subject of the verb *was looking for* and *the person* is the object. Jed (not the person) was doing the action of looking.

- we <u>cannot</u> omit *that* in sentence (b) because *the person* is the subject (not the object) of the verb *had*.

If this is still unclear, it may help to 'unpack' the sentences into their separate parts. For example:

- *Finally, Jed found the person. Jed was looking for the person.* It is now clear that Jed is the subject of both parts. The person is the object of the second sentence.

- *Finally, Jed found the person. The person had the keys.* In contrast, here the person is the subject of the second sentence – and therefore the relative pronoun cannot be omitted.

Watch out for these problems . . .

- **Students use *what* as a relative pronoun:** ✗ *He bought a radio what was broken.*

- **Students use a subject / object pronoun at the end of a relative clause:** ✗ *These are the papers that I was asking about them.*

- **Avoidance:** Students find sentences with relative clauses quite long and cumbersome to construct (and therefore avoid them).

67 Defining and non-defining relative clauses

Form

There are 2 different kinds of relative clause.

Non-defining relative clause

The students, who walked to the top of the hill, saw a large eagle.

We use commas at the beginning and ending of the clause.

The relative clause tells us some extra information about the students but does not define who they are. It answers the enquiry *Can you tell me some more about the students?*

Defining relative clause

The students who walked to the top of the hill saw a large eagle.

The relative clause identifies and defines exactly which students we are talking about. It answers the question *Which students?*

Presentation

The eagle

1) Explain that some students went for a walk in the countryside. Draw the two pictures on the board.

2) Ask what is different between the pictures (In picture A all the students went up the hill. In picture B only some students went up the hill). Ask who saw the eagle (In picture A – all the students. In picture B, only some students).

3) Write the following two sentences on the board.

(a) 'The students, who walked to the top of the hill, saw a large eagle.'

(b) 'The students who walked to the top of the hill saw a large eagle.'

Ask which picture goes with which sentence. Confirm that sentence (a) goes with picture A and (b) with B. In (b) only those *who walked up the hill* saw the eagle.

Practice

Objects around the room

Place various objects in visible locations around the room. For some objects place all of them together – all batteries on the table. For others, place them in a number of different positions (a few toy cars on the floor, some on the bookcase). Write up some sentence starters 'I stepped on . . .' 'I couldn't find . . .' and ask students to work together and write possible endings for each sentence (*I stepped on the cars that were on the floor. I couldn't find the batteries, which were on the table*). Review the answers together afterwards.

Comparing defining and non-defining clauses

Try these pairs of sentences out on your students. Ask the class: *What's the difference in meaning?* Allow lots of discussion – but make sure that you offer a clear explanation by the end (answers are below). Students might think the sentences are identical at first. (Help them to notice the big differences in meaning shown only by a comma (or two).

1(a)   The students who arrived late couldn't get in.

1(b)   The students, who arrived late, couldn't get in.

2(a)   I didn't eat the chocolate which was on his plate.

2(b)   I didn't eat the chocolate, which was on his plate.

Answers

In 1(a) only some of the students couldn't get in. Which ones? The ones who arrived late. This is a defining clause. In 1(b) all of the students couldn't get in. The fact they arrived late is just extra non-crucial information. This is non-defining.

In 2(a) I might have eaten some other chocolate! It's just the chocolate on the plate I deny eating! This is defining. In 2(b) I didn't eat any chocolate. The fact that it was on the plate is just extra information. This is non-defining.

Concept questions

• **My brother, who lives in Mexico, is a lawyer.** How many brothers do I have? (*One*)

- **My brother who lives in Mexico is a lawyer.** How many brothers do I have? (*More than one*) Do the other brothers live in Mexico? (*No, only one brother lives in Mexico – but the speaker must have brothers who live in other countries*)

Meaning and use

Providing key identification = Defining relative clause

A defining relative clause provides essential information that helps us to identify which person or thing is being talked about. For example, on hearing: *The teacher gave the stickers to the boy* we might ask *which boy?* In contrast, this sentence gives us this information:
The teacher gave the stickers to the boy who did the best work.

The relative clause *who did the best work* tells us exactly which boy is being referred to. It identifies and defines the boy. It restricts the meaning down to one specific boy.

Just giving extra information = Non-defining relative clause

A non-defining relative clause does not identify and restrict in that way. It simply gives us some extra information about the noun or noun phrase. For example:
The teacher, who had just come into the room, gave the stickers to the boy.
The relative clause *who had just come into the room* does not define which teacher is involved. It simply offers us some additional interesting information about *the teacher*. We can imagine the information being introduced with *by the way*.
The teacher, who, by the way, had just come into the room, gave the stickers to the boy.
The sentence would still make perfect sense even if the relative was left out
The teacher gave the stickers to the boy.

However . . . have a look at this text:
When I arrived, three teachers were already waiting by the board. The door opened and another came in. The teacher who had just come into the room gave the stickers to the boy.
In the last sentence *who had just come into the room* is now a defining relative clause because it identifies which of the four teachers gave the stickers. If you imagine the same text but without the relative clause it would be unclear which teacher gave the stickers.

Punctuation in non-defining relative clauses

Non-defining relative clauses are usually written with a comma at the beginning and a comma at the end.
Tony, who had been granted leave, was home for several weeks.

If the relative clause comes at the end of a sentence, we use a full stop instead of a second comma, of course.
Bill was a senior police officer, who joined the force back in 1982.

The commas have a similar effect to brackets or dashes, marking off inessential information.

Tony (who had been granted leave) was home for several weeks.

Tony – who had been granted leave – was home for several weeks.

Pronunciation

When spoken, the commas in a non-defining relative clause would typically be heard as two short pauses.

Tony \<pause\> who had been granted leave \<pause\> was home for several weeks.

68 'd better / had better

Form

This is a modal-like fixed form – it is always either *had better* or, more commonly, the contracted form *'d better*. *Had better* never changes for person or tense.

I		give	Mum a ring.
We	'd better	make	sure.
You		take	an umbrella.

Negative

Had better doesn't follow all the normal rules of modals. The negative is made with *not* after *better* (rather than after *had*).
I'd better not waste any more of your time.
We'd better not hang about: it's ten o'clock already.
It's late. I'd better not keep you up any longer.

Questions

Question forms are fairly rare. It is possible to make affirmative questions.
Had you better write to her?
However, it is more common to make negative questions.
Hadn't you better write to her?

Colloquial use

In fast colloquial use, speakers may omit *had*.
You better tell me now.
He better be as good as you say.

Presentation

Help!

1) Prepare short role cards describing a character's problem situations (You have lost your wallet on a bus; You have are lost in the middle of the capital city; Your boyfriend has said your hair is 'a mess').

2) Ask a student to pick a card, read it out and then get suggestions about what to do from the rest of the class. Help students to make the *'d better* structure if they don't use it (*You'd better tell the police; You'd better ask someone for help; You'd better dump him*). There are, of course, no 'right' answers!

3) Distribute the cards to pairs of students and get them to practise giving advice to each other.

Practice

Problem party

Tell school-age students that their parents went away last night and they had a party in their house. Some uninvited guests came and lots of damage was caused. Elicit a list of problems on the board. It's now the morning after. Ask students to come up with a list of things that they'd better do before their parents return.

The best advice

Write a number of life problems on separate cards such as 'I always forget to bring my homework to school.' On another set of cards write a piece of advice for each situation such as 'You'd better put it back in your bag as soon as you finish it.' Mix up each set of cards. In class, randomly give each student one problem and one piece of advice. Students mingle. Each time they meet a new partner they read out their problem and hear the advice from the other person (which in most cases won't match well). They must try to find the best advice for their problem.

Agony aunt

Give students letters describing school problems (*I found answers to a test online – should I cheat? I can't understand the teacher's explanations*). They have to write replies saying what they think the person had better do.

Concept questions

- **Sara had better finish her project.** Does the speaker think it is a good idea for Sara to finish her project? (*Yes*) Does the speaker think that something negative might happen if she does not finish it? (*Yes*)

- **The guests will arrive in an hour so I'd better start cooking.** Is it a good idea to start cooking now? (*Yes*) Might there be some problem if the speaker does not start cooking now? (*Yes*) What? (*We don't know – but maybe the meal will be late. Maybe the guests will be upset etc*)

Meaning and use

Had better has a similar meaning to *should*. When you tell someone that *they'd better do* something, you are giving strong advice about what you think is the best (or right) thing to do in a specific current or future situation.

The most common functions for *had better* are . . .

- advice to others. *You'd better get some sleep. We have an early start tomorrow.*

- advice to self. *I'd better give Mum a ring.*

- warnings. *'You had better be careful,' Dad said, shaking his finger at me.*

- invitations. *You'd better come in or you'll get wet.*

- suggestions, looking for consensus. *I think we'd better ask your mum's opinion first.*

- intention. (Reluctant self-persuasion) *I suppose I had better get back to work.*

There is invariably some suggestion of a negative or even dangerous result if the advised course of action is not followed. Many *had better* sentences could be finished with *or . . .* (stating the possible negative outcome).

- *I'd better phone my wife and tell her I'll be late* (or . . . she'll be angry with me).

- *You'd better be quick* (or . . . you'll miss the deadline).

- *I'm not sure what time the train leaves – we'd better check* (or . . . we might miss it).

- *I'd better make a list, or I'll forget who I've invited.*

- *You'd better take an umbrella – it's going to rain* (or . . . you'll get wet).

Had better is not used to give recommendations, suggestions or general warnings where there wouldn't be a negative outcome if the advice is not followed. We would probably use another modal instead:
✗ *Let's go and see a film and afterwards we had better go for a meal.*
✓ *Let's go and see a film and afterwards we could go for a meal.*

Watch out for these problems . . .

- **Students misinterpret *better*:** The use of the word *better* seems to cause confusion (especially as the *'d* is often hard to hear). There is no comparative meaning here. You are not suggesting that one option is better than another. Similarly, students may see it as a mild suggestion or recommendation (ie *I think it is better if you . . .*) rather than a stronger piece of advice.

- **Students misinterpret *had*:** Expressions with ''d better' are about the present situation (or perhaps a future situation) – but not about the past. The fact that the verb 'had' is in the past is a constant confusion to students ✗ *They arrived late and had better apologise to the hostess.*

- Students use infinitive with *to:* ✗ *You'd better to leave now.*

69 Two-verb structures: *-ing* or infinitive?

Form

After some verbs you have to know whether you should use an *-ing* form or a *to* infinitive.

Pattern A

Some verbs require the use of *-ing*.

admit, adore, avoid, can't stand, celebrate, consider, delay, deny, dislike, enjoy, finish, give up, go, go on, imagine, keep, miss, practise, risk, stop, suggest

✓ *I enjoyed playing tennis.*
✗ *I enjoyed to play tennis.*

Pattern B

Some verbs require the use of the *to* infinitive.

afford, agree, appear, arrange, ask, attempt, choose, claim, decide, expect, fail, forget, hope, intend, learn, manage, need, offer, prepare, pretend, promise, refuse, seem, wait, want, wish

✓ *Her husband failed to pay.*
✗ *Her husband failed paying.*

Pattern C

Some verbs can have either *-ing* or the *to* infinitive and keep the same meaning.

attempt, begin, continue, hate, like, love, prefer, start, try

✓ *The band started playing.*
✓ *The band started to play.*

Some verbs can have either *-ing* or the *to* infinitive but change their meaning.

come, go on, remember, regret

✓ *You remembered buying the milk.*
✓ *You remembered to buy the milk.*

Be careful! The verb *stop* looks as if it should fit into this category:

✓ *She stopped to smoke.*

✓ *She stopped smoking.*

But, in fact the first sentence has an ellipsis (= some omitted words). It means *She stopped doing something in order to smoke*. So, if we expand the sentence, it might, for example, read *She stopped working in order to smoke* ie the verb *stop* actually takes a standard *-ing* verb; it's just that it is hidden!

Presentation

Pattern A or Pattern B?

1) Tell a story that includes a large number of verb + *-ing* and verb + *to* infinitive structures – like this example:

> *Three months ago Marek <u>decided to lose</u> some weight. He <u>wanted to get</u> really slim before summer – and <u>imagined</u> himself <u>lying</u> on the beach – fit and thin! He <u>stopped eating</u> chocolate, <u>gave up drinking</u> beer and <u>refused to eat</u> anything high in fat. This was very difficult for him . . . because he <u>enjoyed eating</u> chocolate and <u>preferred drinking</u> beer to drinking Diet Cola! Luckily, his girlfriend <u>agreed to help</u> him. She <u>promised to buy</u> a lot more fresh foods. She also <u>suggested going</u> swimming every week. He <u>agreed to do</u> this – and he <u>kept following</u> his diet week after week. Two days ago . . . Marek <u>stopped dieting</u>. In all that time . . . he <u>managed to lose</u> half a kilo! Poor old Marek!*

2) Draw two columns on the board and write headings 'Column 1: verb + *to*' 'Column 2: verb + *-ing*.'

3) Briefly explain the grammar point ie that some verbs need either *to* or *-ing* after them. Show a few examples (✓ *I enjoyed playing tennis* ✗ *I enjoyed to play tennis*).

4) Retell your story but pause after the first word of each underlined chunk (*Three months ago Marek <u>decided</u> . . .*) – write the bare infinitive of the next verb on the board (*lose*) and elicit from students which of the two forms (*to lose* or *losing*) they think is correct. When there is an agreed answer, put a note of the word in the correct column (*decide* is added to the + *to* column).

Pattern C: two timelines

1) Draw two timelines on the board, marking *Now* and *Past* on each.

2) Write up one sentence above the first timeline: *You remembered buying the milk.*

Add the other sentence above the second timeline: *You remembered to buy the milk.*

Make pairs. Ask the students to decide if the sentences are both good English. Discuss and establish that they are. Now ask students to think about what the difference in meaning is between the two sentences. Can they explain it to their partner? Can they use the timelines to help make it clear?

3) After some thinking and discussion time, collect ideas. Invite students up to the board to mark their ideas on the timelines. Give clues if they are very stuck or confused ('Think about which happened first – the remembering or the buying'). At an appropriate point, make sure that you establish a clear correct answer. As the timelines below make clear, the sequence of actions is actually quite different in the two sentences!

✓ *You remembered buying the milk* (ie You bought milk – then, afterwards, recalled this).

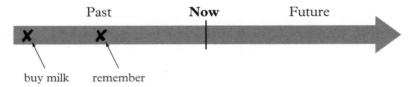

✓ *You remembered to buy the milk* (ie You remembered that you wanted to buy milk).

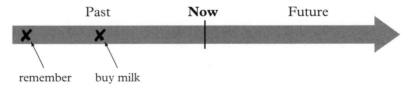

Practice

Guess my secret

Get a student to come out to the front and give them a card with a sentence on (*You love playing tennis* or *You have decided to give up chocolates*). The student should draw one or more simple pictures on the board (a smiley face and a tennis racquet or a box of chocolates with a cross over it) – and / or do a little mime (hitting a tennis ball or looking at a chocolate and then shaking head and saying 'no'). The class must try to guess her original sentence. Repeat with more volunteers and then do in small groups.

Beginning and ending cards

1) Divide a page into three columns and eight rows to make 24 boxes. When cut up, these will make a set of playing cards. On half the cards write sentence beginnings (*Alice's mum won't let her . . . I asked her . . .*) and on the others write the endings of the same sentences (. . . *come with us . . . to marry me*). Photocopy one page for each pair – and cut them up into separate cards.

2) In class, make student pairs, A and B. Hand one set of cards face down to each pair. Tell each student to take five cards. Whenever they play a card, they should take a new card from the pack so that they always have five cards.

3) To play the game, student A should play a card with a sentence beginning. Player B can now play either (a) an ending for that sentence – or (b) a new beginning. If Player B plays an ending, Player A must decide if they agree that is really a good ending for the sentence. If he agrees, then B keeps the two cards (= 2 points). If they disagree, Player B must take back her cards and miss her go. The game continues until all the sentences are complete – or the game is completely stuck! The winner is the person with most points.

4) At the end, lead a discussion, reviewing the sentences and confirming which sentences are possible and which are not, making notes about the grammar on the board. NB there may be possible good answers that were not the original sentences you cut up.

Watch out for these problems . . .

Well . . . fairly obviously . . .

- **Students choose the wrong form:** ✗ *I enjoyed to play tennis yesterday.* ✗ *I like to watching TV.* ✗ *She suggested to visit Berlin.*

70 *In case*

Form

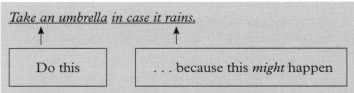

In case is a fixed form. It never changes.

In case + subject + verb phrase

We use *in case* + present tense for sentences about now and the future.
Keep a watch on him in case he gets worse.

In case of + noun phrase

Especially *fire, emergency, accident, problems, difficulty, trouble, dispute, damage, disaster, absolute necessity* etc
A boat will be waiting in case of emergency.

In fast native speaker speech, the word *in* may be dropped (or said so minimally that it is not heard).
A: *Why are you taking the book?*
B: *Case I need to do a repair.*

Presentation

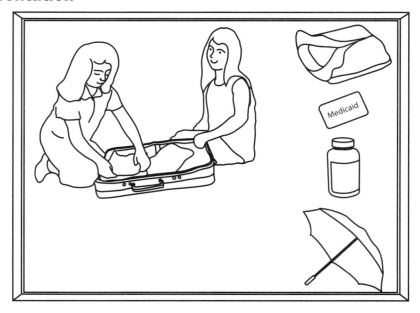

Jenny's holiday

1) Draw a picture of Jenny packing her suitcase for holidays. Her friend Maggie is laughing and asking her about things in the bag: *An umbrella? Why?* Elicit Jenny's reply *I'm taking it in case it rains.*

2) Draw images of other things in the bag and elicit why Jenny is taking them (*Aspirin . . . in case I get a headache. Medical Insurance Card . . . in case I get ill. Jumper . . . in case it's cold*).

3) Get students to look through their bags and tell each other why they have brought some things.

Practice

But Mum . . . I'm grown up now!

Make pairs. A is an 18-year-old, getting ready to leave home and go to university. B is an over-protective parent who is suggesting lots of possible problems, what to take, what not to do (*Take a dictionary in case you can't buy one there. Get insurance for your iPad® in case you lose it. Don't go out after 9 pm in case you get mugged*). Elicit or model one or two examples and then get students to think of more and then role play the scene.

The expedition

Prepare a list of items that might be useful on an expedition to the South Pole (or Sahara, Amazon). Pairs discuss which five items are most important (*We have to take the snake serum in case we get bitten*). Collect ideas in the whole class and reach a compromise solution.

Why do we need them?

Write the names of jobs / professions (doctor, soldier, teacher, cleaner) at the top of separate pieces of paper. Give one to each group. Ask students to think of a reason why we need their profession in our society (*We need doctors in case we get ill*). When they have finished, they pass their paper to another group and get a new one. They should add a new 'in case' ie *not* the same idea as the last one (*We need doctors in case there is a disaster*) – and pass it on one more time (to make three ideas in total on each sheet). When ready, groups read out the three sentences but knocking on the table instead of saying the job name (*We need <knock> in case we get ill*). The other students should guess the missing jobs.

Concept questions

- **I'm taking an umbrella in case it rains.** Am I definitely taking an umbrella? (*Yes*) Will it definitely rain? (*No*) Might it rain? (*Yes*) Is it very likely to rain? (*We don't know*) Will the umbrella be useful if it rains? (*Yes*) Will I be prepared if it rains? (*Yes*) Why am I taking the umbrella? (*So that I will be ready if it rains*)

Meaning and use

All *in case* meanings are connected with the idea of an event that might or might not happen (or have happened).

Present

The main use of *in case* is to say that something is done <u>in preparation for</u> another event that may or may not happen. It helps to explain the *reason* you have for doing something.

Take an umbrella in case it rains.

The speaker does not know if it will rain or not, so takes the umbrella in preparation for the possible rain. Here are some similar examples.

Bring a coat in case it turns cold.
I'll keep Thursday afternoon clear in case we need to meet.
Hold on to the instructions in case you have any problems.

Just in case means the same – but there is a suggestion that the possible event is less likely.

I'll make some sandwiches, just in case we get hungry later on.
Keep your pills handy just in case you feel seasick.

Just in case is often used at the end of a clause, without detailed explanation of the possible event, assuming that the listener will understand what might happen from the preceding conversation.

I'll make some sandwiches, just in case.

Past

When talking about the past, *in case* can be used when you don't know whether something happened, or when you didn't know whether something would happen or not.

In desperation I phoned the hospitals in case there'd been an accident.
I made some sandwiches in case we got hungry.

It can also refer to events that are in the future in the past!

She wouldn't go near the village in case she saw him. (= She wouldn't go near the village <u>because of the possibility that she might</u> see him.)

If / when there is

In case of + noun phrase means *if / when there is*

It's illegal to use the fire alarm except in case of emergency. (= It's illegal to use the fire alarm except <u>if there is</u> an emergency)

Are you prepared to protect yourself in case of attack? (= Are you prepared to protect yourself <u>if there is</u> an attack?)

Watch out for these problems . . .

- **Students use *in case* with an *if* meaning:** ✗ *We'll explain the problem to him in case he comes.*

- **Students use *in case of* with *-ing* form:** ✗ *In case of raining take my umbrella.*

Further reading

When I first started teaching, there was one very thin booklet that I found especially helpful. It was called Situations and Aids for Teaching Structures (1976) by L. Baines, G. Cunningham, J. Lugton, H. Moorwood and B. Haycraft, published by International House. It had very little in it – mainly some ultra-shorthand lists of ideas of possible contexts for teaching different grammatical items – but to a rather confused new teacher it was a godsend as it provided just enough of a seed to allow me to start thinking of my own lessons. I hope that current teachers will find my own book useful in a similar way.

I have looked at many sources in preparing this book. The following titles were the most important:

Aitken, R. (1991), *Teaching Tenses* (London: Nelson ELT).

Bolitho, R. & Tomlinson, B. (2005), *Discover English* (Oxford: Macmillan).

Carter, R. & McCarthy, M. (2006), *Cambridge Grammar of English* (Cambridge: Cambridge University Press).

Clarke, S. (2008), *Macmillan English Grammar in Context – Essential* (Oxford: Macmillan).

Close, R.A. (1992), *A Teachers' Grammar* (Hove: Language Teaching Publications).

Crystal, D. (1996), *Rediscover Grammar* (Harlow: Pearson Longman).

Eastwood, J. (1994), *Oxford Guide to English Grammar* (Oxford: Oxford University Press).

Murphy, R. (2004), *English Grammar in Use* (Cambridge: Cambridge University Press).

Parrott, M. (2000), *Grammar for English Language Teachers* (Cambridge: Cambridge University Press).

Sinclair, J. (1990), *Collins COBUILD English Grammar* (London: HarperCollins).

Sinclair, J. (2004), *Collins COBUILD English Usage* (London: HarperCollins).

Swan, M. (2005), *Practical English Usage* (Oxford: Oxford University Press).

Thornbury, S. (1997), *About Language* (Cambridge: Cambridge University Press).

Vince, M. (2008), *Macmillan English Grammar in Context – Intermediate* (Oxford: Macmillan).

Willis, D. (1991), *Collins COBUILD Student's Grammar* (London: HarperCollins).

Workman, G. (2008), *Concept Questions and Time Lines* (London: Gem Publishing).

Yule, G. (1998), *Explaining English Grammar* (Oxford: Oxford University Press).

Yule, G. (2006), *Oxford Practice Grammar Advanced* (Oxford: Oxford University Press).

I have also used the Macmillan English Dictionary for Advanced Learners (2007) throughout and many of the example sentences are based on the Macmillan corpus.

Macmillan Education
4 Crinan Street
London N1 9XW
A division of Springer Nature Limited
Companies and representatives throughout the world

ISBN 978-0-2307-2321-4

First published 2010

Designed by MPS Limited
Illustrated by MPS Limited
Cover photograph by Ben Welsh/www.photolibrary.com

The publishers would like to thank Martin Hewings, Liz Hunt, Jonathan Marks,
Amos Paran and Michael Swan for their thoughtful insights and recommendations.

Author acknowledgements

This book would have been impossible without the work and support of many
people. I am indebted to editors Jill Florent and Michael Kedward for so many
suggestions, corrections and inspired ideas for rewrites. Many thanks also to
series editor Adrian Underhill for ongoing support and to all the Macmillan
team who worked on this: Helen Kidd, Julie Brett, Rowena Drewett, Matt Kay,
Tor Townsley and Douglas Williamson. At various stages the book was read,
reviewed and sanity-checked by Martin Hewings, Amanda Holmbrook, Liz Hunt,
Jonathan Marks, Amos Paran and Michael Swan, and I am very grateful for all
their comments, criticisms, corrections, groans and suggestions. I'd also like to
thank Bell Educational Trust, my employer, for allowing me the time I needed to
complete this project. And a huge hug and thanks to Noémi, Maisie and Gabriella
for years of putting up with a grumpier than usual man about the house.

Printed and bound by CPI Group (UK) Ltd, Croydon CR0 4YY
2018
12